WORDP
FOR DOS
FOR
DUMMIES™

Quick Reference

by Greg Harvey
Preface by Series Editor Dan Gookin

IDG Books Worldwide, Inc.
An International Data Group Company
San Mateo, California ♦ Indianapolis, Indiana ♦ Boston, Massachusetts

WordPerfect For Dummies Quick Reference

Published by
IDG Books Worldwide, Inc.
An International Data Group Company
155 Bovet Road, Suite 310
San Mateo, CA 94402

Library of Congress Catalog Card No.:93-78447

ISBN 1-56884-009-8

Printed in the United States of America

10 9 8 7 6 5 4 3 2 1

Distributed in the United States by IDG Books Worldwide, Inc.

Distributed in Canada by Macmillan of Canada, a Division of Canada Publishing Corporation; by Woodslane Pty. Ltd. in Australia and New Zealand; and by Computer Bookshops in the U.K. and Ireland.

For information on translations and availability in other countries, contact Marc Jeffrey Mikulich, Foreign Rights Manager, at IDG Books Worldwide; FAX NUMBER 415-358-1260.

For sales inquiries and special prices for bulk quantities, write to the address above or call IDG Books Worldwide at 415-312-0650.

About the Author

Greg Harvey, the author of over 30 computer books, has been training business people in the use of IBM PC, DOS, and software application programs such as WordPerfect, Lotus 1-2-3, and dBASE since 1983. He has written numerous training manuals, user guides, and books for business users of software. He currently teaches Lotus 1-2-3 and dBASE courses in the Department of Information Systems at Golden Gate University in San Francisco. Harvey is the author of *Excel For Dummies, 1-2-3 For Dummies, PC World WordPerfect 6 Handbook, DOS For Dummies Quick Reference,* and *Windows For Dummies Quick Reference,* all from IDG Books.

About the Series Editor

Dan Gookin, the author of *DOS For Dummies, DOS For Dummies, 2nd Edition, WordPerfect For Dummies, WordPerfect 6 For Dummies,* and co-author of *PCs For Dummies* and the *Illustrated Computer Dictionary For Dummies,* is a writer and computer "guru" whose job is to remind everyone that computers are not to be taken too seriously. Presently, Mr. Gookin works for himself as a freelance writer. Gookin holds a degree in Communications from the University of California, San Diego, and is a regular contributor to *InfoWorld, PC/Computing, DOS Resource Guide,* and *PC Buying World* magazines.

Acknowledgments

I want to thank the following people, as well, who worked so hard to make this book a reality:

David Solomon and John Kilcullen for their support for this "baby" Dummies book.

Brandon Nordin and Milissa Koloski for coming up with the original concept of quick references for the rest of us.

Janna Custer and Megg Bonar for straightening out all the contract details.

Diane Steele, Tracy Barr, and Sandy Blackthorn for their editorial assistance.

Michael Partington for the tech review and Beth Baker and Mary Breidenbach in Production.

Last, but never least, I want to acknowledge my indebtedness to Dan Gookin whose vision, sardonic wit, and (sometimes) good humor produced *DOS For Dummies*, the "Mother" of all Dummies books. Thanks for the inspiration and the book that made it all possible, Dan.

Greg Harvey
July, 1993, Inverness, California

(The publisher would like to give special thanks to Patrick J. McGovern, without whom this book would not have been possible.)

Credits

Publisher
David Solomon

Acquisitions Editor
Janna Custer

Managing Editor
Mary Bednarek

Project Editor
Diane Graves Steele

Editors
Corbin Collins
Erik Dafforn
Kezia Endsley

Technical Reviewer
Michael Partington

Production Manager
Beth J. Baker

Production Coordinator
Cindy L. Phipps

Production Staff
Joseph A. Augsburger
Mary Breidenbach
Drew R. Moore
Chris Collins

Preface

DOS For Dummies — and all the books in the *...For Dummies* series — are the ideal computer references. Have a problem? Great, look it up in *...For Dummies,* find out how to get it done right, and then close the book and return to your work. That's the way all computer books should work: quickly, painlessly, and with a dash of humor to keep the edge off.

So why is a WordPerfect quick reference needed? Yikes! Who wants to look at all that stuff? Who cares about the function keys and the reveal codes? Chances are you might, someday.

The way we work with computers is that we often imitate what others do. Fred may hand you a form letter file with a bunch of names and addresses and say, "Run the merge and mail these letters out before you quit work today." Being suspicious — which is always good around Fred — you want to make sure you won't be doing anything disasterous. *WordPerfect For Dummies Quick Reference* can't help you weasel out commands and seldom-used options that are way beyond the reach of the typical Dummy. So what you're left with is the WordPerfect manual or the fuzzy-headed on-line help.

Thank goodness for this book!

Greg Harvey has done the tedious job of transposing all the WordPerfect jargon from crypto-manual speak into a plain language reference we can use during those painful "must look it up in the manual" moments. He's peppered it with information, dos and don'ts, and the splash of humor you've come to expect from any book with *Dummies* on the title.

So tuck this reference in tight somewhere right by your PC. Keep it handy for when you must know the advanced options of some command or to confirm your worst fears about what it is Fred wants you to do to your own PC.

Dan Gookin

About IDG Books Worldwide

Welcome to the world of IDG Books Worldwide.

IDG Books Worldwide, Inc., is a division of International Data Group, the world's largest publisher of computer-related information and the leading global provider of information services on information technology. IDG publishes over 194 computer publications in 62 countries. Forty million people read one or more IDG publications each month.

If you use personal computers, IDG Books is committed to publishing quality books that meet your needs. We rely on our extensive network of publications, including such leading periodicals as *Macworld*, *InfoWorld*, *PC World*, *Publish*, *Computerworld*, *Network World*, and *SunWorld*, to help us make informed and timely decisions in creating useful computer books that meet your needs.

Every IDG book strives to bring extra value and skill-building instruction to the reader. Our books are written by experts, with the backing of IDG periodicals, and with careful thought devoted to issues such as audience, interior design, use of icons, and illustrations. Our editorial staff is a careful mix of high-tech journalists and experienced book people. Our close contact with the makers of computer products helps ensure accuracy and thorough coverage. Our heavy use of personal computers at every step in production means we can deliver books in the most timely manner.

We are delivering books of high quality at competitive prices on topics customers want. At IDG, we believe in quality, and we have been delivering quality for over 25 years. You'll find no better book on a subject than an IDG book.

John Kilcullen
President and C.E.O.
IDG Books Worldwide, Inc.

IDG Books Worldwide, Inc. is a division of International Data Group. The officers are Patrick J. McGovern, Founder and Board Chairman; Walter Boyd, President. International Data Group's publications include: **ARGENTINA's** Computerworld Argentina, InfoWorld Argentina; **ASIA's** Computerworld Hong Kong, PC World Hong Kong, Computerworld Southeast Asia, PC World Singapore, Computerworld Malaysia, PC World Malaysia; **AUSTRALIA's** Computerworld Australia, Australian PC World, Australian Macworld, Network World, Reseller, IDG Sources; **AUSTRIA's** Computerwelt Oesterreich, PC Test; **BRAZIL's** Computerworld, Mundo IBM, Mundo Unix, PC World, Publish; **BULGARIA's** Computerworld Bulgaria, Ediworld, PC & Mac World Bulgaria; **CANADA's** Direct Access, Graduate Computerworld, InfoCanada, Network World Canada; **CHILE's** Computerworld, Informatica; **COLUMBIA's** Computerworld Columbia; **CZECH REPUBLIC's** Computerworld, Elektronika, PC World; **DENMARK's** CAD/CAM WORLD, Communications World, Computerworld Danmark, LOTUS World, Macintosh Produktkatalog, Macworld Danmark, PC World Danmark, PC World Produktguide, Windows World; **EQUADOR's** PC World; **EGYPT's** Computerworld (CW) Middle East, PC World Middle East; **FINLAND's** MikroPC, Tietoviikko, Tietoverkko; **FRANCE's** Distributique, GOLDEN MAC, InfoPC, Languages & Systems, Le Guide du Monde Informatique, Le Monde Informatique, Telecoms & Reseaux; **GERMANY's** Computerwoche, Computerwoche Focus, Computerwoche Extra, Computerwoche Karriere, Information Management, Macwelt, Netzwelt, PC Welt, PC Woche, Publish, Unit; **HUNGARY's** Alaplap, Computerworld SZT, PC World, ; **INDIA's** Computers & Communications; **ISRAEL's** Computerworld Israel, PC World Israel; **ITALY's** Computerworld Italia, Lotus Magazine, Macworld Italia, Networking Italia, PC World Italia; **JAPAN's** Computerworld Japan, Macworld Japan, SunWorld Japan, Windows World; **KENYA's** East African Computer News; **KOREA's** Computerworld Korea, Macworld Korea, PC World Korea; **MEXICO's** Compu Edicion, Compu Manufactura, Computacion/Punto de Venta, Computerworld Mexico, MacWorld, Mundo Unix, PC World, Windows; **THE NETHERLAND'S** Computer! Totaal, LAN Magazine, MacWorld; **NEW ZEALAND's** Computer Listings, Computerworld New Zealand, New Zealand PC World; **NIGERIA's** PC World Africa; **NORWAY's** Computerworld Norge, C/World, Lotusworld Norge, Macworld Norge, Networld, PC World Ekspress, PC World Norge, PC World's Product Guide, Publish World, Student Data, Unix World, Windowsworld, IDG Direct Response; **PANAMA's** PC World; **PERU's** Computerworld Peru, PC World; **PEOPLES REPUBLIC OF CHINA's** China Computerworld, PC World China, Electronics International, China Network World; **IDG HIGH TECH BEIJING's** New Product World; **IDG SHENZHEN's** Computer News Digest; **PHILLIPPINES'** Computerworld, PC World; **POLAND's** Computerworld Poland, PC World/Komputer; **PORTUGAL's** Cerebro/PC World, Correio Informatico/Computerworld, MacIn; **ROMANIA's** PC World; **RUSSIA's** Computerworld-Moscow, Mir-PC, Sety; **SLOVENIA's** Monitor Magazine; **SOUTH AFRICA's** Computing S.A.; **SPAIN's** Amiga World, Computerworld Espana, Communicaciones World, Macworld Espana, NeXTWORLD, PC World Espana, Publish, Sunworld; **SWEDEN's** Attack, ComputerSweden, Corporate Computing, Lokala Natverk/LAN, Lotus World, MAC&PC, Macworld, Mikrodatorn, PC World, Publishing & Design (CAP), DataIngenjoren, Maxi Data, Windows World; **SWITZERLAND's** Computerworld Schweiz, Macworld Schweiz, PC & Workstation; **TAIWAN's** Computerworld Taiwan, Global Computer Express, PC World Taiwan; **THAILAND's** Thai Computerworld; **TURKEY's** Computerworld Monitor, Macworld Turkiye, PC World Turkiye; **UNITED KINGDOM's** Lotus Magazine, Macworld, Sunworld; **UNITED STATES'** AmigaWorld, Cable in the Classroom, CD Review, CIO, Computerworld, Desktop Video World, DOS Resource Guide, Electronic News, Federal Computer Week, Federal Integrator, GamePro, IDG Books, InfoWorld, InfoWorld Direct, Laser Event, Macworld, Multimedia World, Network World, NeXTWORLD, PC Games, PC Letter, PC World Publish, Sumeria, SunWorld, SWATPro, Video Event; **VENEZUELA's** Computerworld Venezuela, MicroComputerworld Venezuela; **VIETNAM's** PC World Vietnam

Introduction

Welcome to the *WordPerfect For Dummies Quick Reference,* a quick reference that looks at the lighter side of WordPerfect commands (such as it is). I mean, how many ways does one person need to get to the same dialog box???

As a means of ferreting out the best possible paths to all the commands, features, and functions of WordPerfect, I offer you the *WordPerfect For Dummies Quick Reference.* This book not only gives you the lowdown on every WordPerfect command, it also rates each command with icons indicating its suitability as well as its general safety (see the "The cast of icons" later in this introduction for a sneak preview).

For your convenience, this book isn't divided into any sections at all! You'll find all the commands listed in alphabetical order from Advance to Zoom.

Each command is handled in a similar way. Below the command name, replete with its suitability and safety icons, you'll find a brief description of its function. If this description reads like stereo instructions, recheck the suitability icon: this command is probably not in your league.

Below the description comes the "Menus" section. Here, you find the path you take to accomplish the task: you start at the command on the main menu, go to the option on the drop-down menu, and then choose the option on the cascading menu or in the dialog box that appears. For each of these steps you'll find a "picturesque" trail to follow and the name of each command and option you need to choose.

Following the "Menus" section, in most cases, you'll find "For function key freaks" to give you the path you follow starting with the function key combination. Sometimes I even throw in a section for "Mouse maniacs." Then you may find steps to help you use the command in real life, lists of other good information that won't fit anywhere else, and a "Secret codes" section that *reveals* the WordPerfect codes.

Bringing up the rear, you'll find a *More stuff* section where I stick in any tips, warnings, reminders, or other trivia that just might come in handy when you use the command.

How do I use this book?

You've all heard of on-line help. Well, just think of this book as on-side help. Keep it by your side when you're at the computer, and, *before* you try to use a WordPerfect command that you're the least bit unsure of, look the command up in the appropriate section. Scan the entry, looking for any warnings (those bomb icons). Follow the "Menus" or "For function key freaks" section to guide you through the options.

The cast of icons

In your travels with the WordPerfect commands in this book, you'll come across the following icons:

Recommended for your average WordPerfect user.

Not recommended for your average WordPerfect user.

Not suitable for your average WordPerfect user but you may get stuck having to use this command anyway.

Safe for your data.

Generally safe in most circumstances unless you really don't follow instructions; then look out!

Potentially dangerous to data but necessary in the scheme of things. Be very careful with this command. Better yet, get somebody else to do it for you.

Safe only in the hands of a programmer or some other totally techy person. Stay clear unless they let you sign a release form and give you hazard pay.

New command in WordPerfect 6.

A tip to make you a more clever WordPerfect user.

Look out! There's some little something in this command that can get you into trouble (even when it's rated safe or generally safe).

Just a little note to remind you of some trivia or other that may someday save your bacon.

A handy-dandy guide to point you straight to the sections in *WordPerfect For Dummies* and *WordPerfect 6 For Dummies* where you can find more examples of how to use this command.

Advance

Positions text precisely on the page without requiring you to monkey around with tabs, spaces, and hard returns.

Menus

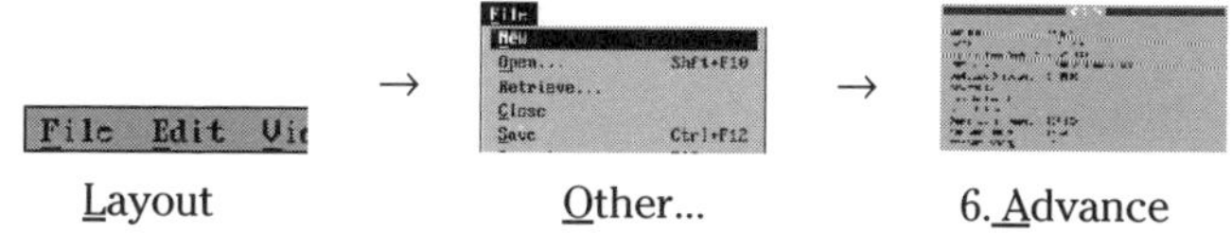

Layout → Other... → 6. Advance

For function key freaks

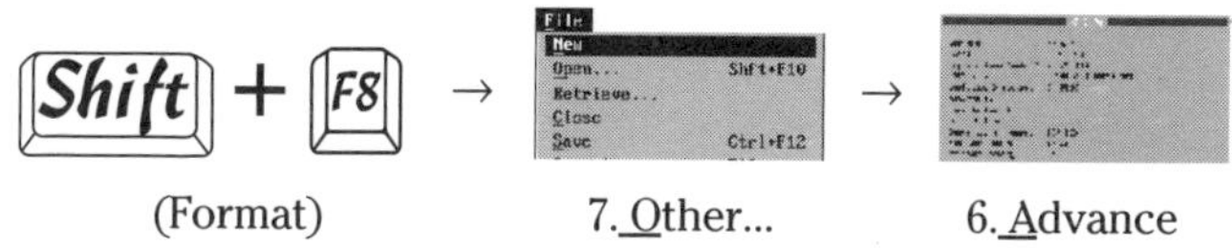

(Format) → 7. Other... → 6. Advance

The Advance dialog box

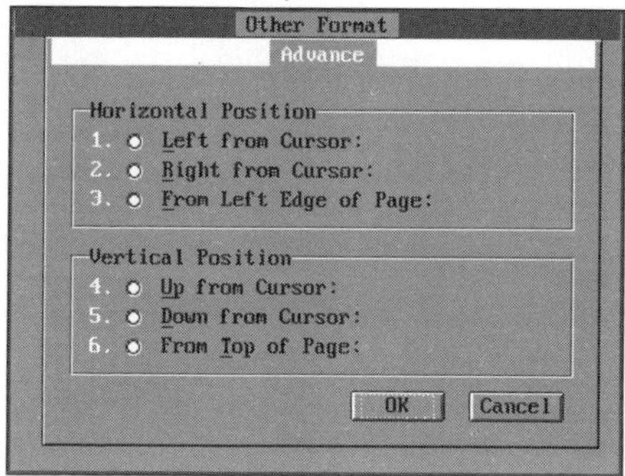

Option or button	Function
1. Left from Cursor:	Adjusts the printing of the text that follows to the left, relative to the cursor's current position, by the amount you specify.
2. Right from Cursor:	Adjusts the printing of the text that follows to the right, relative to the cursor's current position, by the amount you specify.
3. From Left Edge of Page:	Adjusts the text that follows a fixed amount from the left edge of the page.

4. Up from Cursor:	Adjusts the printing of the text that follows up, relative to the cursor's current position, by the amount you specify.
5. Down from Cursor:	Adjusts the printing of the text that follows down, relative to the cursor's current position, by the amount you specify.
6. From Top of Page:	Adjusts the text that follows a fixed amount from the top edge of the page.

Secret codes

Say that you use Advance to position the heading *Fire Sale Today!* 1 1/2 inches in from the left margin and 4 inches down from the top margin of your page. In Reveal Codes, you see

```
[HAdv][VAdv]Fire Sale Today![Hrt]
```

If you highlight the [HAdv] code, it expands to [HAdvToPos:1.5"]. If you highlight [VAdv], it expands to [VAdvToLn:4"].

More stuff

When using the Advance feature to position text, you can use both a Horizontal and Vertical option if you need to. Also, always be sure to position the cursor ahead of the first character you want advanced on the page before you use this command.

Append

Tacks a copy of the block of text you've marked onto the end of a file without requiring you to have that file open in another document window. If you start WordPerfect under the Shell program (see Shell), you can also use Append to add text to one of the Shell's clipboards (it supports up to 80 different ones!) without replacing its current contents.

Menus

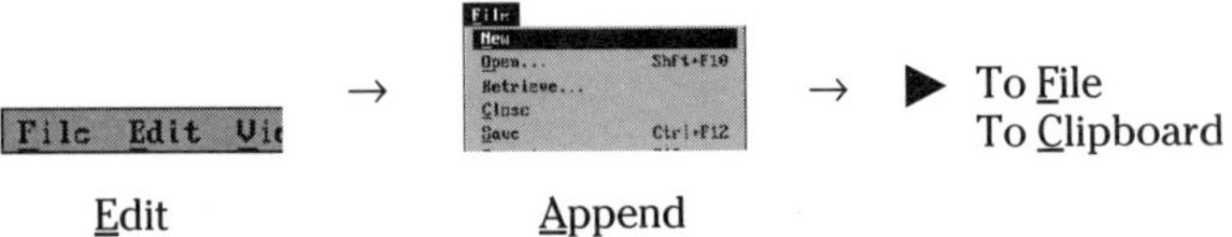

For function key freaks

(Move) 4. Append...

To tack a block onto the tail end of a file

1. Mark the block of the text — see Block (Text) for details — you want to copy onto the file.
2. Choose the Append command on the Edit menu; then choose the To File command on the cascading menu. Or press Ctrl+F4 (Move) and choose the 4. Append option.
3. Type the name of the file you want to add the block onto in the Filename text box of the Append To dialog box. If you don't know the filename, select the file in the File List dialog box by choosing the File List . . . F5 button or press F5 (see File List for details).
4. Choose the OK button or press Enter.

When you next open the file, the block you appended will appear at the very bottom of the document.

To tack a block onto the tail end of the Clipboard

If you start WordPerfect from the Shell program (see Shell), you can add stuff to the end of a clipboard:

1. Mark the text you want to add to the Clipboard (see Cut, Copy, and Paste).
2. Choose the Append command on the Edit menu (instead of Copy) and then choose the To Clipboard command on the cascading menu (repeat this step for each block you want to add to the Clipboard).

When you're ready to dump the total contents of the Clipboard of the document, choose Go To Shell on the File menu or press Ctrl+F1 (Shell). Then choose 5. Retrieve (you can't use Paste on the Edit menu or Ctrl+V to do this).

Auto Code Placement

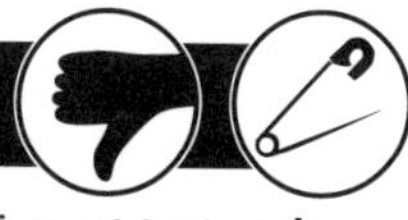

Automatically places certain secret codes that format text at the beginning of their paragraph or page and updates settings without accumulating codes in the Reveal Codes window (thus avoiding that messy code build-up).

Using Auto Code Placement

The secret codes for the WordPerfect formatting features are placed at the beginning of their paragraph when the Auto Code Placement is turned on:

WordPerfect Feature	*Secret Code*
Borders (paragraph)	[Para Border]
Columns	[Col Def]
Delay	[Delay]
Footer	[Footer A] [Footer B]
Header	[Header A] [Header B]
Hyphenation zone	[Lft HZone] [Rgt HZone]
Justification	[Just]
Left and right margins	[Lft Mar] [Rgt Mar]
Line height	[Ln Height]
Leading adjustment	[Leading Adj]
Line numbering	[Ln Num]
Line spacing	[Ln Spacing]
Margins (left and right)	[Lft Mar] [Rgt Mar]
Paragraph spacing	[Para Spacing]
Tab set	[Tab Set]
Watermark	[Watermakr A] [Watermark B]

The secret codes for the following WordPerfect features are placed at the beginning of their page when Auto Code Placement is turned on:

WordPerfect Feature	*Secret Code*
Borders (page)	[Page Border]
Center page	[Cntr Cur Pg] [Cntr Pgs]
Margins (top and bottom)	[Top Mar] [Bot Mar]
Page numbering	[Pg Num Pos]
Page size	[Page Sz/Typ]
Suppress page numbering	[Suppress]

Turning off Auto Code Placement

When you first install WordPerfect 6, Auto Code Placement is turned on in the program. If you want, you can turn off this feature by Choosing the Setup command on the File menu (or press Shift+F1 (Setup). Select Environment and then select the T. Auto Code Placement option to remove the X from its check box. Select the OK button or press Enter.

More stuff

If you turn off Auto Code Placement, it's up to you to make sure that the cursor is positioned correctly in the text before you make any of the formatting changes affected by this feature. Remember, if your cursor is in front of an existing secret code, your change will not go into effect (text is only affected by the secret code that comes immediately before the first character).

Bar Code

Lets you add a POSTNET (Postal Numeric Encoding Technique) bar code when addressing an envelope or creating a mailing label. A bar code uses that funny looking computer script used to mark grocery items that the supermarket scanners can never read. However, using bar codes in your mailing addresses can save you some bucks with the Post Office, so it's worth doing.

Menus

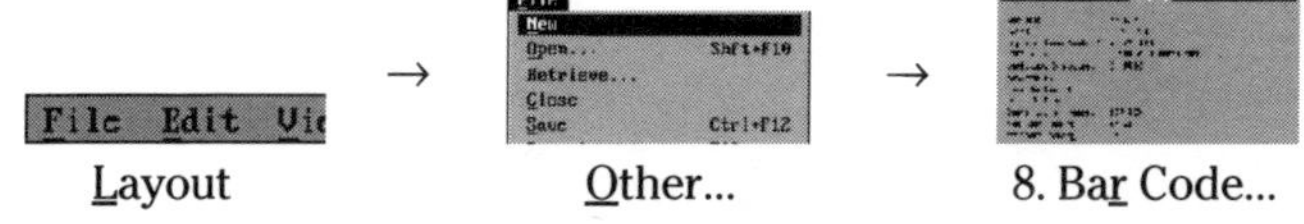

Layout → Other... → 8. Bar Code...

For function key freaks

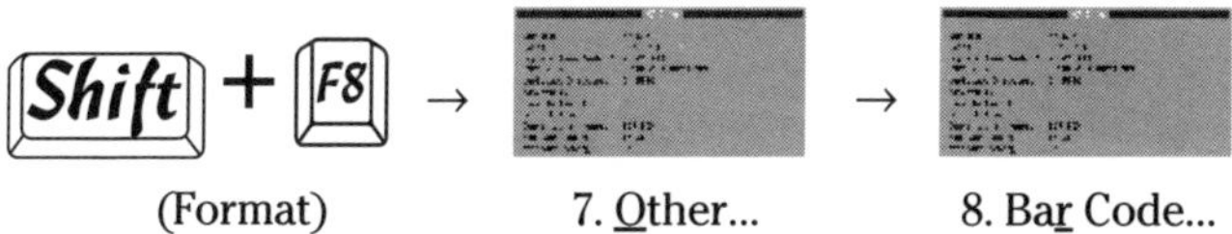

(Format) → 7. Other... → 8. Bar Code...

Belly up to the bar (code)

To insert a bar code in an address (or elsewhere in the document if you're really inclined):

1. Position the cursor where the bar code is to appear.
2. Choose Other on the Layout menu (or press Shift+F8 (Format) and then choose 7. Other.)
3. Choose 8. Bar Code in the Other Format dialog box.

4. Type the five-, nine-, or eleven-digit ZIP code in the POSTNET Bar Code dialog box.
5. Press Enter or choose OK.

When you return to the document, you see the bar code characters in the document if WordPerfect is in graphics or page mode. If the program's in text mode, you need to open the Print Preview window to see the POSNET code before you actually print the document.

Secret codes

Suppose you want to write me a letter telling me how much you love this book (and you do, don't you?). To speed this paean of praise to me, you decide to add a bar code with my ZIP code. When you open the Reveal Codes window, you see the secret code: `[Bar Code]` If you position the cursor on the code in Reveal Codes, this secret code expands to `[Bar Code:949561175]` indicating the English meaning of the gibberish that appears in your document's address.

More stuff

To get rid of a bar code, find its [Bar Code] secret code in the Reveal Codes window and delete it.

You can also add POSTNET bar codes to envelopes when using the nifty new Envelope feature to address them (see Envelope).

Block (Text)

Marks a section of text (called a block) so that you can do all sorts of neat things to it like cut and paste it, spell check it, print it, or even get rid of it.

Menus

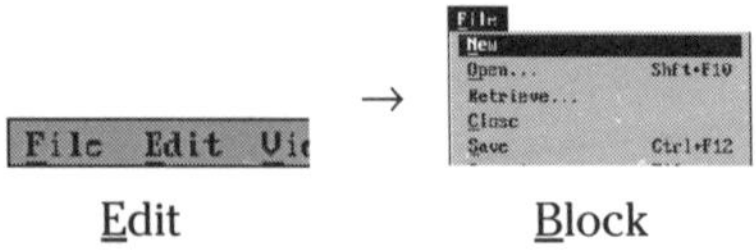

Edit → Block

For function key freaks

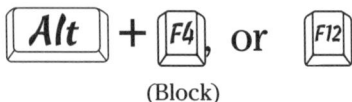

Alt + F4, or F12

(Block)

For mouse maniacs

Position the mouse pointer in front of the first character and then drag through the text to highlight it.

Selecting a particular section of text

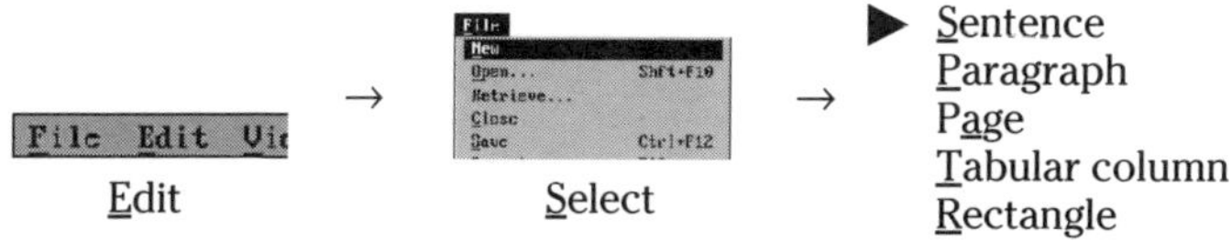

Marking blocks keyboard style

The most direct method for marking a block is to

1. Position the cursor in front of the first character to be included in the block.
2. Choose the Block command on the Edit menu — or press Alt+F4, or F12 (Block). The message `Block on` appears on the status bar.
3. Use the cursor-movement keys (see Cursor Movement) to extend the block. WordPerfect highlights all the text you cover as you move the cursor.

Other slick ways to extend a block

WordPerfect offers all sorts of fast ways to extend a block after you turn on blocking. Here are some you might want to try:

- Press Ctrl+→ to extend a block to the next word to the right or Ctrl+← to extend it to the next word to the left.
- Press ↑ to extend a block up one line or ↓ to extend it down one line.
- Press the Enter key to highlight to the end of the paragraph (that is, to the occurrence of the next hard return).
- Type a particular character to highlight to the next occurrence of that character in the text. For instance, to extend the block to the end of the next sentence, you press the period (.). To extend it to the next occurrence of the letter *t* in the text, type **t**.

Fun things to do with marked blocks

After you've marked your block, you can do all sorts of things with it. Here's a sample of the more common things to do with a marked block:

- Bold its text (F6).
- Underline its text (F8).
- Delete the block (Del or Backspace).
- Center the block (Shift+F6).
- Move the block flush with the right margin (Alt+F6).
- Cut and paste the block (Ctrl+Del).
- Copy and paste the block (Ctrl+Ins).
- Convert the case of the text in the block (Shift+F3). You can uppercase, lowercase, or apply initial caps to the block. If you forget to block the text first, however, Shift+F3 will open a new document.
- Check the spelling in the block (Ctrl+F2).
- Print the block (Shift+F7).
- Save the block as a separate document in its own file (F10).

"Mark It Again, Sam"

After you do something to a marked block, the `Block on` message and the highlighting disappear. If you still need to do something else to the same block, you can mark it again, as follows:

1. Choose the Block command on the Edit menu or press Alt+F4, or F12 (Block).
2. Press Ctrl+Home (Go To) twice. In other words, when the Go To dialog box appears the first time you press Ctrl+Home, you respond by pressing Ctrl+Home again.

Secret codes

After you turn on blocking with the Block command on the Edit menu or Alt+F4, or F12 (Block), if you have Reveal Codes open, the secret code `[Block]` appears right before the Reveal Codes cursor.

More stuff

If you ever find yourself on the wrong block (so to speak), you can cancel the marking operation by pressing Esc or Alt+F4 or F12 (Block).

You can find more about this command in Chapter 6 of *WordPerfect For Dummies* (and *WordPerfect 6 For Dummies*).

Block Protect

Keeps selected text together on the same page at all times no matter what editing changes you make to the document.

Menus

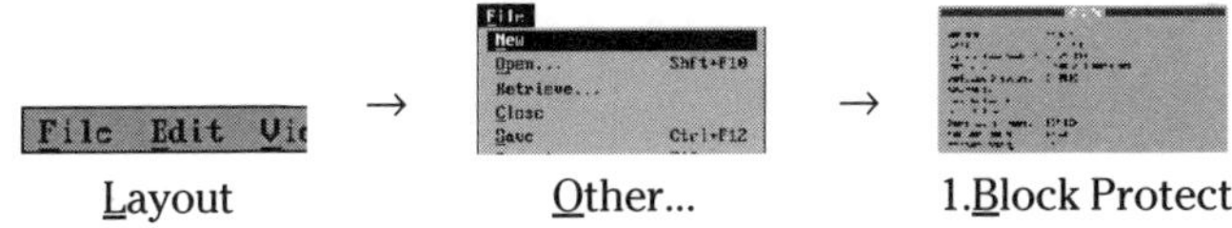

Layout → Other... → 1.Block Protect

For function key freaks

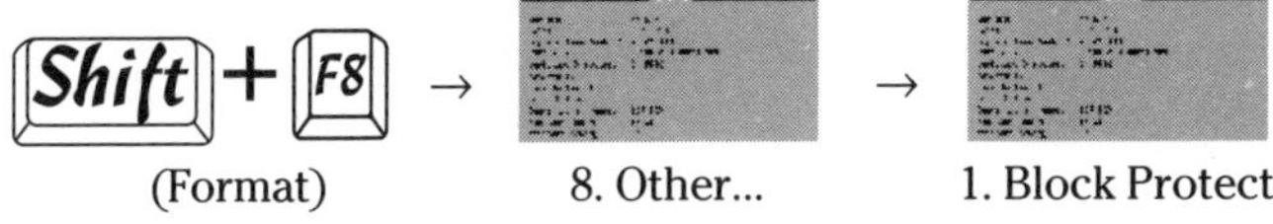

Shift+F8 (Format) → 8. Other... → 1. Block Protect

Using Block Protect

Block protect is one of the easiest ways to ensure that a section of text always stays together on a page, no matter how you edit the document. To protect a block of text:

1. Mark the block of text — see Block (Text) for details — that should always remain on a single page.
2. Choose the Other command on Layout menu; or, press Shift+F8 (Format) and then select 8. Other.
3. Select the 1. Block Protect option.
4. Choose the OK button or press Enter.

Secret codes

Let's say that you block protect the text

```
Let's do lunch as soon as you're in town.
Please let me know when this will be.
```

so that these two sentences don't end up on different pages. In Reveal Codes, you'd then see

```
[Block Pro:On]Let's do lunch as soon as you're
in town. Please let me know when this will
be.[Block Pro:Off]
```

More Stuff

To remove block protection, simply open Reveal Codes and delete either the [Block Pro:On] or the [Block Pro:Off] secret code. See also Conditional End of Page and Widow/Orphan.

You can find more about this command in Chapter 6 of *WordPerfect For Dummies* (and *WordPerfect 6 For Dummies*).

Bold

Prints selected text in boldface type.

Menus

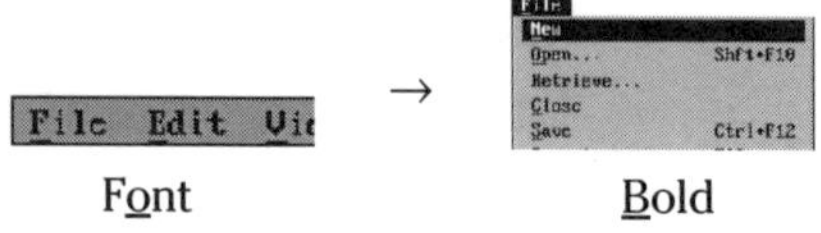

Font → Bold

For function key freaks

(Bold)

Bolding text before you type it

Position the cursor at the place where the first bold character is to appear. Turn on bold by selecting the Bold command on the Font menu or by pressing F6 (Bold). Type the text to appear in bold.

Turn off bold by selecting the Bold command on the Font menu or by pressing F6 (Bold) a second time. You can also turn off bold by choosing the Normal command on the Font menu or by pressing the → key once to move beyond the [Bold Off] secret code.

Bolding existing text

Block the text to appear in bold. Choose the Bold command on the Font menu or press F6 (Bold).

Secret codes

Let's say you bold only the word *Sale* in the heading

Fire **Sale** Today

in your document. In Reveal Codes, you'd see

```
Fire [Bold On]Sale[Bold Off] Today!
```

More stuff

To get rid of bold in text, open Reveal Codes and delete either the [Bold On] or [Bold Off] code that encloses the text.

You can find more about this command in Chapter 8 of *WordPerfect For Dummies* (and Chapter 9 of *WordPerfect 6 For Dummies*).

Bookmark

Marks your place in a document so that you can get right back to it.

Menus

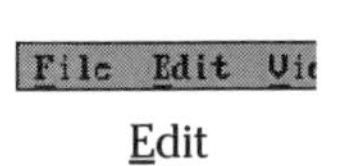

→

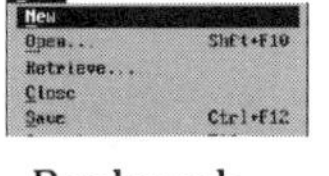

Edit → Bookmark...

For function key freaks

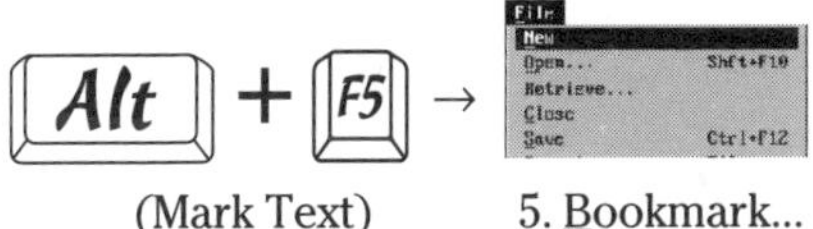

or

(Mark Text) 5. Bookmark... (Bookmark)

The Bookmark dialog box

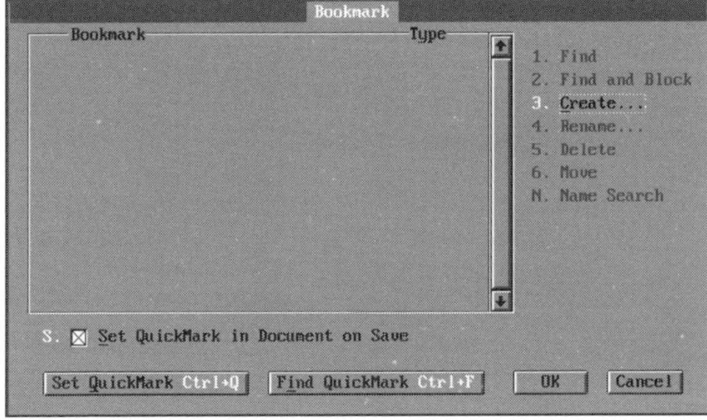

Option or button	Function
1. Find	Locates the bookmark you've highlighted in the Bookmark list box.
2. Find and Block	Locates and marks as a block the bookmark you've highlighted in the Bookmark list box (note that the bookmark must be listed as a Blocked type; otherwise, this option is not available).
3. Create...	Opens the Create Bookmark dialog box where you can name your new bookmark.
4. Rename...	Opens the Rename Bookmark dialog box where you can change the name of the bookmark you've highlighted in the Bookmark list box.
5. Delete...	Deletes the bookmark you've highlighted in the Bookmark list box upon confirmation.
6. Move	Relocates the bookmark you've highlighted in the Bookmark list box to the place where you move the cursor in the document.
N. Name Search	Opens a name search text box where you can type the first few characters of the bookmark you want to highlight in the Bookmark list box.
S. Set QuickMark in Document on Save	When this check box has an X, WordPerfect locates the QuickMark bookmark at the cursor's position each time you save the document.
Set QuickMark Ctrl+Q	Sets the QuickMark bookmark at the cursor's position.
Find QuickMark Ctrl+F	Moves the cursor to the location of the QuickMark bookmark in your document.

Creating a bookmark

1. Position the cursor at the beginning of the text where the bookmark is to be. To create a Blocked bookmark, mark all of the text that you want marked when you select the Find and Block option in the Bookmark dialog box.
2. Choose the Bookmark command on the Edit menu; or, press Alt+F5 (Mark Text) and then select 5. Bookmark option.
3. Choose the 3. Create option to display the Create Bookmark dialog box.

4. To name your bookmark, edit the selected text displayed in the Bookmark Name text box (or you can use the text copied from the document verbatim as the bookmark name).
5. Choose OK or press Enter to return to your document.

Finding a bookmark

1. Choose the Bookmark command on the Edit menu; or, press Alt+F5 (Mark Text) and then select the 5. Bookmark option.
2. Select the name of the bookmark you want to find in the Bookmark list box.
3. To position the cursor at the beginning of the bookmark, choose 1. Find. To highlight the text of a blocked bookmark, choose 2. Find and Block.

Using the QuickMark bookmark

QuickMark is the name of a special bookmark that WordPerfect automatically maintains in your document. Each time you save your document, WordPerfect saves a bookmark named QuickMark at the cursor's position. You can then return to that place in the document by pressing Ctrl+F. If, while working in a document, you want to set the QuickMark bookmark in a particular place without having to save the document, press Ctrl+Q.

Secret codes

Say that you've created a bookmark named Big Money at the beginning of the heading *Projected Profits in 1994.* When you open Reveal Codes, you see

```
[Bookmark]Projected Profits in 1994
```

in the window. When you position the cursor on the [Bookmark] code, it expands to

```
[Bookmark:Big Money]
```

More stuff

Although you can always delete a bookmark that you no longer need by using the 5. Delete option in the Bookmark dialog box, you can also do this quickly by opening Reveal Codes, positioning the cursor on the [Bookmark] secret code, and then pressing the Del key.

You can find more about this command in Chapter 28 of *WordPerfect 6 For Dummies.*

Borders

Lets you put a border around paragraphs, pages, or columns in your document.

Menus

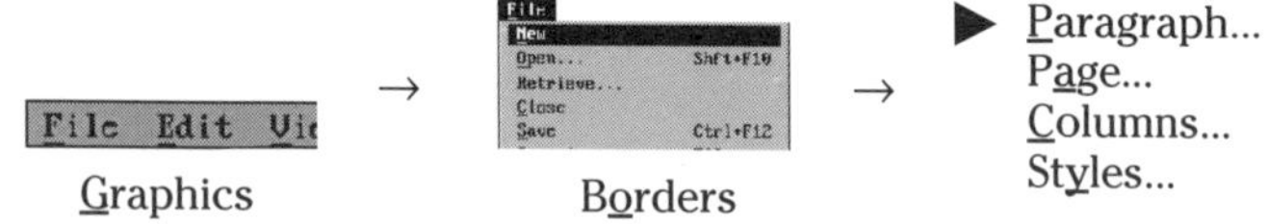

Graphics → Borders → ▶ Paragraph... Page... Columns... Styles...

For function key freaks

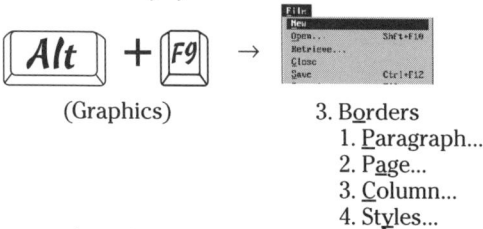

Alt + F9 (Graphics) → 3. Borders
1. Paragraph...
2. Page...
3. Column...
4. Styles...

Adding a border

WordPerfect 6 makes it a snap to put a border around the paragraphs or pages or between the columns in your document:

1. Position the cursor in the paragraph, on the page, or in the columns where you want the borders to start.
2. Choose the Borders command on the Graphics menu; or, press Alt+F9 (Graphics) and choose the 3. Borders option.
3. To put a border around your paragraphs, choose Paragraph. To put a border around your pages, choose Page. To put a border between or around columns in your document, choose Column.
4. To select a different border style, choose the 4. Styles option, highlight the name of the style you want to use in the Border Styles list box, and then choose the Select option or press Enter.
5. To choose a fill pattern for the borders, choose the 4. Fill Styles option, highlight the name of the fill pattern you want to use in the Fill Styles list box, and then choose the Select option or press Enter.
6. Choose the OK button or press Enter.

Turning off borders in a document

Whenever you add paragraph, page, or column borders to a document, WordPerfect adds these borders to all subsequent paragraphs, pages, or columns in the document, You can, however, turn off these borders by following these steps:

1. Position the cursor in the paragraph, page, or columns where the borders are to be turned off.
2. Choose the Borders command on the Graphics menu (or press Alt+F9 (Graphics) and choose the 3. Borders option).
3. To turn off paragraph borders, choose Paragraph. To turn off page borders, choose the Page. To turn off column borders in your document, choose Column.
4. Choose the Off command button.

If you know that you only want a border around a particular paragraph, page, or column, mark its text as a block (see Block (Text) for details) before you create the paragraph, page, or column borders. That way, you don't have to go through the steps for turning off the borders, because WordPerfect automatically turns on borders at the beginning and turns off the borders at the end of the block.

Creating a customized border style

For each type of border (paragraph, page, and column), WordPerfect offers a number of different predefined border styles. If none of these are exactly what you want, you can create your own custom border style as follows:

1. Choose the Borders command on the Graphics menu (or press Alt+F9 (Graphics) and choose 3. Borders).
2. Choose Styles to display the Border Styles dialog box and then choose the 2. Create option.
3. Type the name for the new custom style you want to create in the New Border Style Name dialog box and then choose OK or press Enter.
4. Modify the options you want to change in the Create Border Style dialog box (see next item).
5. If your custom style appears the way you want it in the preview box in the Create Border Style dialog, choose the OK button or press Enter to finish defining the custom style, and then choose the Close button in the Border Styles dialog box.

After creating a custom style, WordPerfect adds its name to the border styles list and you can select it as you would any of the predefined styles when adding borders to your paragraphs, pages, or columns.

The Create Border Style dialog box

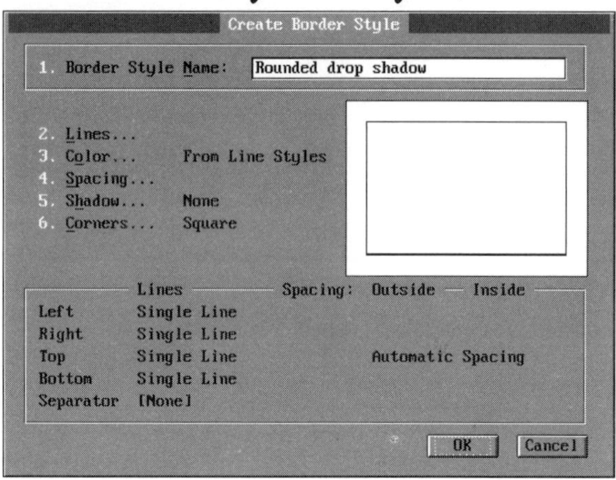

Option or button	*Function*
1. Border Style Name	Choose this option to rename the custom style and then edit or replace the style name and press Enter.
2. Lines	To change the line styles used in your custom border style, choose this option and then choose a new line style for all border lines with 1. Select All, or each of the four line borders individually with 2. Left Line, 3. Right Line, 4. Top Line, 5. Bottom Line, and 6. Separator Line (for column borders).
3. Color	By default, border styles use whatever color is assigned to their particular line styles. To select a new color for all the border lines, choose this option, choose the 2. Choose One Color For All Lines radio button, select the color you want in the Color Selection dialog box, and then choose OK.
4. Spacing	By default, WordPerfect automatically figures out the spacing between the borders and text on the inside and outside. To manually control the spacing between the text and the border lines in your custom border style, choose this option

	and then choose the 1. Automatic Spacing option to remove the X from its check box; then enter the new spacing values in the appropriate Outside Spacing and Inside Spacing check boxes, and choose OK.
5. Shadow	By default, predefined border styles don't use a drop shadow (a drop shadow creates the illusion of depth by adding heavy lines on two of the sides, giving the appearance of shadow). To add a drop shadow to your custom style, choose this option, choose the shadow type, color, and the width of the drop shadow in the Shadow dialog box, and then choose OK.
6. Corners	By default, border styles use square corners. To round the corners for your custom style, choose this option, select 2. Rounded radio button, enter the dimension for the corner radius, and then choose OK.

Secret codes

When you add a border to your document, WordPerfect inserts a [Para Border], [Pg Border], [Col Border] secret code into your document at the beginning of the paragraph, page or column that contains the cursor. Suppose that you block the heading

```
Part I: A New Beginning
```

and then select the thin thick border with no fill pattern for this paragraph. When you open Reveal Codes, you'll find

```
[+Para Border]Part I: A New Beginning[HRt]
[–Para Border]
```

If you position the cursor on the [+Para Border] code that turns on the paragraph border, it expands to [+Para Border]:Thin Thick Border;[None]].

More stuff

You must have the program in graphics mode (see Graphics Mode) to see your borders. If WordPerfect is in text mode (see Text Mode), you must choose the Print Preview command on the File menu to see your borders. If you've used a page border, switch to page mode (see Page Mode) if you want to see the top and the bottom of the border when the top and bottom of the page is in view on the screen.

Button Bar

Button bars let you select commonly used WordPerfect commands or macros simply by clicking their buttons with the mouse.

Menus

To display or hide the currently selected Button Bar:

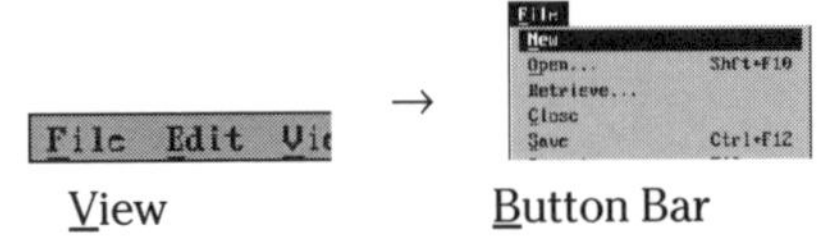

View Button Bar

Changing the display of the button bar

By default, the Button Bar appears at the top of the WordPerfect window, and its icons use both pictures and words. You can change both the position and the style of the buttons by following these steps:

1. Choose the View menu and then select the Button Bar Setup command.
2. Choose Options on the Button Bar Setup cascading menu.

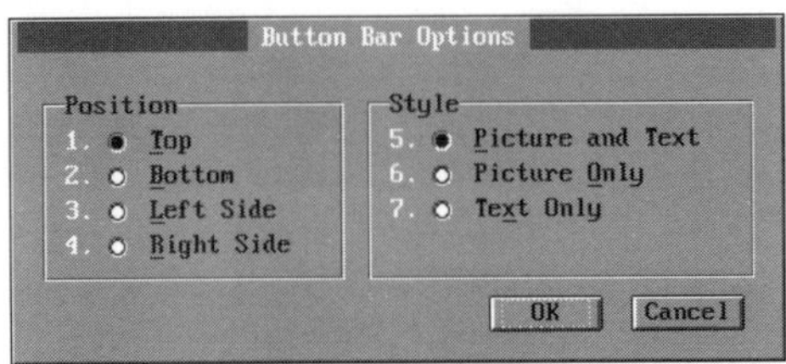

3. To change the placement of the Button Bar, select the appropriate Position radio button (1. Top, 2. Bottom, 3. Left Side, or 4. Right Side).
4. To change the style of the buttons, select the appropriate Style radio button (5. Picture and Text, 6. Picture Only, or 7. Text Only).
5. Select the OK command button or press Enter.

To save room on the screen and still be able to distinguish the buttons easily, select the Text Only Style option. Avoid the Picture Only option unless you are very familiar with the icons used on the Button Bar. The pictures take up more space than the words and are much harder to understand.

Selecting a new button bar

WordPerfect 6 saves button bars in special files located in your Macros/Keyboards/Button which have the WPB (WordPerfect button bar) file extension. To select a new button bar:

1. Choose the View menu and then select the Button Bar Setup command.
2. Choose the Select command on the Button Bar Setup cascading menu.

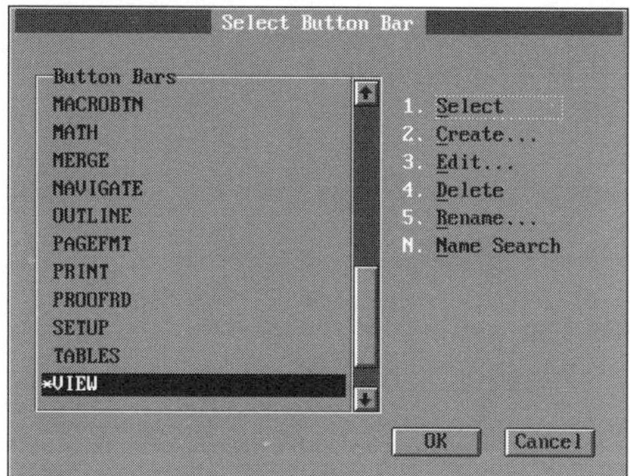

3. Select the button bar file in the Button Bars list box.
4. Choose the 1. Select command button.

Note that the default Button Bar for WordPerfect 6 is called WPMAIN.WPB.

Creating a button bar

WordPerfect makes it easy to create your own button bars:

1. If a button bar isn't already displayed on the screen, choose the Button Bar command on the View command to display it.
2. Choose the View menu and then select the Button Bar Setup command.
3. Choose the Select command on the Button Bar Setup cascading menu.
4. Choose the 2. Create option and then enter the name of the button bar (up to eight characters with no spaces, just like when naming a document). WordPerfect blanks out the currently selected button bar on the screen. As you add buttons to your new bar, they will begin to appear in the area that previously housed the buttons of the current button bar.

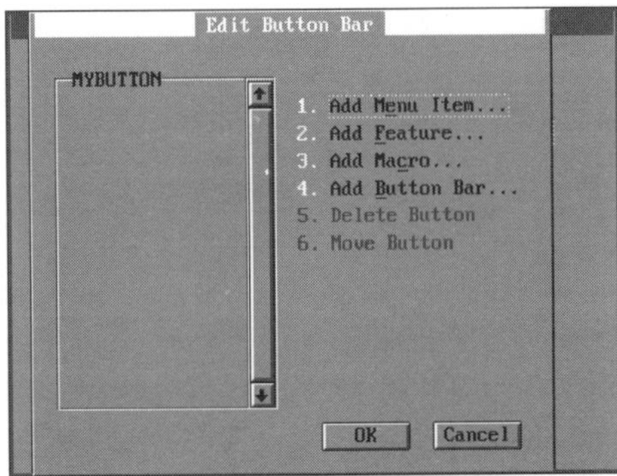

5. To add a button for a particular WordPerfect command, select the 1. Add Menu Item option and then choose the command you want to add on the pull-down menus (you can do this by pressing the arrow keys to highlight the command and pressing Enter or by clicking the command with the mouse).

6. To add a WordPerfect feature that isn't selected from the pull-down menus such as Back Tab, choose the 2. Add Feature option and then highlight the abbreviation for the feature in Feature Button List box and choose the Select button or press Enter.

7. To add a button that plays a macro you've created (see Macros), choose the 3. Add Macro option and then highlight the name of the macro in the Macro Button List box and choose Select or press Enter.

8. To add a button that selects another button bar, choose 4. Add Button Bar option and then name of the button bar in the Button Bar List box and choose Select or press Enter.

9. To delete a button from your button bar, highlight the name of the button in the Edit Button Bar list box and then choose 5. Delete Button option. To remove the button from the button, you must then choose the Yes button in the Delete confirmation dialog box that then appears.

10. To reposition a button in the button bar, highlight the button you want to move in Edit Button Bar list box and then choose the 6. Move Button option. The selected button will then disappear and the 6. Move Button option becomes 6. Paste Button. Highlight the button in the list that should immediately follow the button you're moving and then choose the 6. Paste Button option.

11. When your new button bar appears on the screen the way you want it, choose the OK button to return to the Select Button Bar dialog box.
12. To select your new button bar and display it on-screen, choose the 1. Select option. Otherwise, choose Cancel or press the Esc key.

More stuff

Button bars are for mouse maniacs only. However, they're so much fun and easy-to-use, they almost make it worth your while to start using the little rodents.

You can find more about this command in Chapter 19 of *WordPerfect 6 For Dummies.*

Cancel

Backs you out of the menu or dialog box options or discontinues a procedure before you get yourself into real trouble!

For function key freaks

(Cancel)

For mouse maniacs

If you have a two-button mouse, click both buttons at the same time. If you have a three-button mouse, click the middle mouse button.

More stuff

If you're an old (or young) WordPerfect 5.1 user, you've gotten used to F1 as the Cancel key and the Esc key as the repeat key. If you want to switch these key assignments back to the way they've always been up to now, you choose Setup on the File; then choose Environment and select K. WordPerfect 5.1 Keyboard (F1 = Cancel).

You can find more about this command in Chapter 3 of *WordPerfect For Dummies* (and *WordPerfect 6 For Dummies*).

Center Page

Centers the text on a page vertically between the top and the bottom margins.

Menus

To center to single page:

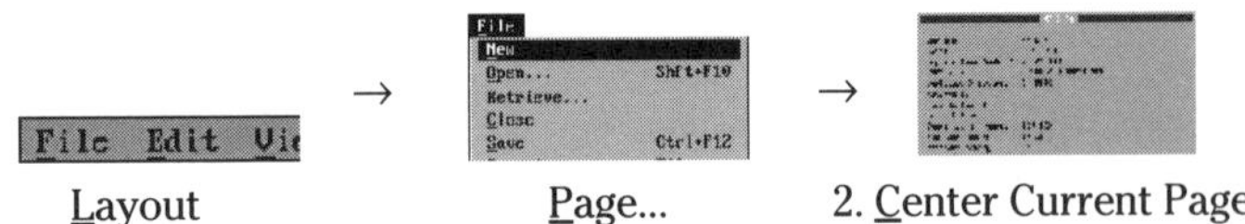

Layout → Page... → 2. Center Current Page

To center to all pages from the current page on:

Layout → Page.. → 3. Center Pages

For function key freaks

To center to single page:

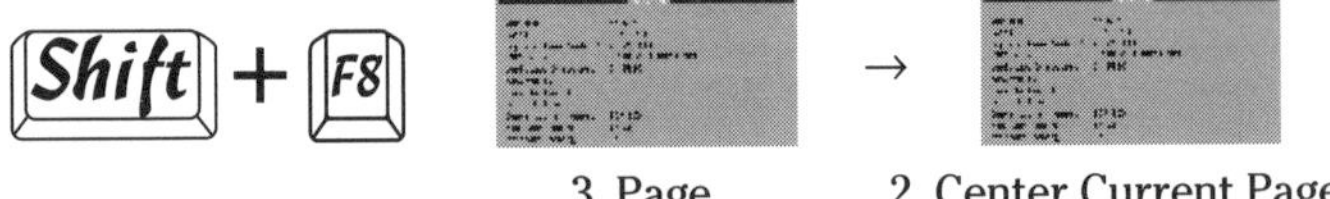

Shift + F8 → 3. Page... → 2. Center Current Page

To center to all pages from the current page on:

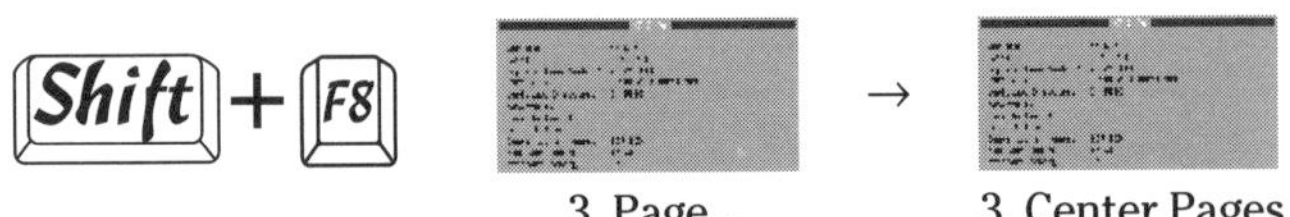

Shift + F8 → 3. Page... → 3. Center Pages

Secret codes

When you choose the Center Current Page option, WordPerfect puts a `[Cntr Cur Pg:On]` secret code at the top of the page. When you choose the Center Pages option, the program puts a `[Cntr Pgs:On]` at the top of the current page. If you then turn off the center page feature on a subsequent page in the document, WordPerfect puts in a `[Cntr Pgs:Off]` secret code at the top of that page.

More stuff

To see the text of a page or group of pages centered vertically on the screen, you have to have WordPerfect in page display mode (see Page Mode).

In WordPerfect 6, Auto Code Placement automatically locates the secret code for centering pages at the very top of the current page, regardless of where your cursor is on that page.

If, when you use the 3. Center Pages option to center all pages from the current one on, you reach a page where the text shouldn't be centered vertically, turn off the page centering by positioning the cursor somewhere on that page and then choosing 3. Center Pages option in the Page Format dialog box to remove the X from its check box; then choose OK.

You can find more information on this command in Chapter 10 of *WordPerfect For Dummies* (and Chapter 11 of *WordPerfect 6 For Dummies*).

Center (Text)

Centers a line of text horizontally between the left and right margins.

Menus

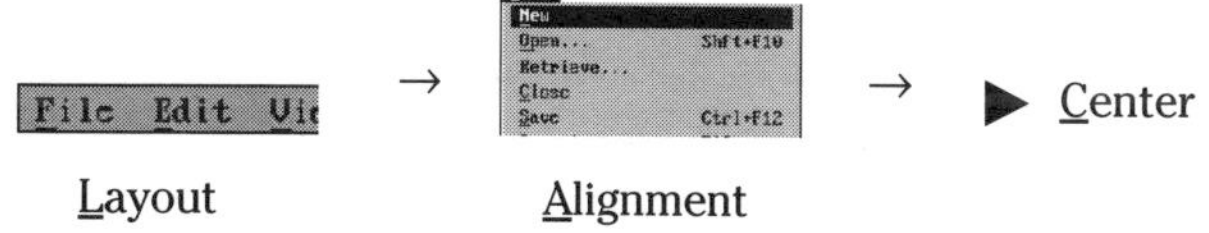

Layout → Alignment → ▶ Center

For function key freaks

(Center)

Centering a line of text

To center a line of text before you type it, position the cursor point at the beginning of the line whose text is to be centered. Choose the Alignment command on the Layout menu and then choose Center (or, better yet, press the Shift+F6 (Center) key). Type your text and then press Enter.

As soon as you press Enter, the cursor returns to the left margin and centering is turned off.

You can center text on a specific column position or tab stop on a line. To do this operation, press the spacebar or Tab key until you reach the place where the text is to be centered; then choose the Alignment command on the Layout menu and Center (or just press the Shift+F6 (Center) key).

Centering a block of text

To center more than one line of text, mark the lines as a block and then choose the Alignment command on the Layout menu and Center or press the Shift+F6 (Center) key.

Secret Codes

If you centered the title *My Life and Welcome to It!* as you typed it, when you open Reveal Codes, you see

```
[Cntr on Mar]My Life and Welcome to It![HRt]
```

On the other hand, if you had marked this title as a block and then centered it afterward, you'd see

```
[+Just]My Life and Welcome to It![HRt][-Just]
```

When you position the cursor on the first [+Just] code it would expand to [Just:Cntr]. When you position the cursor on the second [—Just] code, it would expand to [Just:Left].

More stuff

You can also center text by changing the justification of the document from normal left to center justification. For more information on this method, see Justification.

You can find more information on this command in Chapter 9 of *WordPerfect For Dummies* (and Chapter 10 of *WordPerfect 6 For Dummies*).

Columns

Allows you to lay out text in multiple columns in a document. You can choose between newspaper columns, where text flows up and down each column, or parallel columns, where text flows across the page.

Menus

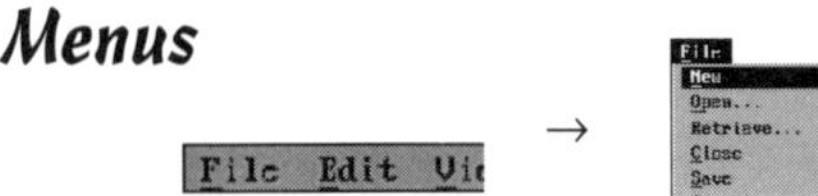

Layout → Columns...

For function key freaks

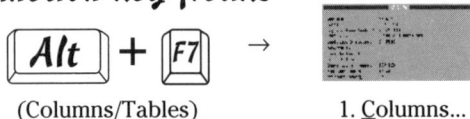

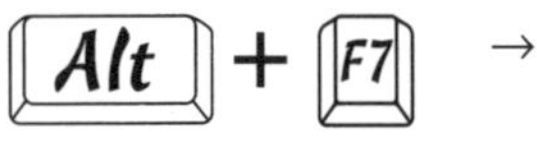

(Columns/Tables) → 1. Columns...

For mouse maniacs

If necessary, display the ribbon by choosing Ribbon on the View menu and then click the Column button on the ribbon (the one with 1 Col in it) to open its drop-down list box; then click the number of (newspaper) columns you want to create (between 2 and 24).

To turn off newspaper columns later in the document from the ribbon, click 1 Col in the Column button drop-down list box.

The Text Columns dialog box

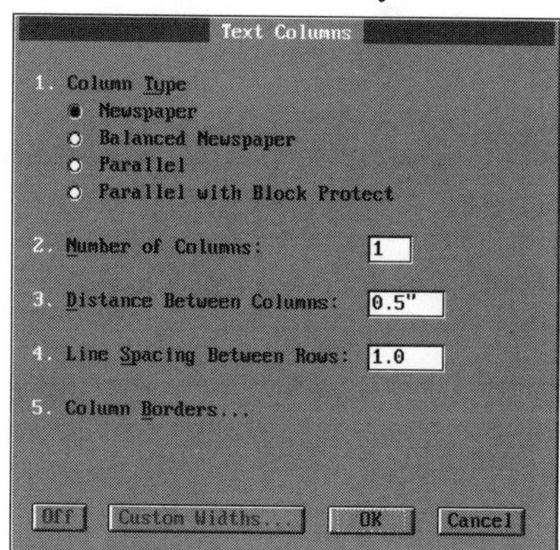

Option or button	*Function*
1. Column Type	Choose 1. Newspaper when you want the text to be read up and down with the columns across the page, 2. Balanced Newspaper when you want WordPerfect to create even newspaper columns, 3. Parallel when you want the text to read across and then down the columns, or 4. Parallel with Block Protect when you want parallel columns that always stay together on a page.
2. Number of Columns	Selects the number of newspaper or parallel columns to create (between 2 and 32).
3. Distance Between	Changes the distance between columns Columns(0.5" by default).
4. Line Spacing Between Rows	Changes the line spacing between rows (single spacing). You change the spacing in half line increments as in 1.5 for line-and-a-half spacing between the rows of text set in columns.

5. Column Borders...	Allows you to add a border between (the default) or around your columns in the Create Column Border dialog box (see Borders).
6. Custom Widths	Allows you to modify the widths and/or the space between specific newspaper or parallel columns (by default, WordPerfect creates uniform columns with the same amount of space between them).

Turning off columns

1. Position the cursor at the place where the text should be set once again in a single column.
2. Choose Columns on the Layout menu.
3. Choose the Off command button.

Entering text in columns

You can enter text before you define the columns or after. Usually, when using the newspaper columns, you'll find it easier to type the text first in the normal single-column layout and then define the newspapers columns and reset the text. If you create columns before you type the text of newspaper columns, just keep in mind that you press Ctrl+Enter (Hard Page) when you need to break a column early so that you can start entering at top of the next column.

With parallel columns, you'll usually want to define the columns first before you type the text. When you complete an entry in one column, you need to press Ctrl+Enter (Hard Page) to advance to the next column to the right. When you enter the text for the last column in a row, pressing Ctrl+Enter (Hard Page) returns the cursor to the first parallel column below. If you want to insert a blank column, press Ctrl+Enter (Hard Page) twice in a row.

Editing Columns

When you create text columns in your document, the status bar changes to include a Col indicator, which tells you the column position of the cursor. To move the cursor in columns and edit text, you use the following keystrokes:

Keystrokes	*Function*
Ctrl+Enter	Breaks a column and advances to the next column.
Ctrl+Home, →	Moves the cursor to the next column to the right.
Ctrl+Home, ←	Moves the cursor to the next column to the left.

Home, ↑	Moves the cursor to the top of the current column.
Home, ↓	Moves the cursor to the bottom of the current column.
Ctrl+End	Deletes from the cursor to the end of the line within the current column.
Ctrl+PgDn	Deletes from the cursor to the end of the current column.

Secret codes

Suppose that you've set the text on the page in two balanced newspaper columns. If you open Reveal Codes, you'll see two [Col Def] secret codes, one where two-column format begins and the second where it stops. If you position the cursor on the first [Col Def] code, it expands to

```
[Col Def:Newspaper with Balance:2]
```

If you then position the cursor on the second [Col Def] code, it becomes

```
[Col Def:Off]
```

More stuff

Instead of trying to deal with parallel columns and the Ctrl+Enter (Hard Page) keystrokes, try using tables (see Tables) instead. On the whole, they're not only more versatile but a lot easier to deal with.

You can find more information on this command in Chapter 12 of *WordPerfect 6 For Dummies.*

Comments

Adds comments to your text that will appear in a text box on-screen but will not be printed as part of the document.

Menus

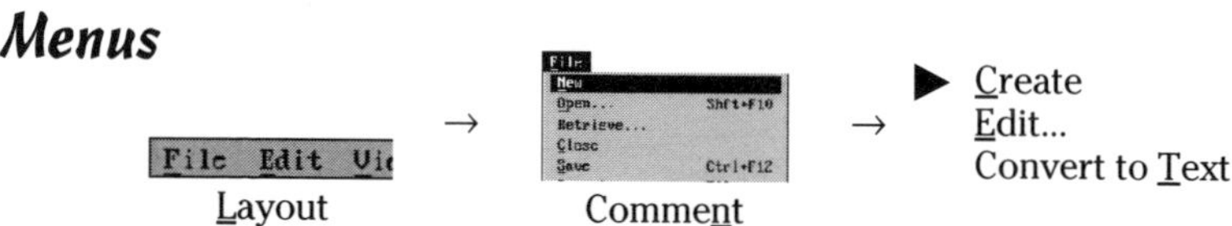

For function key freaks

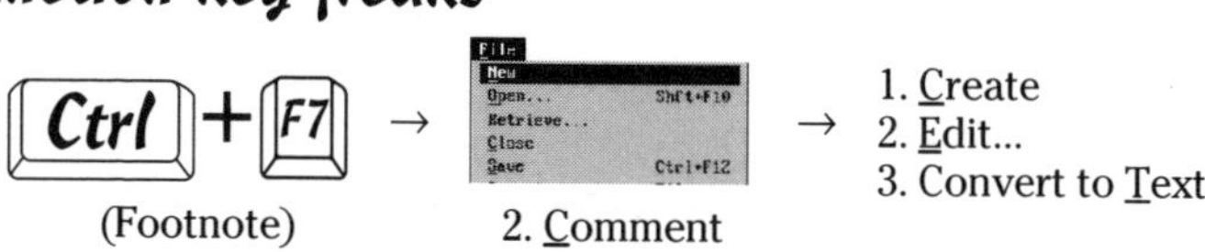

Creating a comment

1. Place your cursor in the document where you want the comment to appear.
2. Choose Comment from the Layout menu and then choose Create on the cascading menu (or press Ctrl+F7 (Footnote); then select the 2. Comment and 1. Create options).
3. Type the text of comment in the blank document editing window and then press the F7 (Exit) key to return to your document.

Editing a comment

1. Position your cursor just after the comment you want to edit.
2. Choose Comment from Layout menu, choose Edit on the cascading menu (or press Ctrl+F7 (Footnote), and then select the 2. Comment and 2. Edit options).
3. Edit the text of the comment as you would any other text; then press F7 (Exit) to return to your document.

Converting a comment to document text

1. Place your cursor just after the comment you want to convert to text.
2. Choose Comment from the Layout menu, choose Convert to Text on the cascading menu (or press Ctrl+F7 (Footnote), and then select the 2. Comment and 3. Convert to Text options).

Converting document text to a comment

1. Mark the text you want to convert as a block (see Block (Text) for details).
2. Choose Comment from the Layout menu, choose Create (or press Ctrl+F7 (Footnote), and then select the 2. Comment and 1. Create options).

Secret codes

When you create a comment in your document, WordPerfect inserts the secret code

```
[Comment]
```

at the cursor's position. Unlike a lot of other secrets codes, however, when you put the cursor on this code in the Reveal Codes window, it does not expand in any way.

More stuff

You can locate comments in your document by searching for its [Comment] secret code (see Search and Replace).

If you add a comment to your document but it doesn't show up on the document screen, someone has turned off the display of comments in WordPerfect. To turn them back on, choose Screen Setup on the View menu, choose 4. Window Options and 6. Display Comments to put an X back into its check box, and then choose OK.

Compare Documents

Compares the copy of the document in the current document editing window with the version of the document saved on disk. Text added to the document on-screen that no longer exists in the document on disk gets redlined, while text deleted from the document on the screen that still existing in the document on disk is copied to the version on-screen as strikeout text (see Redline/Strikeout).

Menus

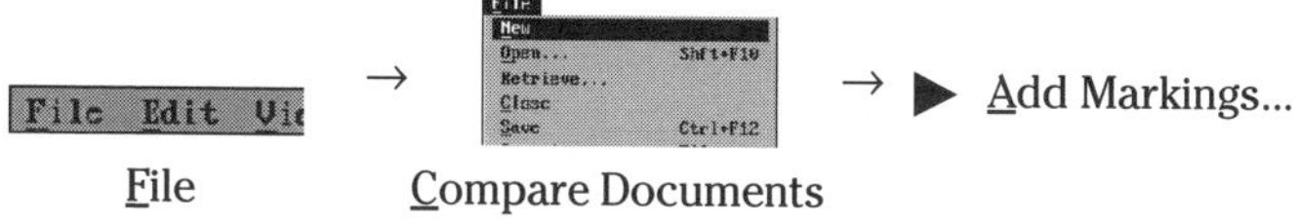

File → Compare Documents → ▶ Add Markings...

For function key freaks

Alt + F5 (Mark Text) → 8. Add Markings...

The Compare Documents dialog box

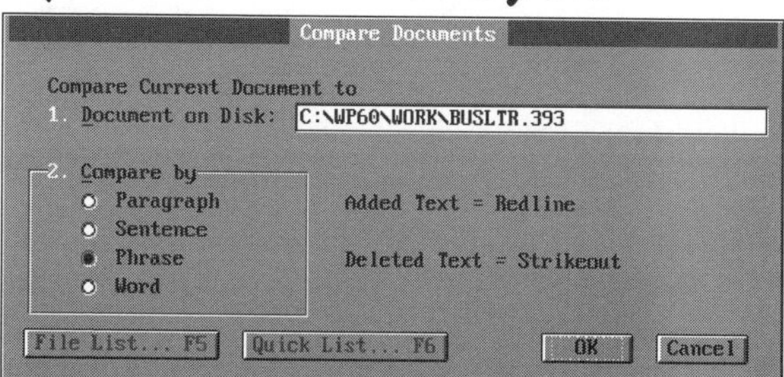

Option or Button	*Function*
1. Document on Disk	Specifies which file on disk should be compared to the one in the current document window. By default, WordPerfect suggests the name of the same document you're working on (assuming that you've saved the file at least once). If you don't want to use this file in the comparison and need help finding the file you do want to use, choose this option and then select the File List... F5 button or press F5 (see List Files for details).
2. Compare by	Specifies how WordPerfect should compares the documents. Choose 1. Paragraph to compare them paragraph by paragraph, 2. Sentence to compare them sentence by sentence, 3. Phrase to compare them phrase by phrase (the default — WordPerfect considers a phrase to be any text between two marker such as punctuation, hard returns, hard pages breaks, and the like), or 4. Word to compare them word by word.

Removing the redline and strikeout markings

After WordPerfect finishes comparing the document on-screen with the file you specified on disk, you can remove the redline markings and the strikeout text.

Select the Compare Documents command on the File menu, choose Remove Markings on the cascading menu (or press Alt+F5 (Mark), and then select the 9. Remove Redline/Strikeout option). Select the Yes button in the dialog box asking you to confirm the deletion of all redline markings and strikeout text.

Secret codes

When you open the Reveal Codes window after comparing documents, text added in the document appear surrounded by a pair of [Redln On] and [Redln Off] secret codes. Text deleted from the document on-screen that still exists in the one on disk is surrounded by a pair of [StkOut On] and [StkOut Off] codes.

More stuff

If a section of the document on disk has been moved, WordPerfect marks the relocated text with strikeout and inserts the message `THE FOLLOWING TEXT WAS MOVED` before the text and the message `THE PRECEDING TEXT WAS MOVED` after the text.

Conditional End of Page

Tells WordPerfect to keep a specified number of lines together on one page no matter how your editing changes affect the paging of the document.

Menus

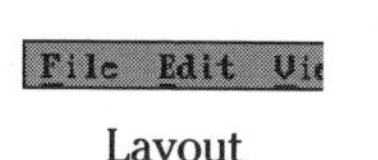 → 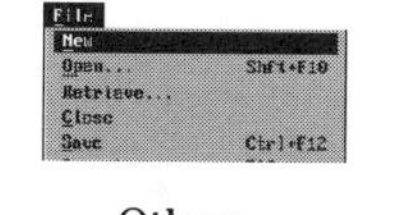 → 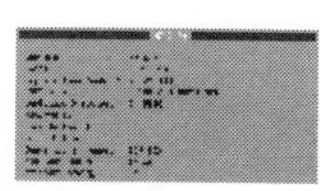

Layout | Other... | 2. Conditional End of Page Number of Lines to Keep Together:

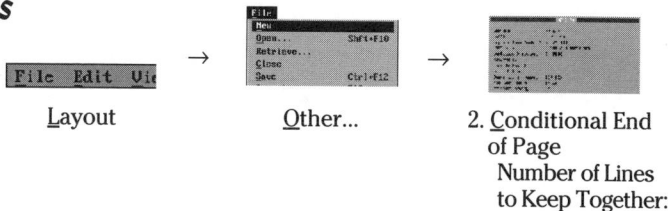

For function key freaks

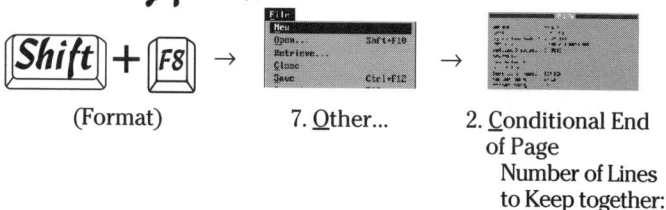

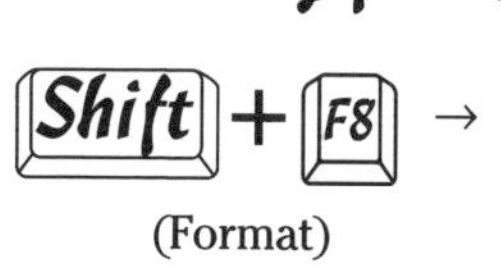 →  → 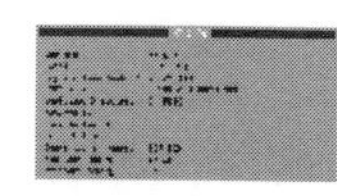

(Format) | 7. Other... | 2. Conditional End of Page Number of Lines to Keep together:

Using Conditional End of Page

1. Move the cursor to the beginning of first line of the group you want to stay keep together on a page.
2. Choose the Other command on the Layout menu (or press Shift+F8 (Format) and choose 7. Other.
3. Select the 2. Conditional End of Page option to put an X in its check box and select the Number of Lines to Keep Together text box.
4. Enter the number of lines to stay together in Number of Lines to Keep Together text box and press Enter. When counting lines, be sure to include any blank lines between the ones you want to stay together.
5. Select the OK button or press Enter.

Secret codes

Suppose that you want to make sure that a single-line section heading, the blank line below it, and all five lines of the first paragraph of that section to stay together on a page, so you select the Conditional End of Page feature and designate 7 as the number of lines. When you open Reveal Codes, you see the `[Condl EOP]` secret code at the beginning of the section heading. When you put the cursor on this code, it expands to `[Condl EOP:7]`.

Convert Case

Changes the text you've marked as a block to all uppercase, all lowercase, or initial capital letters.

Menus

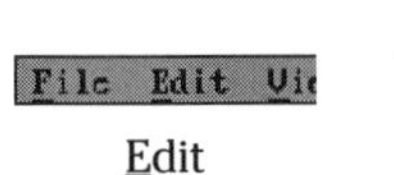

Edit

→

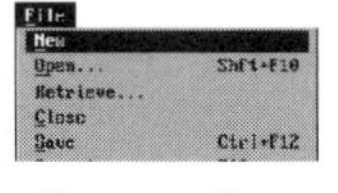

Convert Case

→

▶ Upper
Lower
Initial Caps

For function key freaks

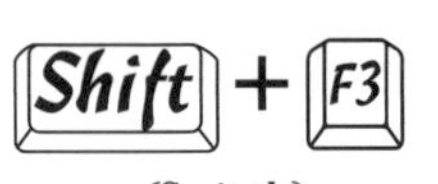

(Switch)

→

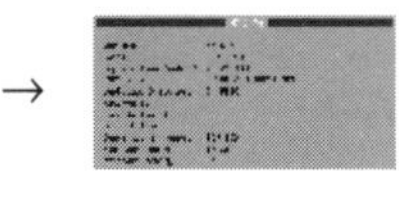

→

1. Uppercase
2. Lowercase
3. Initial Caps

More stuff

Before you can use this command to convert the case of existing text, you must first mark it as a block (see Block (Text) for details).

You can find more information on this command in Chapter 8 of *WordPerfect For Dummies* (and Chapter 9 of *WordPerfect 6 For Dummies*).

Cursor Movement

Before you edit the text of your document, you need to position the cursor in the correct place in the text. Note that WordPerfect restricts cursor movement to existing text in a document and never lets you move it beyond the last character in the document.

Cursor movement with the keyboard

WordPerfect offers a variety of ways to move the cursor with the keyboard as shown in this table:

Keystrokes	*Cursor Movement*
←	Next character or space to the left.
→	Next character or space to the right.
Ctrl+←	Beginning of the next word to the left.
Ctrl+→	Beginning of the next word to the right.
Ctrl+↑	Beginning of the current or previous paragraph.
Ctrl+↓	Beginning of the next paragraph.
Home, ↑, or — (gray minus key on the numeric keypad)	Top of the current screenful of text.
Home, ↓, or + (gray plus on the numeric keypad)	Bottom of the current screenful of text.
Home, ←	Left edge of the current screen or beginning of the current line.
Home, →	Right edge of the current screen or the end of the current line.
Home, Home, ←	Beginning of the line just after any secret codes.
Home, Home, Home, ←	Beginning of the line just before any secret codes.
Home, Home, → or End	End of the current line (off screen, if necessary).
Home, Home, ↑	Beginning of the document.
Home, Home, Home, ↑	Beginning of the document in front any secret codes you add to the document.
Home, Home, ↓	End of the document.
Ctrl+Home, ↑	Top of the current page.
Ctrl+Home, ↓	Bottom of the current page.
PgUp	Top of the previous page.
PgDn	Top of the next page.
Ctrl+Home, *character*	Next occurrence of the *character* you enter after pressing the Ctrl+Home (Go To) key. For instance, pressing Ctrl+Home and typing a period (.) moves the cursor to the end of the current sentence.
Ctrl+Home, *page number*, Enter	Top of the page with the specified *page number*.
Ctrl+Home, Ctrl+Home	Cursor position before the last cursor-movement command.

For mouse maniacs

If you use the mouse, you can reposition the cursor in the document text by placing the mouse pointer on the character or space and clicking the left mouse button.

More stuff

In WordPerfect, the shape of the cursor depends upon which display mode you're in. If you're in text mode (see Text Mode), the cursor appears as a blinking underscore under the character or space. If you're in graphics or page mode (see Graphics Mode or Page Mode), the cursor appears as a flashing vertical bar in front of the character or space.

You can find more information on this command in Chapter 2 of *WordPerfect For Dummies* (and *WordPerfect 6 For Dummies*).

Cut, Copy, and Paste

Allow you to move or copy blocks of text to new places in the same document to different documents open in other document windows.

Menus

To cut the marked block of text and copy it to Clipboard; then paste it elsewhere in a single procedure:

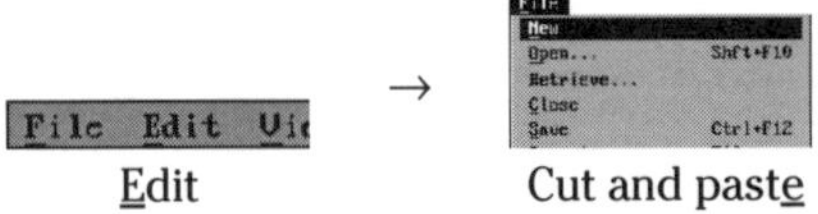

Edit → Cut and paste

To copy the marked block of text to the Clipboard; then paste it elsewhere in a single procedure:

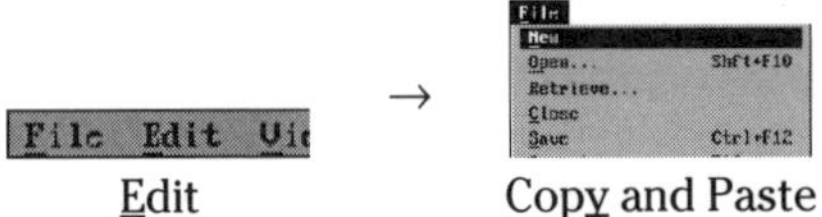

Edit → Copy and Paste

To just cut the marked block of text and copy it to the Clipboard:

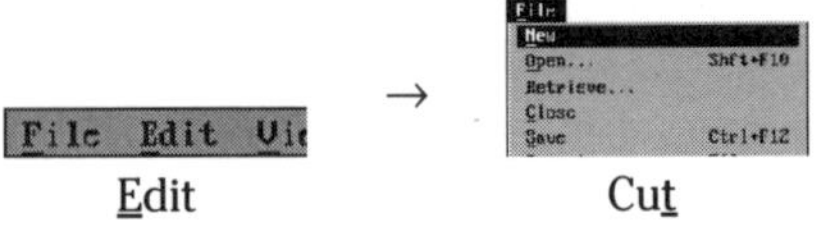

Edit → Cut

To just copy the marked block of text to the Clipboard:

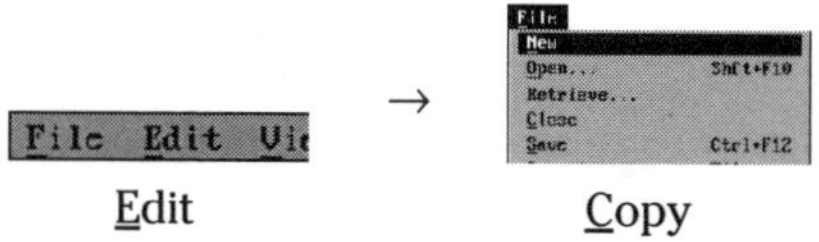

Edit → Copy

To paste the block of text stored in the Clipboard:

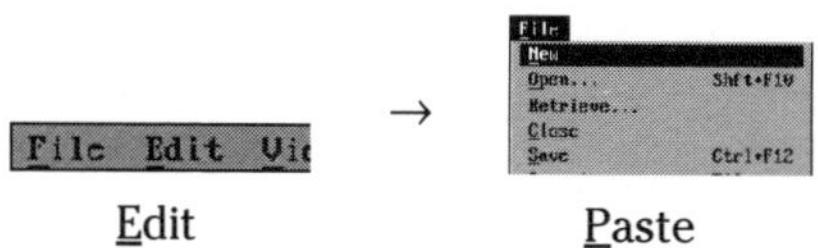

Edit → Paste

WordPerfect 6 employs a number of keystroke shortcuts for the various cut, copy, and paste procedures that you can use instead of the pull-down menus: Ctrl+Del to cut and paste a block of text, Ctrl+Ins to copy and paste a block of text, Ctrl+X to cut the block, Ctrl+C to copy the block, and Ctrl+V to paste the contents of the Clipboard.

For function key freaks

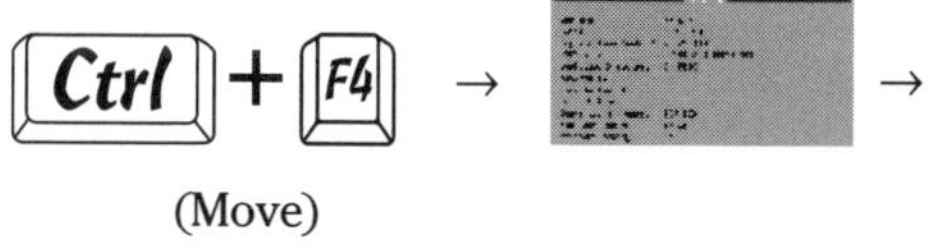

(Move)

Using Cut, Copy, and Paste

In WordPerfect 6, the procedure for moving document text is called *cut and paste*, while the procedure for copying text is called (what else) *copy and paste*. Both procedures use a special area of memory called the *Clipboard* that temporarily holds the information to be moved or copied.

When using Cut, Copy, and Paste, keep in mind the Clipboard normally holds only one block of text at a time. Therefore, that any new block that you copy to the Clipboard completely replaces the one that was there already. The only way to add information to the Clipboard is with the To Clipboard option of the Append command (see Append for details). However, because the block that you place in the Clipboard stays there until you replace it with another one or you exit WordPerfect, you can use the Paste command to copy it over and over again in the same or a different document.

To move or copy a block in one operation

1. Mark the block of text you want to move (cut) or copy (see Block (Text) for details).
2. To move the block, choose the Cut and Paste command on the Edit menu (or press the Ctrl+F4 (Move) key and choose the 1. Cut and Paste option) To copy the block, choose the Copy and Paste command on the Edit menu (or press the Ctrl+F4 (Move) key and choose the 2. Copy and Paste option) instead. Note that if you choose Cut and Paste, the highlighted text disappears from the document and in both cases, the message `Move cursor; press Enter to retrieve` appears on the status bar.
3. Move the cursor to the place in the document where you want to paste the text and then press the Enter key. If you want to move or copy the text to a different document, press the Shift+F3 (Switch) key or the Home, 0 (Switch To) key to select the window containing the document; then position the cursor at the proper place in its text before you press the Enter key.

If you decide that you don't want to complete the cut and paste or copy and paste operation that you've started, press the Esc key instead of Enter to terminate the operation. Note, however, that the block you just cut or copied to the Clipboard remains there even when you use this option so that you can later paste the block simply by positioning the cursor in the text and selecting the Paste command on the Edit menu (Ctrl+V).

To move or copy text in separate operations

WordPerfect 6 does not require you to cut and paste or copy and paste a block of text in a single operation. If you prefer, you can mark the block and then cut it with the Cut command (Ctrl+X) or copy it with the Copy command (Ctrl+C) on the Edit menu as one operation. Then, later, when you're ready you can move the cursor to the proper place in the document and paste it with the Paste command on the Edit menu (Ctrl+V).

More stuff

If you ever goof up and cut a block that you'd meant to copy, just go ahead and paste the block without moving the cursor (either by pressing the Enter key if you choose Cut and Paste or, otherwise, by choosing the Paste command on the Edit menu). After restoring the cut block in this manner, move the cursor to the place where you need a copy of the block and just choose the Paste command on the Edit menu (Ctrl+V) a second time.

Date

Puts today's date into your document either as text or as a secret code that WordPerfect updates each time you open the document.

Menus

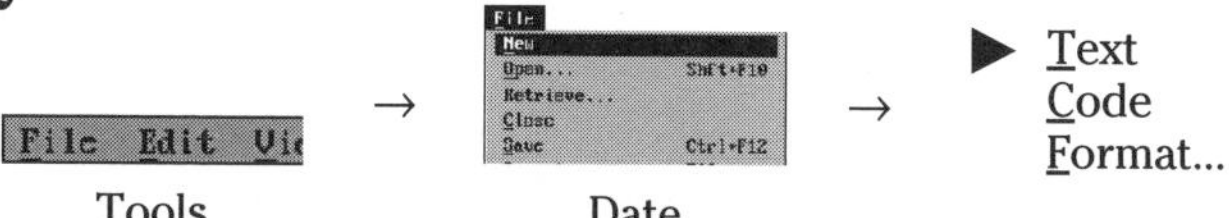

Tools → Date → ▶ Text / Code / Format...

For function key freaks

(Date) →

1. Insert Date Text
2. Insert Date Code
3. Date Format...

Inserting the date

To insert the current date as text (that doesn't change unless you get in there and edit it), Position the cursor where you want to the date to appear. Choose Date from the Tools menu and then choose Text. Or, press Shift+F5 (Date) and then choose the 1. Insert Date Text option.

To insert the date as secret code that WordPerfect automatically keeps up-to-date for you, Position the cursor where you want to place the secret date code. Choose Date from the Tools menu and then choose Code. Or, press Shift+F5 (Date) and then choose 2. Insert Date Code.

To select a new date format choose Date from the Tools menu and then choose Format. Or, press Shift+F5 (Date) and then choose 3. Date Format. Choose the radio button for the predefined format (between 1 and 8) in the Date Formats dialog box that best fits your needs. Then choose OK or press Enter.

Secret codes

When you select the Date Code command, WordPerfect inserts the secret code `[Date]` in the text at the cursor's position. If you position the cursor on this code in the Reveal Codes screen, WordPerfect expands the code to display the current date (using whatever format is currently in effect).

If you select a new date format, WordPerfect inserts a `[Date Fmt]` in the document at the cursor's position. If you position the cursor on this code in Reveal Codes, WordPerfect expands the secret code to display the codes used in the selected date format.

More stuff

Changing the date format for a document has no effect on the dates that you've already inserted into the text with the Date Text and Date Code commands.

Delete (Text)

WordPerfect provides loads of ways to get rid of text. The easiest way to delete text is to mark it as a block — see Block (Text) for details — and then press the Del or Backspace key. However, you can also delete text with the keyboard, using any of the following keystrokes:

Keystroke	*Deletion*
Backspace	Character to the left of the cursor.
Del	Character or space the cursor is on.
Ctrl+Backspace	The word cursor is on, including the space after.
Home, Backspace	From the cursor left to the beginning of a word.
Home, Del	From the cursor right to the end of a word, including the space after.
Ctrl+End	From the cursor to the end of the current line.
Ctrl+PgDn	From the cursor to the end of the current page.

Directory Tree

Enables you to choose the directory you want to use by selecting it from a *tree* diagram, showing the structure of the current drive with subdirectories appearing as branches of each directory above it. Don't forget the Undelete (Esc) command at those times when you make a boo-boo and blow away text that you shouldn't have blown away.

The Directory Tree dialog box

To display Directory Tree dialog box, choose the Directory Tree... F8 button (this button appears in a few different file-related dialog boxes, most noticeably in the Specify File Manager List dialog box — see File Manager).

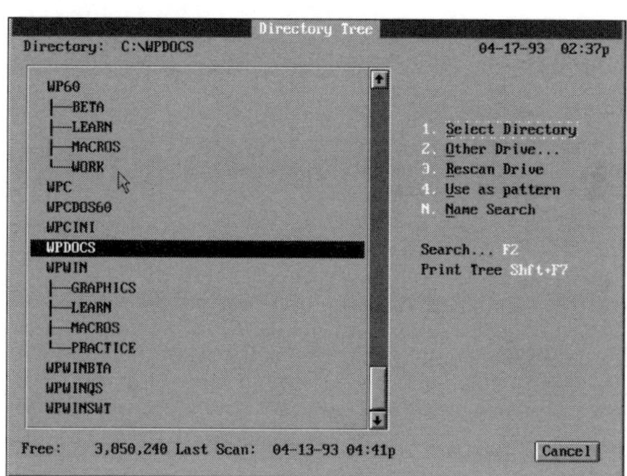

Option or Button	*Function*
1. Select Directory	Displays the File Manager dialog box showing the files in the directory currently highlighted in the Directory Tree dialog box (see File Manager for information on what you can do with these files).
2. Other Drive...	Displays the Other Drive dialog box where you can select the letter of the new drive you want to use.
3. Rescan Drive	Reads the selected drive and updates the directory tree shown in the Directory list box.
4. Use as pattern	Inserts the complete directory path, including the directory currently selected in the Directory Tree dialog box into the Specify File Manager List dialog box.
N. Name Search	Displays an empty text box where you can type the first few characters of the name of the directory you want to select in the Directory Tree dialog box.

Search... F2	Displays a Search for Directory dialog box where you can type the directory name (all or part of it) as the search text that you want WordPerfect to locate. To search backward from the currently highlighted directory, choose the Backward Search check box. To find the first occurrence of the search text, choose the Search F2 button or press F2. To find the next occurrence of the search, press F2 twice in a row.
Print Tree Shft+F7	Prints the tree diagram with all of the directories on the current drive.

More stuff

The Directory Tree provides the most visual means of selecting the directory that you want to work with because it diagrams the relationship between directories and their subdirectories. After the Directory Tree dialog box is displayed, you can use the Name Search or the Search... F2 option to quickly find the location of the desired directory in the tree. See File Manager for more information on what you can do with a directory and its contents after you've found it!

Display Modes

Enables you to choose between the faster text mode (which doesn't show fonts and graphics as they will print) and the slower graphics and page (which both show fonts and graphics more or less as they will print).

Menus

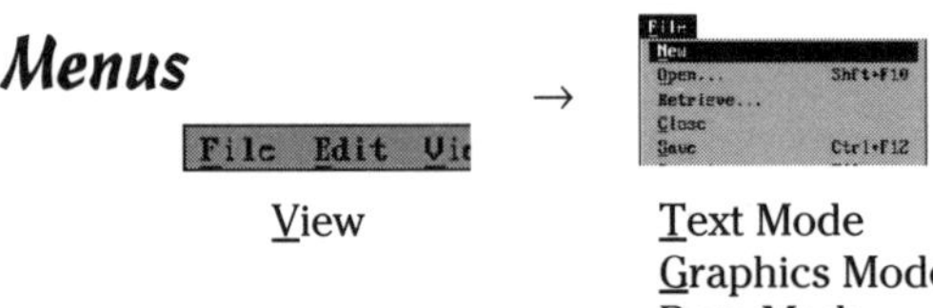

View → Text Mode
Graphics Mode
Page Mode

For function key freaks

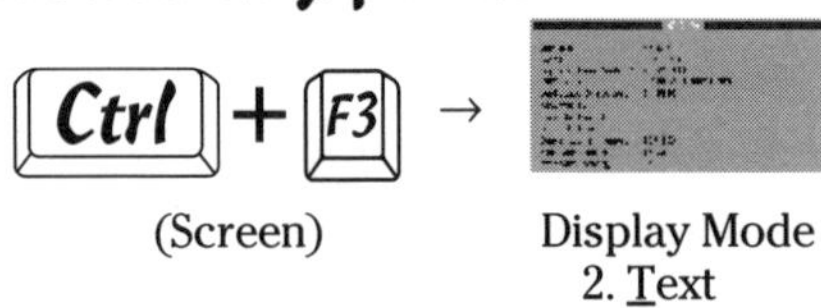

(Screen) → Display Mode
2. Text
3. Graphics
4. Page

More stuff

Choose page mode over graphics mode when you need to see the page's margins and any special page elements like page numbers, headers, footers, and footnotes. Note that even when these special page elements are visible on your screen, you still can't edit them (although you can edit anything in the body of the document in either graphics or page mode). Also, when WordPerfect is in graphics or page mode, you can use the Zoom command on the View menu to zoom in and out on the document page. When the program is in text mode, you can't zoom in and out.

Document Information

Gives you oodles of statistics about your document, such as how many characters, words, lines, sentences, and paragraphs it contains, as well as the average word length and average number of words per sentence.

Menus

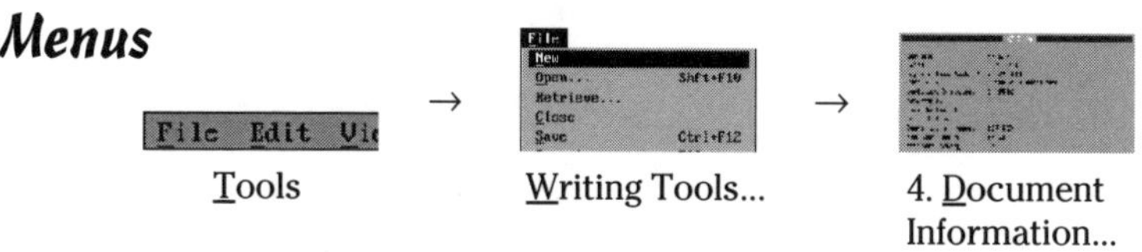

Tools → Writing Tools... → 4. Document Information...

For function key freaks

(Writing Tools) → 4. Document Information...

More stuff

To get information about a particular part of a document, mark the section as a block — see Block (Text) for details — before you open the Writing Tools dialog box and choose the Document Information command (as indicated earlier).

Document Summary

The document summary crams together a bunch of information that you can use later on to identify the document for editing. This feature is very helpful when you're dealing with lots and lots of documents that use similar names. If you add document summaries to all of them, you can use this information with the Look or Find feature in the File Manager (see File Manager) to locate the one you need to edit.

Menus

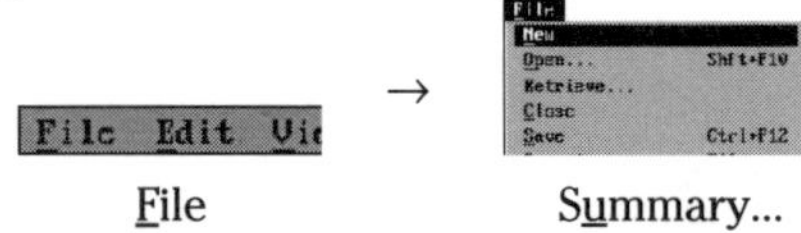

File → Summary...

The Document Summary dialog box

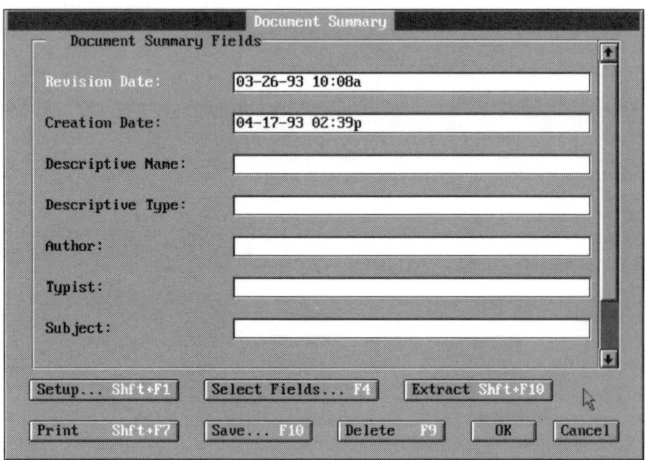

Option or Button	*Function*
Revision Date	Indicates the last date the document was revised. WordPerfect automatically enters the date you created the document summary in this text box. If the revision date is incorrect, enter the correct date here (following the format 01/11/94 or 01-11-94).
Creation Date	Indicates the date the document was first created. WordPerfect automatically enters the date you created the document summary in this text box. If the date is incorrect, enter the correct date here (following the format 01/11/94 or 01-11-94).
Descriptive Name	Allows you to enter a long name for the file. You can list and sort files by their descriptive names in the File Manager by choosing the Descriptive Names and Type radio button in the File Manager Setup dialog box.

Descriptive Type	Enables you to enter a classification or category for the document, such as *legal brief* or *contract*. You can enter a default descriptive type to be used in each document summary (see Setup... Shift+F1). You can list and sort files by descriptive type in the File List window of the WordPerfect File Manager.
Author	Identifies the document's author. Use Extract Shft+F10 to enter the name or initials of the author from the last document summary you created.
Typist	Identifies the document's typist. Use Extract Shft+F10 to enter the name or initials of the typist from the last document summary you created.
Subject	Identifies the subject of the document. Use Extract Shft+F10 to enter the first part of the document text that follows the word or phrase identified as the Subject Search Text (*RE:* is used by default — to change, see Setup... Shft+F1).
Account	Identifies the account number for the document.
Keywords	Enables you to add terms that you can later search for with the File Manager's Find feature when trying to locate the document for editing.
Abstract	Enables you to add a brief synopsis of the document's contents. Choose Extract Shft+F10 to enter the first part of the document text as the document summary abstract.
Setup... Shft+F1	Enables you to change various document summary setup options, including modifying the Subject Search Text (*RE:* is used by default), adding a default descriptive type, and having WordPerfect automatically display the Document Summary screen whenever you first save a new document.
Select Fields...F4	Enables you to modify which fields (tags) appear in the document summary screen. You can delete default fields or rearrange them as well as add new fields.

Extract Shft+F10	Extracts the Author, Typist, and Subject information from the last document summary you created and the Abstract information from the first part of the document's text.
Print Shft+F7	Prints the document summary information.
Save... F10	Saves the document summary as a separate file (after you indicate the filename)
Delete F9	Deletes the document summary from the current document.

More stuff

You can edit a document summary from anywhere in the document by choosing the Summary command on the File menu. You can use the Find command in the File Manager to search documents quickly with the summary information. You can also view document summary information at the top of the document by choosing the 3. Look command in the File Manager (see File Manager for details).

Drag and Drop (Text)

Enables you mouse maniacs to move or copy text marked as a block to a new place in the document by dragging the block to its new position and then dropping it in place by releasing the mouse button.

Moving and copying a block with drag and drop

To move a block of text with drag and drop, select (highlight) the text you want to move as a block either by clicking (remember that you can select the current word by double-clicking it, the sentence by triple-clicking it, and the paragraph by quadruple-clicking it) or dragging through it. Or, block it with cursor movement keys — see Block (Text) for details. Then position the mouse pointer somewhere within the highlighted block and hold down the mouse button. Drag the mouse pointer (a small rectangle appears under it as you drag, indicating that drag and drop is happening) to the place in the document where the block is to move to and then release the mouse button to insert the block of text in its new position in the document.

To copy text rather than move it, follow the preceding procedure except hold down the Ctrl key as you click on the marked block and begin to drag it.

If you hold down the Alt key as you drag a block of text, WordPerfect not only moves the blocked text when you release the mouse button but also keeps it blocked.

Double Indent

Indents the current paragraph one tab stop on both the left and right side without making you go through the trouble of changing the left and right margins in the document.

Menus

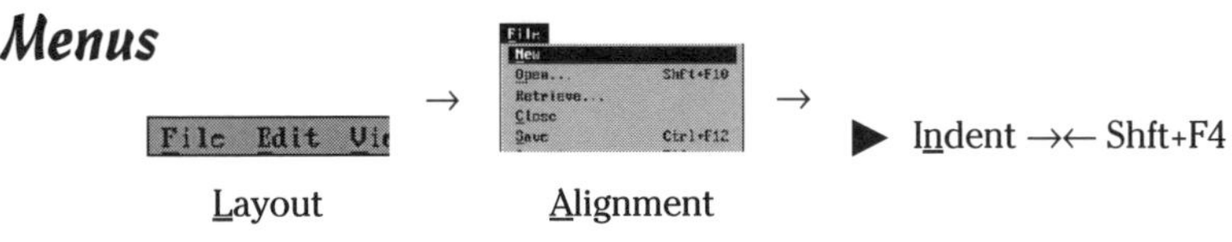

Layout → Alignment → ▶ Indent →← Shft+F4

For function key freaks

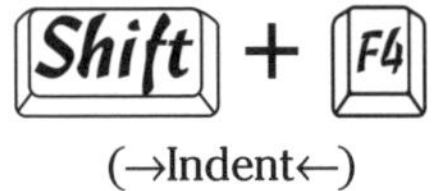

(→Indent←)

Using Double Indent

Double Indent enables you to indent a paragraph of text on both sides (thus it is also known as a left/right indent) in a single command. Before you use this command, you must position the cursor at the beginning of the paragraph, and WordPerfect must be in Insert Mode (make sure Typeover has replaced the font on the filename on the status bar).

Secret codes

When you use Double Indent to set off a paragraph on the left and right sides, WordPerfect puts a `[Lft/Rgt Indent]` secret code in the text at the cursor's position.

Envelopes

Enables you to quickly address an envelope for the letter in the current document editing window. When you use Envelope, WordPerfect locates the mailing address in the letter and automatically copies it to the Mailing Address part of the Envelope dialog box for you.

Menus

Layout → Envelope...

For function key freaks

(Envelope)

For mouse maniacs

If necessary, select the WPMAIN button bar by choosing the Button Bar Setup command on the View menu and then choosing the Select command on the cascading menu. Highlight WPMAIN in the Button Bar's list box and then choose the 1. Select option or OK. Then click the Envelope button.

The Envelope dialog box

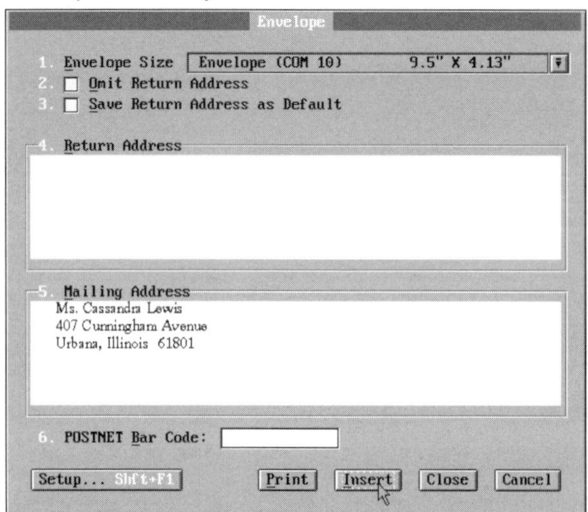

Option or Button	*Function*
1. Envelope Size	Enables you to select the envelope size you want to use (the 9 by 4⅛-inch business envelope is selected by default).

2. Omit Return Address	Omits the return address shown in the Return Address area of the Envelope dialog box from the envelope you're creating (use this option when you're using envelopes that have the return address preprinted on them).
3. Save Return Address as Default	Saves the return address shown in the Return Address area of the Envelope dialog box as the default to be automatically entered in this area in all future envelopes that you create.
4. Return Address	Enables you to enter or edit the return address to be printed on the envelope.
5. Mailing Address	Enables you to edit the mailing address picked from the letter in the current document window or enter one if none can be located in the current document.
6. POSTNET Bar Code:	Enables you to edit the ZIPcode to create an extended ZIPcode (the so-called ZIPcode plus four) that WordPerfect then prints as a bar code above the mailing address on the envelope.
Setup... Shft+F1	Enables you to modify the envelope setup options, including the default envelope size, the position of the return and mailing address on a given envelope size, and whether or not a POSTNET bar code is created (or whether the bar code option is displayed).
Print	Prints the envelope using the information in the Envelope dialog box.
Insert	Inserts the envelope as a separate page tacked onto the end of the document in the current document window.

Secret codes

When you choose the Insert button to tack the envelope onto a new page at the bottom of your document, WordPerfect inserts a bunch of secret codes at the top of that page for formatting your new envelope, including: [Lft Mar], [Rgt Mar], [Top Mar], [Bot Mar], [Just], [Paper Sz/Typ], [VAdv], and [Bar Code]. To see exactly what new format settings are in effect on this page, just position the cursor on each of these codes in the Reveal Codes window to expand them.

Exit (Document)

Closes the current document and prompts you to save the file in case you are about to blow some of your work away.

Menus

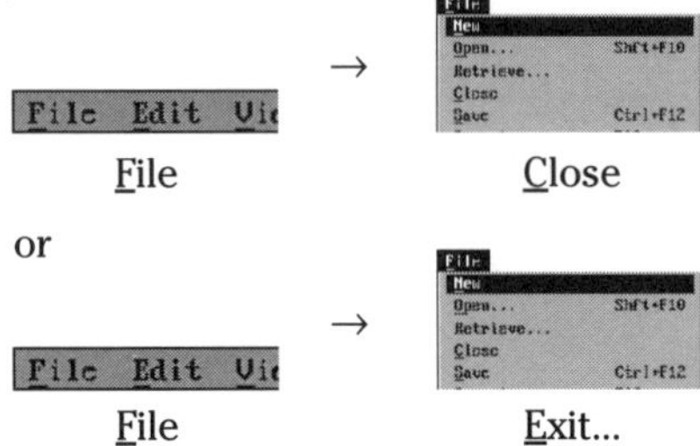

File → Close

or

File → Exit...

For function key freaks

(Exit)

For mouse maniacs

If you frame the current document editing window (with the Frame command on the Window menu), you can close the current document by clicking the Close button, which appears as a dot in a small rectangle in the upper left-hand corner of the window frame.

More stuff

When you close a document that's never been saved before, WordPerfect displays the Document dialog box with the message `Save (untitled)? Document has been modified.` To save the document, choose the Yes button or the Save As button, or press Enter and then name the document in the Save Document dialog box. To dump the document, choose the No button. If no other documents are open, WordPerfect displays the Exit WordPerfect? dialog box. To quit WordPerfect when it displays the Exit WordPerfect? dialog box, choose the Yes button. To stay in WordPerfect, choose the No button. To return to the document you're about to dump, choose the Cancel button or press Esc or Enter.

When you close a document that contains changes that haven't been saved, WordPerfect displays the same Document dialog box except that the Save prompt shows the current name of the document, indicating that the document has been modified. To save changes with the same name, choose the Yes button or press Enter. To change the filename, choose the Save As button and modify the name in the Save Document dialog box. To abandon your changes, choose the No button.

When you close a document for which all changes have been saved, WordPerfect displays the Document dialog box with a message asking you if you want to save the document without the `Document has been modified` message.

When you have more than one document open and you try to close the current document, WordPerfect displays an Exit dialog box (rather than an Exit WordPerfect dialog box), asking you whether you want to exit the current document editing window. To close the current document and display the document in the next window, choose the Yes button. To close the document and remain in the current document window (in other words, to clear the window), choose the No button or press Enter. To return to the document in the current window without closing it, choose the Cancel button or press Esc.

Exit (WordPerfect)

Quits WordPerfect and returns you to wherever you started the program (that is, to either that ugly DOS prompt or the confusing Windows desktop).

Menus

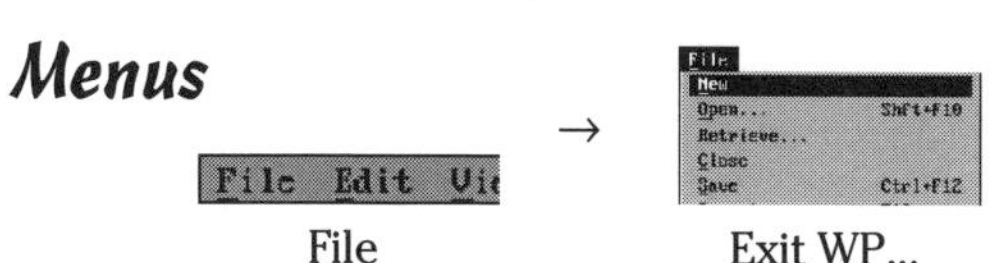

File → Exit WP...

For function key freaks

(Exit)

The Exit WordPerfect dialog box

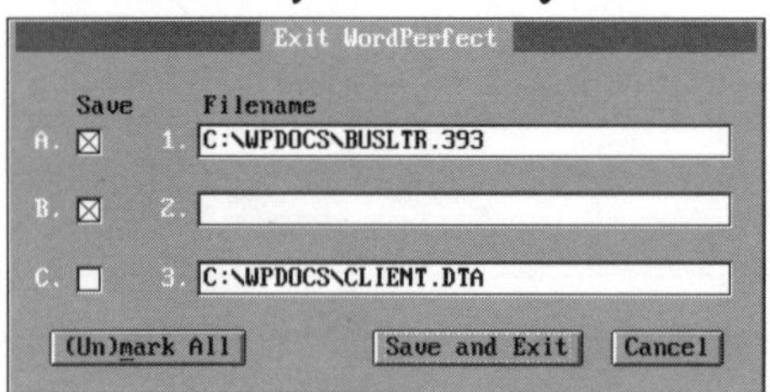

When you choose the Exit WordPerfect command, the Exit WordPerfect dialog box shows you all the documents that are currently open in different document windows. If a particular document contains changes that haven't been saved, the check box for that document (in the Save column) contains an X and the normal Exit button changes to Save and Exit.

To save changes to all of the files, choose the Save and Exit button. If you see a document you don't want to save, choose its letter (A, B, C, and so on) to remove the X from its check box before choosing the Save and Exit button. If you don't want to save *any* of the changes in *any* of the documents with Xs in their Save check boxes, choose the (Un)mark All button and then choose the Exit button.

More stuff

Be sure that you really, *really* mean to dump a file before you remove the X in its Save check box or before you, heaven forbid, use the (Un)mark All button and then choose the Exit button.

File Manager

Enables you to do all sorts of nifty file-oriented tasks that you normally wouldn't be caught dead doing, such as changing the directory, finding, copying, moving, and deleting files; you can do all of this without ever once having to resort to using the horrible DOS operating system.

Menus

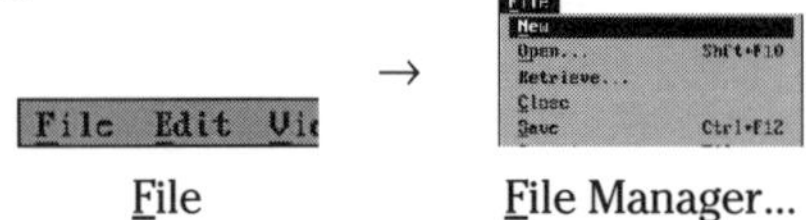

File → File Manager...

For function key freaks

(File Manager)

The Specify File Manager List dialog box

When you first choose the File Manager command on the File menu or press the F5 (File Manager) key, WordPerfect displays the Specify File Manager List dialog box (shown next) where you can select a new directory to use or specify what types of files you want to work with before opening the File Manager dialog box. You can also use this dialog box to change the default directory (the default directory is the one that WordPerfect keeps choosing every time you do something file-related, such as opening or saving a file) or even to create a brand new directory.

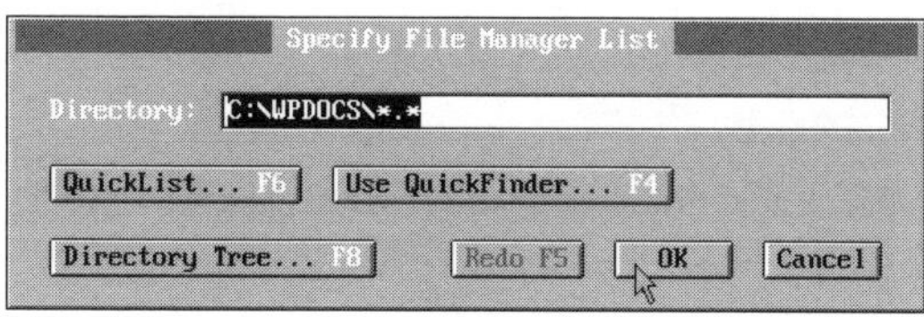

Option or Button	*Function*
Directory	Lists the path and name of the default directory. To select a new default directory, type = (equal sign) and enter the pathname of the new directory in the Change Default Directory dialog box. Then choose OK or press Enter. To select another directory without changing the default directory, edit the pathname in the Directory text box of the Specify File Manager List dialog box. To display all files in the directory shown in the Directory text box and open the File Manager dialog box, choose OK or press Enter. To display just certain files in the File Manager, modify the *.* pattern in the pathname shown in the Directory text box to indicate the type of files to be listed (such as ***.ltr** to display only the files with the extension .LTR) before you choose OK or press Enter.

QuickList... F6	Displays the QuickList dialog box where you can select a new directory using a straightforward alias, such as *Letters and correspondence,* instead of the normal DOS gobbledygook like C:\WP6\LETTERS (see QuickList).
Use QuickFinder... F4	Displays the QuickFinder File Indexer dialog box where you can create indexes and use them to quickly find the file you want to use (see QuickFinder).
Directory Tree... F8	Displays the Directory Tree dialog box where you can view the directory structure of your computer's hard disk and select a new directory (see Directory Tree).
Redo F5	Enables you to display the contents of the directory you last selected in the File Manager dialog box, even when that directory is not the current one.

The File Manager dialog box

When you choose the OK button or press Enter in the Specify File Manager List dialog box, WordPerfect opens the File Manager dialog box (shown next) where you can do all sorts of nifty file-related things, such as open, move, copy, delete, or even search for the file you want to use.

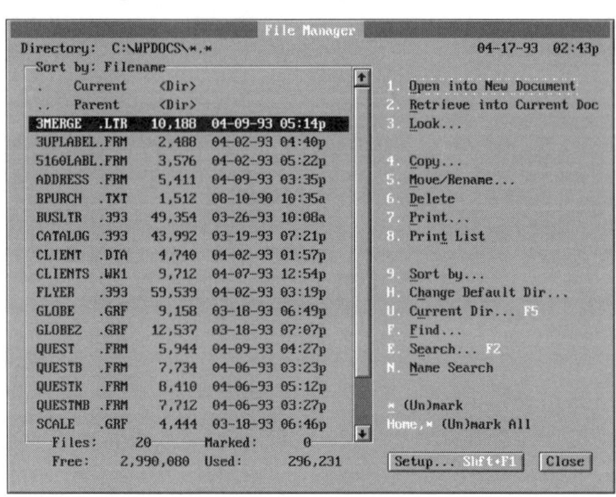

Option or Button	*Function*
1. Open into New Document	Opens the file that's highlighted in the Sort by list box into a new document editing window. If more than one file is marked in the list box, WordPerfect asks you whether you want to open the marked files. If you choose the Yes button, the program opens all marked files, each in its own window (provided that you don't try to open more than nine files total and that your computer has enough memory). If you choose the No button, WordPerfect asks you whether you want to open the document currently highlighted in the list box.
2. Retrieve into Current Doc	Opens the file that's highlighted in the Sort by list box into the current document editing window, inserting its text at the cursor's position. If more than one file is marked in the list box, WordPerfect asks you whether you want to retrieve the marked files. If you choose the Yes button, the program retrieves all marked files in the current document editing window. If you choose the No button, WordPerfect asks you whether you want to retrieve the document currently highlighted in the list box.
3. Look...	Displays the contents of the highlighted document in a special Look at Document non-editing window. If the document contains a document summary (see Document Summary), WordPerfect shows you the summary in a Look at Document Summary window (choose 6. Look at Text option to see the text). To scroll continuously through the text, choose the Scroll option (choose it again when you want to stop). To see the next file in the list, choose 1. Next. To see the previous file, choose 2. Previous. If you find that the document is the one you want, choose 3. Open to open it in a new window or choose 4. Delete to get rid of it or 5 * Mark to mark it.

4. Copy...	Copies the files that you've marked or the one that's currently highlighted to the drive and directory that you specify in the Copy dialog box.
5. Move/Rename...	Moves the files that you've marked to whatever drive and directory you specify in Move Marked Files to text box in the Move/Rename dialog box. When no files are marked, this option enables you to move and/or rename the one that's highlighted. To move the file, edit the directory path in the New Name text box. To rename the file, edit the filename in this text box.
6. Delete	Deletes the files that you've marked or the one that's currently highlighted. Be very careful with this option — think before you choose the Yes button to confirm the file deletion because once you zap your files, WordPerfect offers no undelete feature to bring them back.
7. Print	Prints the files that you've marked or the one that's currently highlighted. When you print multiple files, WordPerfect puts them into a print *queue* (a two-dollar word for line) which you can control with the options in the Control Printer dialog box (see Print).
8. Print List	Prints a directory listing of all the files in the directory selected in the File Manager dialog box.
9. Sort by...	Displays the File Manager Setup dialog box where you sort the files in some way other than by filename (the default). The files are sorted in the File Manager dialog box. Sort choices include 1. Filename, 2. Extension, 3. Date/Time, 4. Size, and 7 No Sort. When you choose the Descriptive Names and Types radio button, WordPerfect makes the 5. Descriptive Name option the default and enables you to choose the 6. Descriptive Type option as well.

H. Change Default Dir...	Makes the directory you select in the Change Default Directory dialog box the new default directory. This directory remains the default until you exit WordPerfect or use this option later on to make another directory the default. If you enter a directory that WordPerfect can't find, the program displays a dialog box asking you whether you want to create that directory. Choose Yes if you want to add the directory. Otherwise, choose No if you simply made a mistake.
U. Current Dir...F5	Changes the directory to the one you select in the Specify File Manager List dialog box and displays its contents in the File Manager dialog box without changing the default directory (see preceding H. Change Default Dir...).
F. Find...	Enables you to search for a file by entering a word or phrase found in the filename (1. Filename), the document summary (2. Document Summary), the first page of the document (3. First Page), or in the text of the entire document (4. Entire Document). Choose the 5. Conditions option to enter a search condition (see following section, Making Up Search Patterns). Choose the 6. Indexed Find option to use the QuickFinder (see QuickFinder). Choose the 7. Undo option to restore the list of files in the File Manager dialog box to its state before you conducted the search (you can move back through the three previous states).
E. Search...F2	Enables you to search for a file by its filename by entering a search pattern (see following section, Making Up Search Patterns).
N. Name Search	Enables you to select a file in the File Manager list box by entering all or part of its filename.

Setup... Shft+F1	Enables you to change the way files are listed in the File Manager dialog box. You can change the way files are sorted, list the descriptive names and types (see Document Summary), and display only WordPerfect documents. In addition, you can specify that the directory list be printed in compressed (tiny) print whenever you choose the 8. Print List option (see previous 8. Print List).

Making up search patterns

You can make up search patterns when trying to locate a file with the F. Find and E. Search...F2 options in the File Manager dialog box. These search patterns can contain wildcard characters (? and *) to stand in for missing letters, as well as the semicolon (;) or space to create an *and* condition, the comma (,) to create an *or* situation, and the hyphen or dash (-) to exclude a particular word pattern. Refer to the following table for examples of how these characters can be used in search patterns.

Search Pattern	*WordPerfect Finds*
promotion	All files in the directory that contain the word *promotion.*
h?re	All files in the directory that contains words like *hire, hare,* and *here.*
"make work"	All files in the directory that contain the exact phrase *make work* (note that you must leave a space after the word *work*).
"make work"	All files in the directory that contain phrases like *make work, make workers, make workdays* (note that you must leave no space after the word *work*).
"make*work"	All files in the directory that contain phrases that start with *make* and end with *work* such as *makeup work* or *make too much work.*
overdue bill	All files in the directory that contain both the words *overdue* and *bill.*
overdue;bill	All files in the directory that contain either the word *overdue* or the word *bill.*

overdue,bill;credit	All files in the directory that contain either the words *overdue* and *credit* or the words *bill* and *credit.*
overdue "final notice"	All files in the directory that contain both the word *overdue* and the phrase *final notice.*
—overdue	All files in the directory that don't contain the word *overdue.*
"non-credit"	All files in the directory that contain the hyphenated term *non-credit.*

Finding files by dates

If you've added document summaries to your WordPerfect files (see Document Summary) and know when (exactly or approximately) you created or last revised the document you want to find, you can search for the file by dates as follows:

1. Choose the F. Find option in the File Manager dialog box and then choose the 5. Conditions option in the Find dialog box to open the File Manager Find Conditions dialog box.
2. Choose the 5. Show Default Summary Fields Only option.
3. Choose the Date pop-up list button for the Revision Date in the 4. Document Summary Fields option. If you want to search by creation date instead, press Tab or ↓ to select the Date pop-up list button for the Creation Date.
4. When the right Date button is selected, press Enter to display the Find Conditions Date dialog box.
5. If you want to find a file created or a revised on a particular date, type the date in Dates text box, following the pattern 11/24/94.
6. If you want to find a file created before or after a particular date, or somewhere between two dates, select the Dates pop-up list button (press the Esc key to display the command letter) and then select the Before, After, or Between option and enter the appropriate date(s).
7. Choose the OK button to close the Find Conditions Date dialog and then fill out any other necessary search conditions in the File Manager Find Conditions dialog. Then choose its OK button to start the search.

8. WordPerfect redraws the File Manager dialog box, showing only the files that have been created or revised on, before, after, or between the dates you specify. To find the exact file you want to work with, you can use the 3. Look option to review their document summaries or text.

More stuff

Searching through the text of hundreds of documents to find the one you need to edit can eat up a lot of precious time. To speed up searches, attach document summaries to the documents you create and restrict the searches you conduct with the F. Find option to particular document summary fields (see Document Summary).

Flush Right

Aligns a short line of text flush with the right margin.

Menus

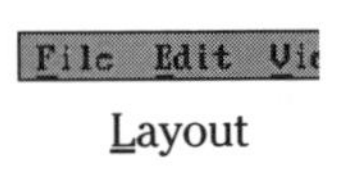

Layout

→

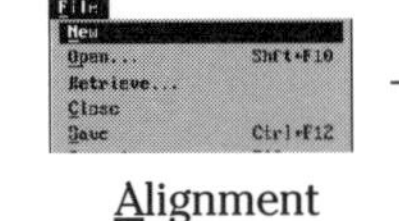

Alignment

→ ▶ Flush Right Alt+F6

For function key freaks

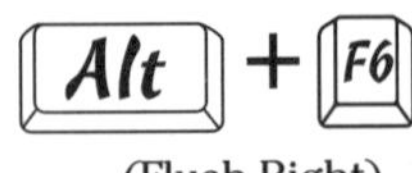

(Flush Right)

Flushing text to the right before you type it

You can align a line of text with the right margin as you type it by following these steps:

1. Position the cursor at the beginning of the line that should be flush right.
2. Choose the Alignment command on the Layout menu and then choose the Flush Right command — or better yet, press the Alt+F6 (Flush Right) key. WordPerfect pushes the cursor to the right margin.

3. Start typing the line of text to appear right-aligned in the document (as you type, characters are inserted backwards from right to left instead of in the normal left-to-right direction).

4. When you finish entering the phrase or short line, press the Enter key to insert a hard return to move the cursor to the beginning of the next line and return to normal left alignment.

Flushing existing text to the right

You can also use the Flush Right feature to align existing text with the right margin. You can use this technique to right align a bunch of short lines (like a return address) with the right margin in one fell swoop:

1. Block the text to be right aligned — see Block (Text) for details.

2. Choose the Alignment command on the Layout menu and then choose the Flush Right command (or press the Alt+F6 (Flush Right) key. WordPerfect then aligns the entire cursor up with the right margin in your document.

Secret codes

If you right aligned the company name *Moving Maniacs* as you typed it, when you open Reveal Codes, you see

```
[Flsh Rgt]Moving Maniacs[HRt]
```

On the other hand, if you marked this name as a block and then centered it afterward, you see

```
[+Just]Moving Maniacs[HRt][—Just]
```

When you position the cursor on the first [+Just] code, it expands to [Just:Right]. When you position the cursor on the second [—Just] code, it expands to [Just:Left].

More stuff

You can also right align text by changing the justification of the document from the normal left to right justification. For more information on this method, see Justification.

Font

Enables you to select a new font, font size, text color, and appearance or relative size attribute.

Menus

To select a new font, font size, appearance or relative size attribute, or text color in the Font dialog box:

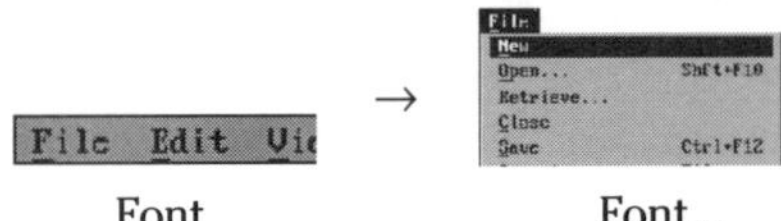

Font → Font...

To select a new relative font size or to superscript or subscript text with the Font pull-down menu:

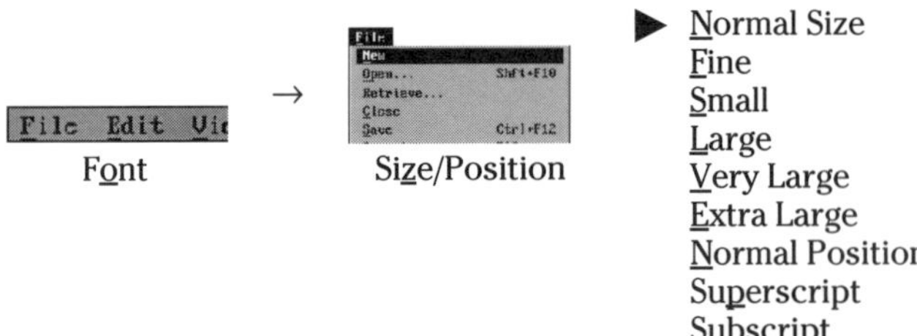

Font → Size/Position ▶ Normal Size
Fine
Small
Large
Very Large
Extra Large
Normal Position
Superscript
Subscript

To choose a new attribute with the Font pull-down menu:

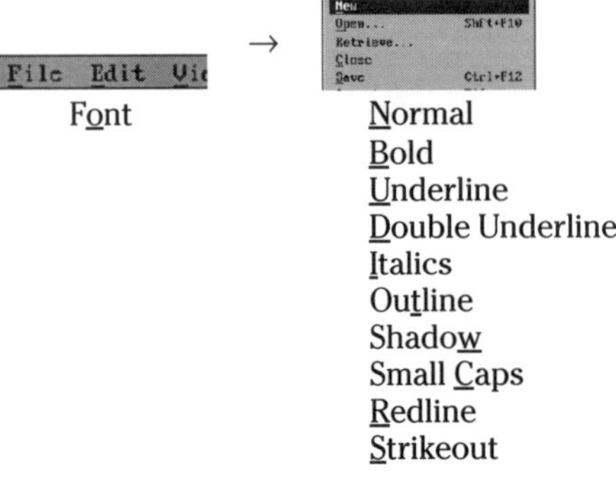

Font → Normal
Bold
Underline
Double Underline
Italics
Outline
Shadow
Small Caps
Redline
Strikeout

For function key freaks

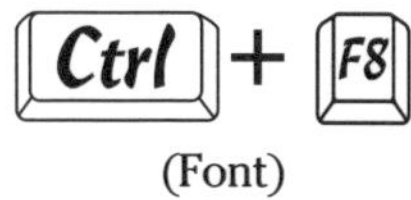

(Font)

For mouse maniacs

To select a new font for your document, display the ribbon with the Ribbon command on the View menu and then select the font by clicking the Font button and highlighting the font name or by dragging to the font name in the drop-down list.

To select a new font size, click the Font size button at the end of the ribbon and then type in the new size (in points) or click its drop-down button and highlight the new size or drag to the new size in the drop-down list.

The Font dialog box

WordPerfect lets you change the font, font size, appearance and relative size, and color, all in one operation in the Font dialog box. When changing the font or its attributes, be sure to position the cursor at the place in the text where the change is to take place before you use the options in the Font dialog box. If you only need to apply the font or font attribute to a portion of the text (such as a heading), first block the text (see Block (Text)) before you select your options in the Font dialog box.

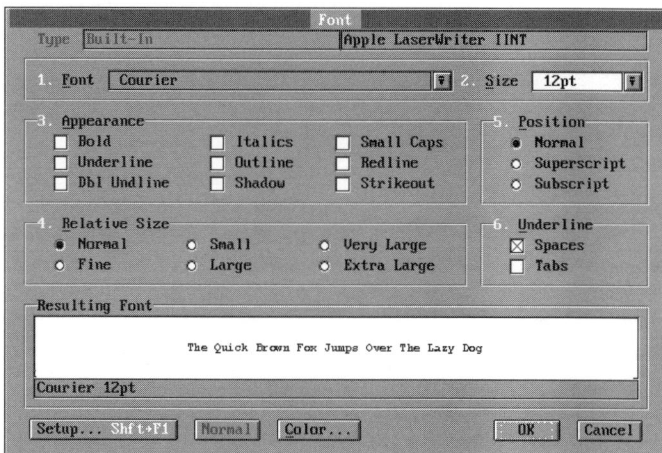

Option or Button	Function
1. Font	Enables you to choose a new font from the list.
2. Size	Enables you to choose a new point size for the font. If you're using a laser printer such as an HP LaserJet III or Apple Laserwriter that can scale your font to create new sizes, you can type the point size (like 100) in the Size text box if the size you want to use isn't listed.
3. Appearance	Enables you to choose a new style for the font, such as bold, underline, italics, and so forth.
4. Relative Size	Enables you to choose a new size for your font which is based entirely on a set percentage of the size of initial font. For example, if the initial font for your printer is 10-point Courier, choosing Large gives you 12-point Courier because this size is 120% of the 10-point initial font.
5. Position	Enables you to superscript or subscript the text.
6. Underline	By default, WordPerfect underlines the spaces between words. To remove underlining from spaces, choose 1. Spaces to remove the X from its check box. To add underlining between tabs, choose 2. Tabs to put an X in its check box.
Setup... Shft+F1	Enables you to install fonts, edit the initial font for your printer, as well as change the percentages for the various relative size options.
Normal	Turns off all appearance and size attributes that are turned on in the text.
Color...	Enables you to specify a new color for your text (besides the default of basic black).

Selecting a new text color

If you're lucky enough to have a color printer, you can use the Print Color command on the Font menu or the Color button in the Font dialog box to select a new color for your text. Obviously, you won't see the color that you select on the screen unless you have a color monitor (likewise, if you try to print colors on a black and white printer, you only get black and white — however, colors printed on a black and white laser printer do appear as shades of gray).

To select a new color, follow these steps:

1. Position the cursor at the place in the document where the new color is to begin. If you only need to apply the color to a section of text (such as a heading), select the text as a block instead — see Block (Text) for details.
2. Choose the Font menu and then select the Print Color option or open the Font dialog box and choose the Color button.
3. To use a predefined color like white, red, or blue, select the color in the Palette Colors list box and then choose the Select button.
4. To vary the shade (tint) of the color, choose the 2. Shade (% of Color) option and then enter the percentage of the shade you want to use in its text box (or click ↑ or ↓ until you have the shade you want — watch the sample color box in the lower right corner of the Color Selection dialog box to see how the new shade will appear on the screen).
5. To create a custom color, choose the 3. Custom Color option to open the Custom Color dialog box. You can choose the Red, Green, and Blue options and enter the appropriate percentages of each color in their various text boxes. Or you can drag the little square on the color bar up or down until you have the approximate color you want and then fine-tune it by slightly varying the red, green, and blue percentages. If you want to add this color to the color palette so that you can use it in the future, select the 2. Add to Palette option. Then choose the 1. Color Name option and enter a name for your custom color in its text box. When you're through defining the custom color, choose the OK button to close the Custom Color dialog box and return to the Color Selection dialog box.
6. Assuming that the color you want your text to be now appears in the Resulting Font box, select the OK button to close the Font dialog box .

Secret codes

Let's say that you want the first heading in your document, *Profits for the Making,* to stand out and that you're using a printer where 12-point Courier is the initial font. After marking this heading as a block, you choose Bodoni-WP Bold as the font and 24 points as the font size for this text. When you open Reveal Codes, you'll see

```
[+Font:Bodoni-WP Bold][+Font Size:24pt]
Profits for the Making[-Font Size:12pt]
[-Font:*Courier][HRt]
```

Note that the asterisk before Courier in `[-Font]` secret code indicates that this font is built into the printer. Also note that after making this font change, when the cursor is somewhere on this heading, the left side of the status bar lists the current font and font size as `Bodoni-WP 14pt Bold (Type 1)` that is, at least until you save the document for the first time. After you save it, the filename replaces the font information. However, if you display the ribbon (see Ribbon), you see the current font name and size in the Font and Font size buttons on the right side of this bar.

More stuff

The new fonts, font sizes, and font attributes that you select for your dialog box stay in effect from the cursor's position forward in the document until you turn them off. To turn off a font change, you must choose the original font. To turn off a size change, you must select the original size. To turn off a color change, you must select the original color (usually black). To turn off an appearance or relative size change, select the Normal command on the Font menu (you can also turn off appearance attributes like bold and underlining by choosing that attribute again). However, if you mark your text as a block — see Block (Text) for details — before you choose the new font, font size, color, appearance or relative size attribute you want to use, WordPerfect automatically turns these things off at the end of the block so that you don't have to remember to do it yourself.

To see fonts, font sizes, and font attributes on your screen more or less as they appear when printed, you must put WordPerfect in graphics or page display mode (see Graphics Mode and Page Mode for details). If you run the program in text mode, you have to use the Print Preview command on the File menu to see the text as it will appear in the printout.

Because bold and underlining are so commonly used in documents, WordPerfect dedicates function keys — F6 (Bold) and F8 (Underline) — that you can use to turn these attributes on and off (see Bold and Underline).

Footnotes and Endnotes

Enables you to add footnotes that appear throughout the text at the bottom of the page or endnotes which are grouped together at the end of a section within the document or at the end of the document itself. WordPerfect automatically numbers both types of notes so that you don't have to drive yourself crazy renumbering the darn things by hand when you have to add a note or take one out.

Menus

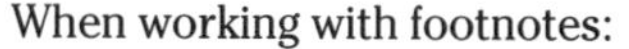

When working with footnotes:

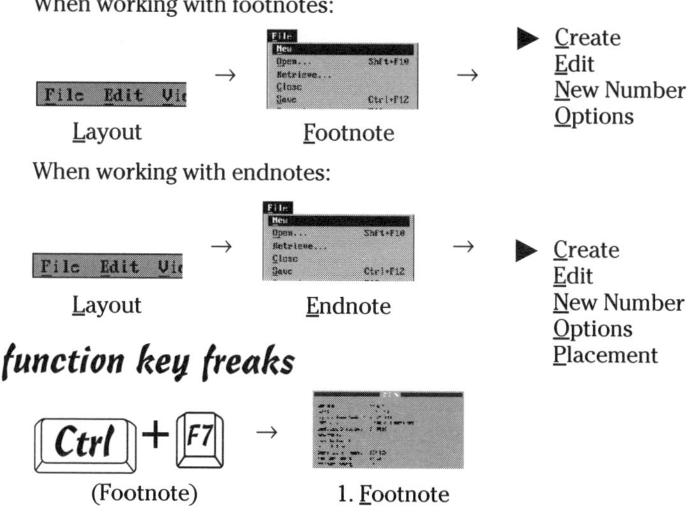

Layout → Footnote → ▶ Create / Edit / New Number / Options

When working with endnotes:

Layout → Endnote → ▶ Create / Edit / New Number / Options / Placement

For function key freaks

Ctrl + F7 (Footnote) → 1. Footnote or 3. Endnote

Creating a footnote or endnote

To create a footnote or an endnote in the text of your document:

1. Position the cursor at the place in the document's text where the footnote or endnote number is to appear.
2. Choose the Layout menu and then select the Footnote or Endnote option. Or press the Ctrl+F7 (Footnote) key and then select 1. Footnote or 3. Endnote.
3. Select the Create option. WordPerfect opens a Footnote or Endnote window that contains the next available note number.
4. Type the text of your footnote or endnote and then press the F7 (Exit) key. When entering the text of your note, you can use the WordPerfect pull-down menus to select the editing and formatting commands that you need to edit the text, including the Speller and Thesaurus.

To edit the text of a footnote or endnote, choose the Footnote or Endnote command on the Layout menu or in the Notes dialog box. Select Edit and enter the number of the footnote or endnote you want to edit in the Footnote or Endnote Number dialog box. The program displays the Footnote or Endnote window where you make your editing changes. When you are finished editing, press the F7 (Exit) key to return to your document.

Changing the footnote or endnote numbering

WordPerfect automatically numbers your footnotes and endnotes starting with the number 1. If you ever need to restart the numbering of your footnotes or endnotes at a particular place in the document (like at a section break), follow these steps:

1. Position the cursor in front of the first footnote or endnote number in the text that is to be renumbered. To renumber all the footnotes or endnotes in your document, move to the beginning of the document.
2. Choose the Layout menu and then select the Footnote or Endnote option. Or press the Ctrl+F7 (Footnote) key and then select 1. Footnote or 3. Endnote.
3. Select the New Number command on the Layout menu or the 3. Number option in the Notes dialog box to have WordPerfect open the Set Footnote or Endnote Number dialog box.
4. To restart the numbering, select the 1. New Number option and then type in the new starting number for your footnotes or endnotes in the text box and press Enter.

5. By default, WordPerfect uses Arabic numerals (the Numbers option) as the numbering method. To change the numbering method, choose the 2. Numbering Method option and then choose between Lower Letters, Upper Letters, Lower Roman, Upper Roman or Characters. If you choose Upper or Lower Letters, your footnote or endnotes are lettered consecutively from A through Z (letters are doubled, as in aa, bb, or AA, BB and so on, if you have more than 26 footnotes or endnotes). If you choose Characters, your footnotes or endnotes are marked with asterisks (the first with one, the second with two, and so on). When you select this type, you can then use the 6. Characters option to specify which characters are to be used.
6. To have each number, letter, or character increase with each subsequent footnote or endnote, choose the 3. Increment Number option by putting an X in its check box.
7. To have each number, letter, or character decrease with each subsequent footnote or endnote, choose the 4. Decrement Number option by putting an X in its check box.
8. If for some reason you don't want the footnote or endnote numbers to be displayed in the document, choose the 5. Display in Document option to remove the X from its check box.
9. If you choose Characters as the numbering method, select the 6. Characters option and enter up to 5 different characters (without any spaces between them) in its text box that you want used in marking footnotes and endnotes. After the characters you specify here are all used up, WordPerfect doubles, and, if necessary, triples these characters.
10. When you're finished setting the footnote or endnote numbering, choose the OK button.

If you've put both footnotes and endnotes in the same document (that must be *some* document!), be sure to modify the Numbering Method for one or the other. Otherwise, no one except for yourself (and maybe not even you) will be able to tell which numbers in the text refer to the footnotes at the bottom of the page and which refer to the notes at the end of the section or document, because WordPerfect numbers both the footnotes and endnotes in your document in the same superscript style and starting with 1.

Changing the footnote and endnote options

WordPerfect offers a number of options for changing the way footnote and endnote numbers and text appear in the document. To change the way footnote or endnote reference numbers appear in the text or the way the text of the notes are laid out, you must open the Notes dialog box by pressing the Ctrl+F7 (Footnote) key. To change the way reference numbers appear, choose the 1. Footnote or 3. Endnote option. Then select the 5. Edit Style in Document option and edit the secret codes used by footnote or endnote style in document. To change the way text of the note is formatted, choose the 1. Footnote or 3. Endnote option. Then select the 6. Edit Style in Note option and edit the secret codes used by footnote or endnote style in note (see Styles for details).

In addition to editing the style for the footnote text, you can also change the way they are positioned on the page with the options in the Footnote Options dialog box. To open this dialog box, choose the Footnote command on the Layout menu. Then select Options on the cascading menu — or press the Ctrl+F7 (Footnote) key — and then choose 1. Footnote and 4. Options. In this dialog box, you have the following choices:

Option or Button	*Function*
1. Spacing Between Footnotes	By default, WordPerfect uses a line height of 0.167 inch between each footnote (comparable to the height of a typical 12-point font). To change the space between notes, enter a new value in this text box.
2. Amount of Footnote to Keep Together	WordPerfect keeps at least ½- inch of the text of a footnote together on the bottom of a page. To change the amount of text that remains together, enter a new measurement in this text box.
3. Footnote Separator Line	WordPerfect prints a 2-inch horizontal line separating body text from the footnotes on a page. To omit this separator, select this option. Then choose 1. Line Style and change the setting from Single Line to [None]. You can also select any other line style as well as modify the alignment, length, and spacing above and below the separator line.

4. Restart Footnote Numbers each Page	Select this check box to have each Page your footnotes renumbered, starting with 1 on each page of the document.
5. Footnotes at Bottom of Page	WordPerfect prints footnotes at the bottom of the page even when the text does not fill up the whole page. Remove the X from this check box if you want your footnotes to be printed immediately below the text on a short page.
6. Print Continued Message	If a footnote is too long, WordPerfect continues its text on the next page. Select this check box to have "`(continued)...`" printed on the last footnote line of the first page and "`...(continued)`" printed on the first footnote line of the next page.

You can also change endnote options in the Endnote Options dialog box. To open this dialog box, choose the Endnote command on the Layout menu and then select Options on the cascading menu. Or press the Ctrl+F7 (Footnote) key and then choose 3. Endnote and 4. Options. In this dialog box, you have the following two choices:

Option or Button	*Function*
1. Spacing Between Endnotes	By default, WordPerfect uses a line height of 0.167 inch between each endnote. To change the space between endnotes, enter a new value in this text box.
2. Minimum Amount of Endnote to Keep Together	WordPerfect keeps at least ½ inch of the text of any endnote together that falls at the bottom of the page. To change the amount of text that remains together, enter a new measurement in this text box.

Repositioning endnotes

Endnotes are automatically grouped together on their own page at the end of the document unless you specify otherwise (like putting them together on their own page at the end of a section within the document). To change the placement of endnotes, follow these steps:

1. Position the cursor at the place in the document where the endnotes are to be printed.
2. Choose the Endnote command on the Layout menu and then select the Placement command on the cascading menu (or press Ctrl+F7 and then select the 4. Endnote Placement option). WordPerfect displays a dialog box asking whether you want to restart the numbering of endnotes (you renumber your notes when your document is divided into sections, and you want the note numbers to start with 1 in each section).
3. Select the Yes button to have WordPerfect renumber your endnotes or select No if you want the numbering to remain consecutive from the beginning of the document or the last section. If you're in text or graphics mode, WordPerfect inserts an Endnote Placement comment in the text followed by a hard page break to mark the placement of the notes.
4. To have the text of the endnotes appear in your document instead of the silly Endnote Placement comment, switch to page mode by selecting the Page Mode command on the View menu or, if this isn't possible, open the preview document window by selecting the Print Preview command on the File menu.

Secret codes

When you create a Footnote or Endnote in the document, its number appears in the regular document while a `[Footnote]` or `[Endnote]` secret code appears in the Reveal Codes window. If you put the cursor on this secret code in Reveal Codes, it expands to show you not only the text of the note but also what numbering style is used.

When you reposition endnotes in your document, WordPerfect inserts both an `[Endnote Placement]` and a `[HPg]` (hard page break) secret code at the cursor's position in the document.

More stuff

Remember: to see the text of the footnotes and endnotes that you add to your document, you must have WordPerfect in page display mode (see Page Mode) or you must select the Print Preview command on the File menu.

Go To

Moves the cursor to specific places in the document, such as to a particular character in the text or to the top of particular page.

Menus

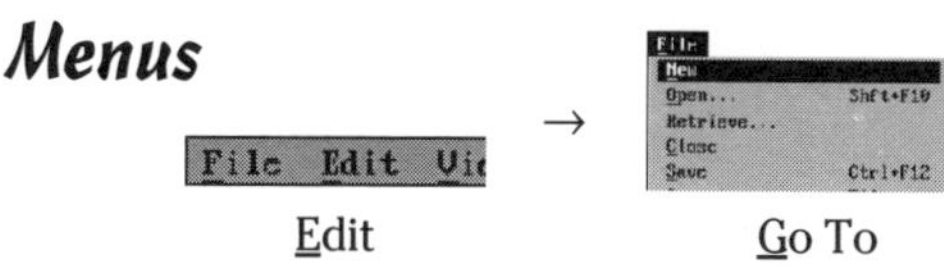

Edit → Go To

For function key freaks

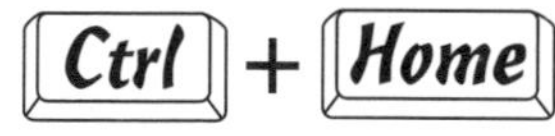

Go To it

To jump the cursor to the top of a particular page number, type the page number in the Go to dialog box and press Enter. To jump to the next occurrence of a particular character in the text, type the character. For instance, to move to the next period in the text, type **.** or to move to next capital letter B, type **B**, or to move to the next tab in the document, press Tab, or to move to the end of the paragraph, press Enter (you get the idea).

To return the cursor to its last known position in the document, press Ctrl+Home (the shortcut keys would then be — Ctrl+Home, Ctrl+Home — twice in a row).

More stuff

You can't use Go To to move to a particular number in the text of your document because WordPerfect interprets any number you enter in the Go to dialog box as a page number and tries to take you to that page! Also, if you ever type a character or press a key in the Go to dialog box and WordPerfect beeps at you (how rude), you know that either the character doesn't exist in the document or it's too far away for WordPerfect to get to it (2,000 characters or more down the line).

Go To Shell

Enables you to return temporarily to DOS (yuk!) or to the WordPerfect Shell program (a utility included with WordPerfect 6.0 that you can use to run different programs and switch and transfer information among them).

Menus

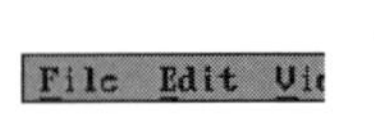

→

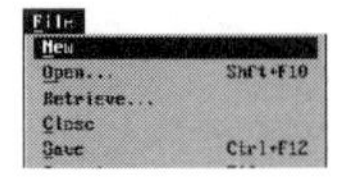

File Go To Shell...

For function key freaks

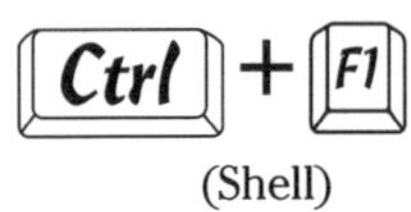

(Shell)

Go to DOS — do not collect $200

WordPerfect's Go To Shell command takes you to different places, depending upon how you're running the program. If you start WordPerfect under plain old DOS, you get a dialog box that basically gives you only two choices: 1. Go to DOS or 6. DOS Command — all the rest of the Shell options are dimmed, meaning that they're hands off (unless you're running the program on a network).

If you're brave enough to choose 1. Go to DOS, you end up getting thrown out into DOS with only the message `Type 'EXIT' to return to program` and the DOS prompt, something like `C:\WPDOCS>`.

While you're at the DOS prompt, you can enter DOS commands until the cows come home (just be sure that you have your *DOS for Dummies Quick Reference* at your side). When you're ready to go back home to WordPerfect, just click your heels together three times... But seriously, just type the word **exit** and press Enter and, voila, you'll be safely back home in the WordPerfect document editing window.

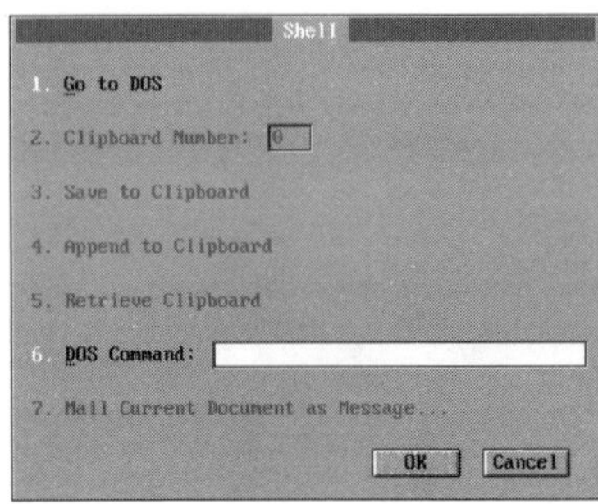

If you know what DOS command you want to run, you don't even have to leave WordPerfect to execute it. Instead, you can choose 6. DOS Command and then type the command in the text box (just as though you were actually at the DOS prompt — a sort of virtual DOS) and press Enter. WordPerfect then hands off the DOS command to DOS, which runs the command (provided you entered the command correctly). After doing whatever the command is supposed do, however, DOS hands you back to WordPerfect and returns you to the document editing screen, without your having to type **exit** or anything like that.

The Shell game

WordPerfect 6.0 ships with a nifty utility program called the Shell (Version 4.0, if you care). The Shell Enables you to do all sorts of neat things like start a bunch of different programs (if you have enough memory) and switch between them. In addition, the Shell gives you access to more than one clipboard (up to 80 to be exact), and the information that you copy into one of these clipboards in one program can be pasted into a document in a completely different program that you're also running under the Shell.

When you choose the Go to Shell command in WordPerfect after you've started the program under the Shell, you get a slightly different bunch of options in the Shell dialog box. You still get to go to DOS (6. Go to DOS) or issue a DOS command from WordPerfect (7. DOS Command). In addition, however, you get to switch between the programs you're running (1. Active Programs) and save, append, and retrieve stuff from different Shell clipboards. Choose 2. Clipboard Number to select the clipboard to use (between 0 and 79). Choose 3. Save to to copy the block of text you've marked to the clipboard you've selected. Choose 4. Append to add the block of text you've marked to the selected Shell clipboard. And, choose 5. Retrieve to paste the contents of the selected Shell clipboard into your document.

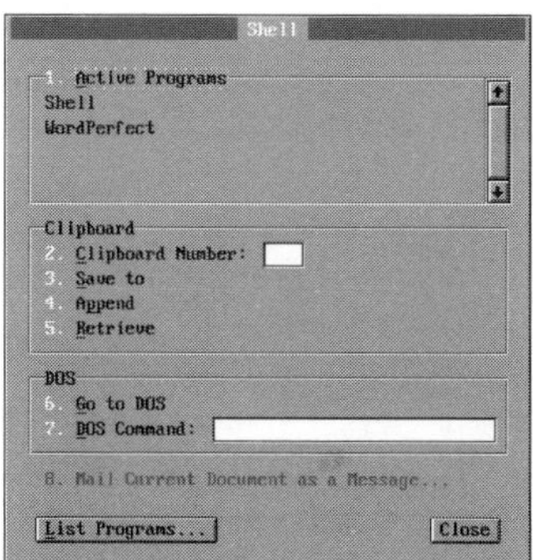

More stuff

If you ever use the Go to DOS option in the Shell dialog box, be sure that you don't do something stupid like turn off the computer from the DOS prompt without bothering to return to WordPerfect and properly exit the program. Remember that to get back to WordPerfect from DOS, you have to type **exit** and press Enter.

Graphics (Boxes)

Enables you to dress up a document with clip art, charts and graphs, scanned photographs, as well as special elements like sidebar text and equations.

Menus

To retrieve a picture in your document:

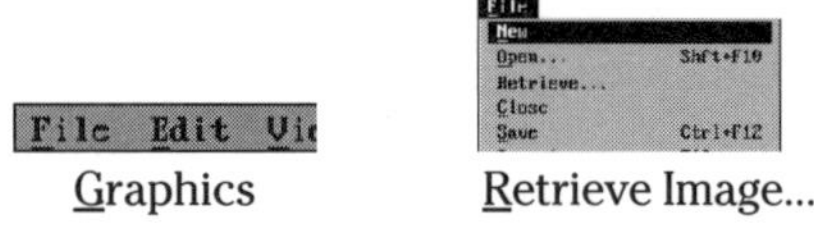

Graphics Retrieve Image...

To work with a graphics box:

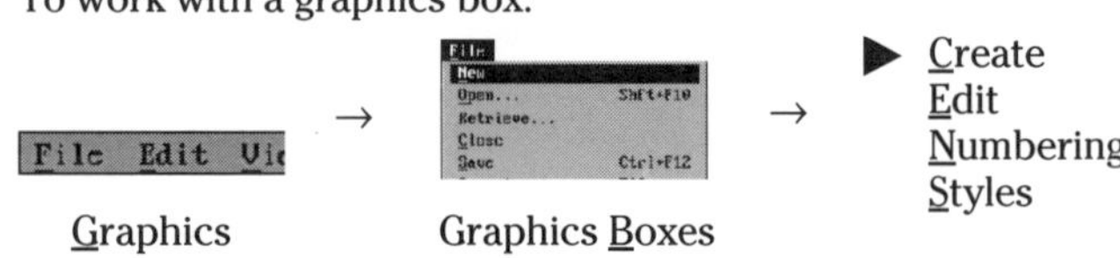

Graphics Graphics Boxes

▶ Create
Edit
Numbering
Styles

For function key freaks

To retrieve a picture in your document:

(Graphics) Retrieve Image...

To create a graphics box:

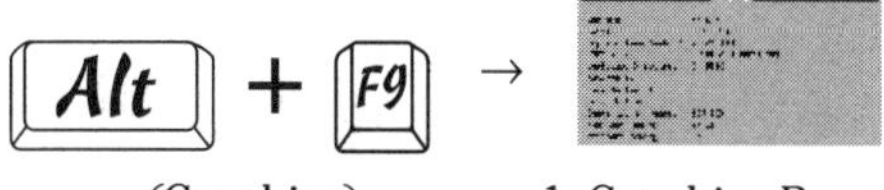

(Graphics)

1. Graphics Boxes
    1. Create
    2. Edit
    3. Numbering
    4. Styles

Retrieving an image

To retrieve a piece of clip art or a scanned image saved in a disk file into your document, simply choose the Retrieve Image command on the Graphics menu and then enter the filename in the Retrieve Image File dialog box and press Enter. WordPerfect then puts the image in a figure box attached to the current paragraph.

If WordPerfect is in text mode, you see only the box number with the outline showing where the graphic image will appear. If WordPerfect is in graphics or page mode, however, you have the supreme pleasure of actually seeing the artwork you retrieved into your document!

Little boxes

When you retrieve an image into your document as outlined in the previous section, WordPerfect puts the graphics file into a Figure Box (which uses a single line border and is attached to the current paragraph). In addition to a Figure Box, WordPerfect offers a host of other box styles that you can choose from, each of which offers slightly different options.

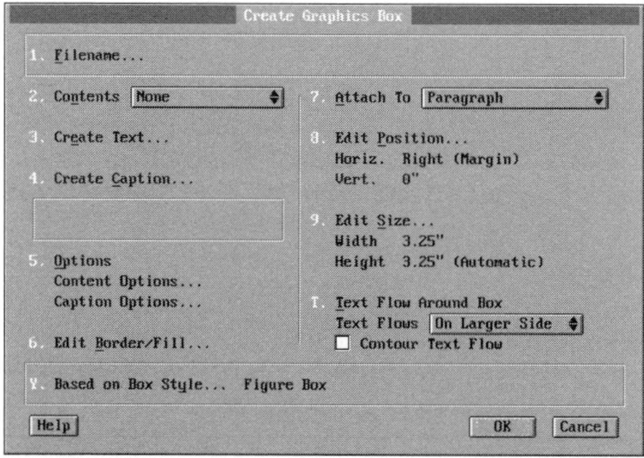

To use another type of graphics box (or any other graphics options, for that matter) for the image or text you want to add to your document, you need to go through the folderol of creating a graphics box by selecting the appropriate options in the Graphics dialog box.

Option or Button	*Function*
1. Filename...	Enables you to indicate the name and location of the graphics file you want to put in the graphics box you're creating.
2. Contents	Enables you to indicate the type of contents you want to put in the graphics box (Image, Image on Disk, Text, Equation, or None). Choose Image on Disk rather than Image when you're dealing with a humongous graphics file that you don't want to save as part of your document.
3. Create Text...	This option varies according to the Contents selected: it is Create Text when None or Text is chosen, Image Editor when Image or Image on Disk is chosen, and Create Equation when Equation is chosen. Use this option to add or edit text to appear in the graphics box when it appears as Create Text. Use it to edit your graphic image when it appears as Image Editor. Or use it to add or edit an equation when it appears as Create Equation.
4. Create Caption...	Enables you to add a caption that appears with the graphics box. Note that WordPerfect automatically adds the next available box number as part of this caption. If you don't want this number to appear in the caption, highlight it and then delete it.
5. Options 1. Contents Options... 2. Caption Options...	Enables you to modify the position of the contents within the graphics box by choosing 1. Contents Options or to modify the position and format of the caption by choosing 2. Caption Options.
6. Edit Border/Fill...	Enables you to change the borders used by the box style you've chosen and/or to add a fill pattern for the graphics box.
7. Attach To	Enables you to change how the graphics box is anchored in the document (Fixed Page Position, Paragraph, Page, or Character Position). The way the graphics

	box is attached determines whether or not it moves with the text. For example, when attached to a paragraph, the graphic moves with the paragraph from page to page.
8. Edit Position...	Enables you to change the position of the graphics box. The actual options and dialog boxes that appear vary according to the Attach To option that's been selected.
9. Edit Size...	Enables you to set the height and the width of the graphics box (normally done automatically by WordPerfect).
T. Text Flow Around Box 1. Text Flows 2. Contour Text Flow	Enables you to change the way surrounding text flows in relation to the graphics box. Use 1. Text Flows to change which side or sides of the box the text flows on (On Larger Side, On Left Side, On Right Side, On Both Sides, On Neither Side, or Through Box). Use 2. Contour Text Flow to have WordPerfect wrap the text so that it follows the contour of the graphic (and not the graphics box) on the side or sides selected.
Y. Based on Box Style...	Enables you to select a new graphics box style that determines how the contents appear in the graphics box and how the graphics box appears in the document.

Moving and resizing graphics boxes

Once you've got your graphics box in the document, you may find that you need to move it around or make it bigger or smaller. If you're a mouse maniac, WordPerfect 6 makes this a snap. To move the box, just drag the box to its new position in the document. To resize the box, click on the box to make the *sizing handles* appear (the black boxes at the corners and the midpoints of each side), then pick a sizing handle and start dragging it until the box is the size and shape you want before you release the mouse button.

Note that this is one area where mouse users have it all over you keyboard users. If you want to move or resize a graphics box with the keyboard, you have to edit the graphics box and then use those silly 8. Edit Position and 9. Edit Size options to enter the *exact* measurements of the new vertical and horizontal position and the width and height of the graphics box.

Secret codes

Any time you insert a graphics box in the document, WordPerfect inserts a secret Box code that identifies the style, number, and contents of the graphics box. For example, suppose that you retrieve the grizzly bear graphic that comes with WordPerfect as the first graphic image in your document. When you open the Reveal Codes window, you'll see the secret code

```
[Box (Para):1;Figure Box]
```

where the grizzly should be. If you position the cursor on the secret code, it expands to

```
[Box (Para):Edit Num 1;Figure
Box;GRIZZLY.WPG;]
```

giving you even more details about the box and its contents (the most helpful of which is the filename).

More stuff

To get rid of a graphics box, open the Reveal Codes window (Alt+F3) and then position the cursor on the Box secret code and press Del. If you're in graphics or page mode and you use a mouse, you can also dispose of a box by clicking on it, pressing Del, and then choosing Yes in the message dialog box that asks you to delete the selected graphics box.

To edit a graphics box, position the cursor somewhere in front of the Box secret code and then open the Graphics menu. Choose Graphics Boxes, followed by Edit. WordPerfect displays a Select Box to Edit dialog box showing the number of the next graphics box in the document. Assuming that this dialog box contains the correct box number, simply choose the Edit Box button to open the Edit Graphics Box dialog box, showing the current settings for that graphics box. If you use the mouse, you can skip all of this because double-clicking the graphics box opens the Edit Graphics Box dialog box with the current settings. After changing all the settings that need changing, choose OK to close the Edit Graphics Box dialog box and update the graphics box in your document.

Graphics (Lines)

Enables you to liven up your document with vertical or horizontal lines (also known as rules).

Menus

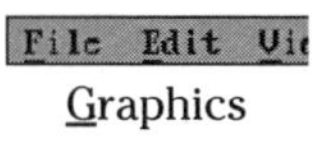

Graphics →

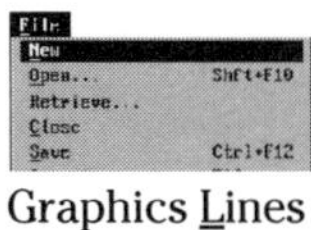

Graphics Lines →

▶ Create...
Edit...
Styles...

For function key freaks

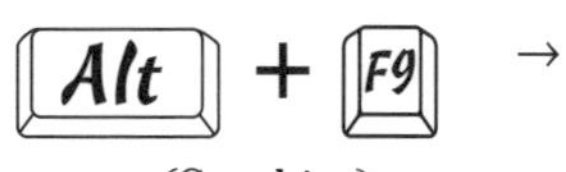

(Graphics)

→

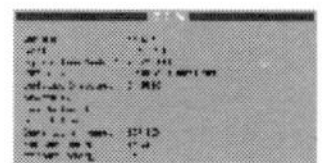

2. Graphics Lines
   1. Create...
   2. Edit...
   3. Styles...

The Create Graphics Line dialog box

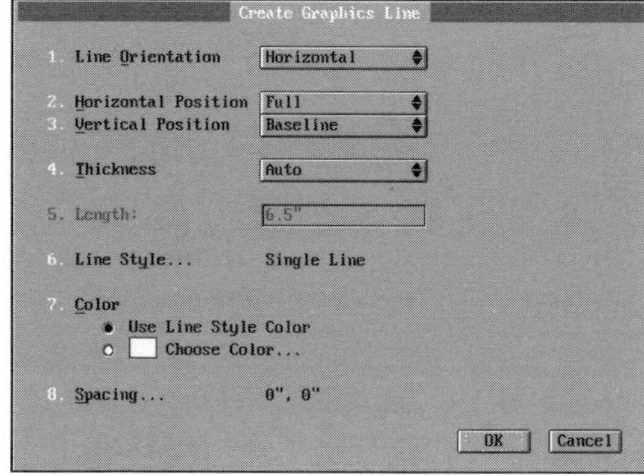

Option or Button	*Function*
1. Line Orientation	Enables you to choose between a Horizontal and a Vertical graphics line.
2. Horizontal Position	Enables you to choose the horizontal position for the graphics line which determines where it goes in relation to the left and right margins. If you're creating a horizontal line, you can choose between Set, Left, Right, Centered, and Full (default). If you're creating a vertical line, you can choose between Set, Left (default), Right, Centered, and Between Columns. Use Set to specify the distance from the left edge of the page.
3. Vertical Position	Enables you to choose the vertical position for the graphics line which determines where it goes in relation to the top and bottom margins. If you're creating a horizontal line, you can choose between Set and Baseline

	(default). If you're creating a vertical line, you can choose between Set, Top, Bottom, Centered, and Full (default). Use Set to specify the distance from the top edge of the page.
4. Thickness	Enables you to specify the thickness of the graphics line.
5. Length	Enables you to specify the length of the line — except when you're creating a horizontal line with a horizontal position of Full or a vertical line with a vertical position of Full.
6. Line Style...	Enables you to select a new line style for the graphics line (Single Line is the default).
7. Color	Enables you to specify a color for the line.
8. Spacing...	Enables you to specify the amount of space above and below a horizontal graphics line or between the margin and a left- or right-aligned vertical graphics line.

Secret codes

When you add a graphics line to your document, WordPerfect inserts a Graph Line secret code that describes the line's number and orientation. For example, if the first graphics line you add to a document is a horizontal line using all the default settings, you see the secret code

```
[Graph Line:1;Horiz]
```

in the Reveal Codes window. When you position the cursor on this code, it bulks out to

```
[Graph Line:Edit Num 1;Horiz;Single
Line;Full;Baseline;6.5";Auto]
```

More stuff

The only way to see a graphics line when the program is in text mode is with the Print Preview feature. To get rid of a graphics line, open the Reveal Codes window (Alt+F3), position the cursor on the Graph Line secret code, and press Del. If you're in graphics or page mode and you use a mouse, you can also dispose of a graphics line by clicking on it, pressing Del, and then choosing Yes in the message dialog box that asks you to delete the selected graphics line.

To edit a graphics line, position the cursor somewhere in front of the Box secret code and then open the Graphics menu. Choose Graphics Lines, followed by Edit. WordPerfect displays a Select Graphics Line to Edit dialog box, showing the number of the next line in the document. Assuming that this dialog box contains the correct line number, simply choose the Edit Line button to open the Edit Graphics Line dialog box, showing the current settings for the line.

If you use the mouse, you can skip all of this because double-clicking the graphics lines opens the Edit Graphics Line dialog box with the line's current settings. After changing all the settings that need changing, choose OK to close the Edit Graphics Line dialog box and update the graphics lines in your document.

Note that you can also move and size a graphics line with the mouse when WordPerfect is in graphics or page mode. To move the line, drag it to its new position and then release the mouse button. To change the length of the line, drag one of the sizing handles at each end of the line. To change the thickness of the line, drag one of the sizing handles on the top or bottom of the midpoint of the line.

Graphics Mode

Enables you to see the fonts, graphics, and text layout in your document pretty darn close to the way they'll appear when you print the document. Graphics mode can slow WordPerfect down to a crawl, however.

Menus

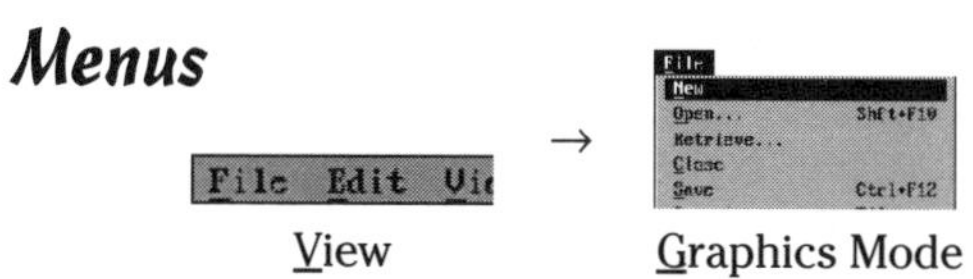

View → Graphics Mode

For function key freaks

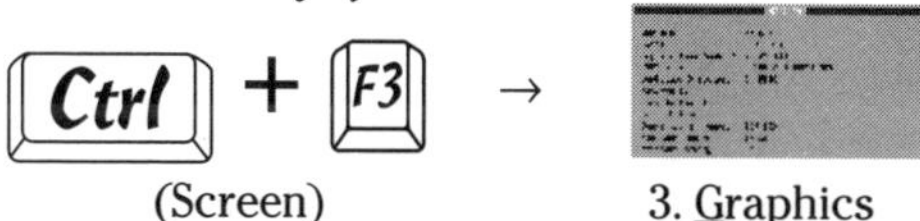

Ctrl + F3 (Screen) → 3. Graphics

Hanging Indent

Sets off the first line of an indented paragraph by releasing it to the left margin. Be sure that the cursor's at the beginning of the first line of the paragraph before you choose the Hanging Indent command.

Menus

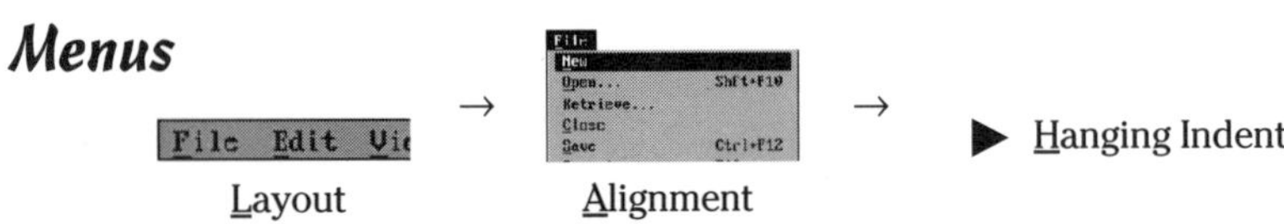

Layout → Alignment → ▶ Hanging Indent

For function key freaks

F4 (Indent) Shift + Tab (Margin Release)

Secret codes

When you choose the Hanging Indent command, WordPerfect inserts these two Secret codes back to back:

```
[Lft Indent][Back Tab]
```

If you open the Reveal Codes window and zap the [Back Tab] secret code (this is the same code that WordPerfect inserts when you press the Shift+Tab or Margin Release key) without bothering the [Lft Indent] code, the entire paragraph is indented on the left to the first tab stop. If you delete the [Lft Indent] secret code without zapping the [Back Tab] code, the paragraph returns to the left margin, but the beginning of the first line disappears off the left side of the screen (as the line is released to the tab stop in front of the left margin).

Header/Footer

Adds a header to the document that prints the same information at the top of each page or a footer that prints the same information at the bottom of each page.

Menus

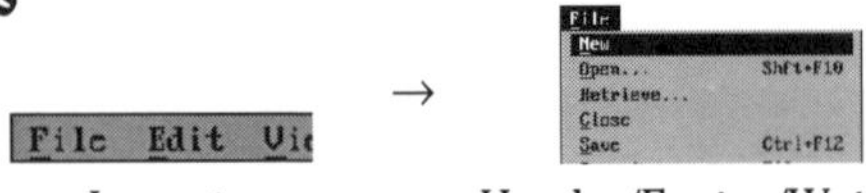

Layout → Header/Footer/Watermark...

For function key freaks

Shift + F8 (Format) → 5. Header/Footer/Watermark...

Creating a header or footer

WordPerfect enables you to create up to two different headers and footers for a document (you can put one header on even pages and another on odd pages, for example). To create a header or footer for the document, follow these steps:

1. Position the insertion point somewhere on the first page of the document where the header or footer is to appear. If you want the header or footer to appear on every page of the document, make sure that your cursor is on page 1. If you don't want the header or footer to appear on the first page, make sure your cursor is on page 2 (or whichever page should be the first).
2. Choose the Layout menu and then select the Header/Footer/Watermark command — or press Shift+F8 (Format). Choose the 5. Header/Footer/Watermark option to open the Header/Footer/Watermark dialog box.
3. To create a header, choose the 1. Headers option. To create a footer, choose the 2. Footers option.
4. If you choose 1. Headers option, choose 1. Header A option if you're creating your first header; otherwise, choose the 2. Header B option. By default, WordPerfect separates the body of the document from the header text with 0.167 inch of space (12 points). If you want to increase or decrease this spacing, choose the 3. Space Below Header option and then enter the new value in its text box (to enter this value in points, type a *p* after your value, as in **18p** when you want to designate 18 points as the space). Do this before you choose the 1. Header A or 2. Header B option to create your new header.
5. If you choose 2. Footers option, choose 1. Footer A option if you're creating your first footer, otherwise, choose the 2. Footer B option. By default, WordPerfect separates the body of the document from the footer text with 0.167 inch of space (12 points). If you want to increase or decrease this spacing, choose the 3. Space Above Footer option and then enter the new value in its text box before you choose the 1. Footer A or 2. Footer B option to create your new footer.
6. In the Header A (or B) or Footer A (or B) dialog box, choose the pages on which the header or footer should appear. By default, the 1. All Pages radio button is selected. To have the header or footer appear on only even-numbered pages, choose the 2. Even Pages option. To have the header or footer appear on only odd-numbered pages, choose the 3. Odd Pages option.
7. Choose the Create button or press Enter.

8. WordPerfect opens a new document window in which you can enter the text of header or footer on as many lines as you need. Format the text of your header or footer using the same WordPerfect commands as you would to format normal document text. To insert the page number in the header or footer, open the Layout menu and then choose Page. Choose the 1. Page Numbering option (see Page Numbering). To insert the current date in the header or footer, choose the Date command on the Tools menu and then select the Text or Code (if you want WordPerfect to keep updating the date or time). To insert the filename, open the Layout menu and then choose Other and 5. Insert Filename (see Insert Filename).
9. When you've finished entering and formatting the header or footer text, press F7 (Exit) to return the document.

Secret codes

When you create a header for footer, WordPerfect inserts a [Header] or [Footer] secret code at the top of the current page that identifies the letter of the header or footer. For example, if you add a single footer to all pages that inserts the name of the document (called MYJUNK.DOC) flush with the right margin, you see the secret code `[Footer A]` when you open the Reveal Codes window. When you position the cursor on the secret code, it then expands to

```
[Footer A:All Pages;[FlshRgt]
[Filename;MYJUNK.DOC]]
```

which tells you that this footer shows up on all pages and gives a whole bunch of details about its contents.

More stuff

To see your header or footer on the screen, you must put WordPerfect into page mode or open the Print Preview window (by choosing Print Preview on the File menu). To edit a header or footer, you must open the Layout menu and choose Header/Footer/Watermark. Choose 1. Headers or 2. Footers and then choose 1 Header A or 2 Header B or 1. Footer A or 2 Footer B. Finally, choose Edit to have WordPerfect open the Header or Footer editing window. Make your changes and then press F7 (Exit) to return to your document.

To discontinue a header or footer from a certain page onward to the end of the document, open the dialog box for the particular Header or Footer (A or B) and then choose the Off button. To suppress the display of a header or footer on just one particular page, open the Layout menu, choose Page, and then choose 9.

Suppress... (Page Numbering, Headers, and so on). Then select the option for the header or footer you don't want printed on that page (see Suppress for details).

To get rid of a header or footer from the entire document, go to the top of the first page on which it occurs and open the Reveal Codes window (Alt+F3). Then position the cursor on the [Header] or [Footer] secret code and press Del.

Note that WordPerfect 6.0 also enables you to create a watermark, which is kinda like a header or footer.

Help

Gets you help on using a particular WordPerfect feature just as you're valiantly trying to figure out how to get WordPerfect to do what you want.

Menus

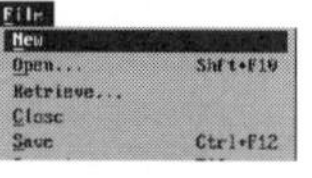

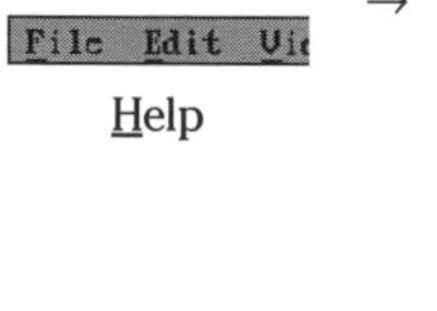

Help → Contents... F1
Index...
How Do I...
Coaches...
Macros...
Tutorial...
WP Info...

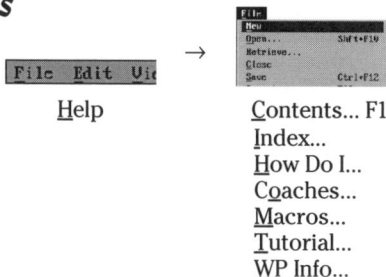

For function key freaks

(Help)

The Help menu commands

Help Command	Function
Contents...	Displays the Contents Help dialog box in which you can select the help index, help on particular tasks, a glossary of terms, function key template, or a list of common keystrokes, shortcut keys, or error messages.
Index...	Displays an alphabetical index of help topics. To display the online help, highlight the topic and press Enter.

How Do I...	Displays a list of common tasks that you perform with WordPerfect, organized by the categories Basics, Basic Layout, Advanced Layout, Writing Tools, Graphics/Equations, Macros, and Merge. To get help on a particular task, highlight it and press Enter.
Coaches	Displays an alphabetical list of topics on which WordPerfect can coach you. To have the program coach you through performing a particular task, highlight it and press Enter.
Macros...	Displays a Contents Help dialog box in which you can get all sorts of help on creating and using macros.
Tutorial	Starts an online tutorial that you can use to learn the basics of using WordPerfect.
WP Info...	Displays a list of boring statistics on WordPerfect (such as the version number, date, and registration number) and how its using your hardware (such as memory available and the printer you've selected).

More stuff

To get help on a particular menu or dialog box option while you're trying to use the darn things, press F1 (Help) after highlighting the particular menu command or opening the particular dialog box. Some dialog boxes also have a Help button that you can use in the same way as the F1 key to get help on the use of the dialog box options.

Hypertext

Enables you to jump to a bookmark (see Bookmark) elsewhere in the same — or even a different — document or to run a favorite macro (see Macros).

Menus

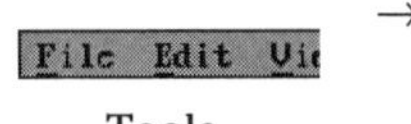

Tools

→

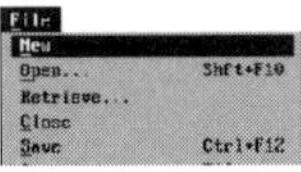

Hypertext...

For function key freaks

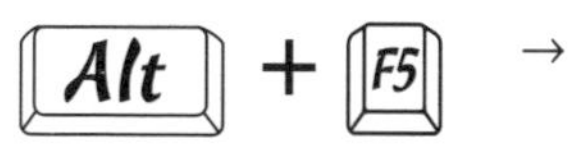

(Mark Text)

→

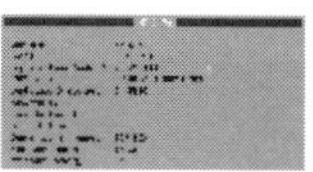

6. Hypertext...

The Hypertext dialog box

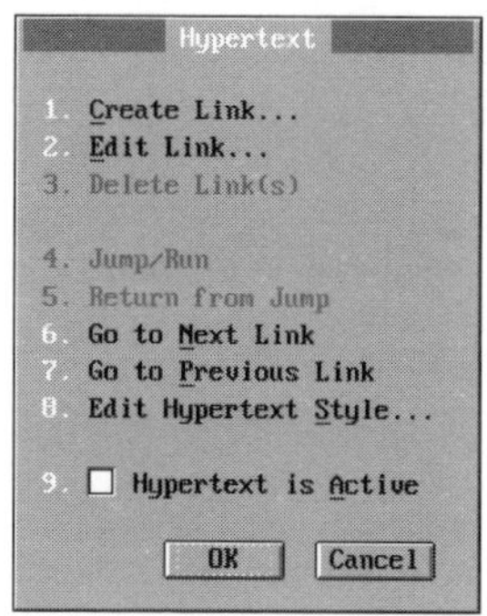

Option or Button	*Function*
1. Create Link...	Enables you to create a link to a particular bookmark you've created in this or another document, or to a macro that you want to run. When creating a link to a bookmark or macro, you can also indicate whether the hypertext should appear as highlighted text or in a button (which shows up only in graphics or page display mode).
2. Edit Link...	Enables you to edit a particular hypertext link.
3. Delete Link(s)	Enables you to get rid of a particular hypertext link.
4. Jump/Run	Jumps you to the bookmark that's linked to the hypertext, or runs the macro that you've linked to it.
5. Return from Jump	Returns you to the hypertext from which you jumped to the current bookmark.

6. Go to Next Link	Takes you to the next hypertext link in the document.
7. Go to Previous Link	Takes you to the previous hypertext link in the document.
8. Edit Hypertext Style...	Enables you to edit the Hypertext Style used to highlight hypertext in the document. Normally, WordPerfect displays hypertext as bold and underlined. You can edit the Hypertext Style to include any kind of formatting that you see fit (such as Very Large italicized text or whatever).
9. Hypertext is Active	Enables you to activate the Hypertext feature in your document, so that you jump and return from a linked bookmark or run a linked macro.

More stuff

Before you can create a hypertext link, you must create the bookmarks (see Bookmark for details) or macros (see Macros) that you want to link to. Then you must locate the text you want to designate as hypertext (meaning that this text activates the link to the bookmark or macro) and mark it as a block.

After you create a hypertext link, you can jump to the linked bookmark or run the macro by locating the cursor on the hypertext (shown in the document highlighted according to the Hypertext Style or within a button) and then pressing Enter (or clicking on it with the mouse), provided that the Hypertext is Active check box in the Hypertext dialog box is checked.

If the Hypertext is Active option is not checked, you can jump to the bookmark or run the linked macro by opening the Hypertext dialog box: choose Hypertext on the Tools menu and then choose 4. Jump/Run. To return to the hypertext in the document open the Hypertext dialog box and choose 5. Return from Jump.

Hyphenation

Automatically hyphenates words in a paragraph to reduce the raggedness of the right margin (when using Left justification) or the white space between words in the lines (when using Full justification).

Menus

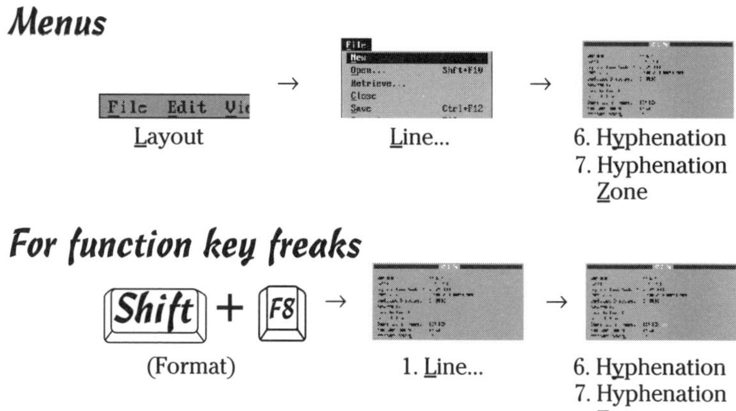

Layout → Line... → 6. Hyphenation
7. Hyphenation Zone

For function key freaks

(Format) → 1. Line... → 6. Hyphenation
7. Hyphenation Zone

Manual hyphenation or all hyphens are not created equal

Normally, WordPerfect inserts a soft return (with the secret code [SRt]) in front of any word at the end of a line that extends beyond the right margin, which it then wraps to the beginning of the next line in the paragraph. If you are using left justification in the document, word wrap can create an extremely raggedy right margin if you're using lots of big words that WordPerfect has to wrap to the beginning of new lines. If you are using full justification, word wrap can create big areas of white space in a paragraph because it pads the lines in a paragraph with white space to fill out each line and make its text flush right.

To reduce the raggedness of the right margin or amount of space between words in a line, you can hyphenate words that WordPerfect wraps. In WordPerfect, you can hyphenate text manually or you can use the program's automatic Hyphenation feature to do the job for you. When hyphenating text manually, you need to be aware of the different types of hyphens and their function in the document. The following table shows you these hyphen characters, along with some other special characters that you can use to indicate when and how words can break when they fall at the end of a line.

Keystroke	*Secret Code*	*What It's Good For*
-	[- Hyphen]	Hyphen placed in document when you press the hyphen (-) key that indicates where WordPerfect may break the word when it falls at the end of the line.
Ctrl+Shift+-	[- Soft Hyphen]	Soft hyphen placed in document when WordPerfect hyphenates a word or when you type Ctrl+Shift+-. A soft hyphen disappears if the word no longer falls at the end of the line and needs to be hyphenated.
Home,- (hyphen)	- (non bold)	Hard hyphen that binds the two words so that WordPerfect does not separate the two words when they fall at the end of a line.
Home+Spacebar	[HSpace]	Hard space that binds two words and the space between them so that WordPerfect does not separate the words when they fall at the end of a line.
Home, Enter	[Hyph SRt]	Hyphenation Soft return that indicates where WordPerfect can break a word, without inserting a soft hyphen, when the word falls at the end of a line.

Automatic Hyphenation

If you want, you can have WordPerfect do all of the hard work of hyphenating your text for you. To have the program hyphenate your words according to its dictionary, follow these steps:

1. Position the cursor at the place in the document where you want to turn on hyphenation. To hyphenate the entire document, press Home, Home, Home ↑ to move the cursor to the beginning of the document.

2. Choose the Line command on the Layout menu — or press Shift+F8 (Format) — and then choose the 1. Line option.
3. Select the 6. Hyphenation option to put an X in its check box and then choose OK or press Enter. WordPerfect inserts the [Hyph On] code in the document and, from that point on, hyphenates the document as required by hyphenation zone.
4. As you add text from the cursor's position or scroll through the document, WordPerfect displays the Position Hyphen dialog box, prompting you to confirm its suggested hyphenation of the word (if that word isn't in the spelling dictionary).
5. To accept the position of the hyphen, select the 1. Insert Hyphen option. To reposition the hyphen in the word before hyphenating it, press the ← or → until the word is hyphenated correctly and then choose the 1. Insert Hyphen option. To insert a space rather than a hyphen in the word, choose the 2. Insert Space option. To insert a hyphenation soft return to break the word without inserting a space, choose the 3. Hyphenation SRt option. To temporarily suspend the hyphenation (so that you can do something else like scroll the text or spell check it), choose the 4. Suspend Hyphenation option. To have WordPerfect wrap the entire word to the next line rather than break with a hyphen, space, or hyphenation soft return, choose the 5. Ignore Word option.
6. To turn off hyphenation at beginning of the paragraph where the cursor is positioned in the document, choose the Line command on the Layout menu — or press Shift+F8 (Format) — and then choose the 1. Line option. Select the 6. Hyphenation option to remove the X from its check box and then choose OK or press Enter. WordPerfect inserts an [Hyph Off] code at the beginning of the current paragraph, and from this point on WordPerfect simply word wraps the words at the end of your lines that extend beyond the right margin.

Secret codes

WordPerfect inserts a [Hyph On] secret code where you turn on hyphenation in the document and a [Hyph Off] secret code where you turn it off. When WordPerfect prompts you to hyphenate a word, and you choose the 5. Ignore Word option, the program inserts a [Cancel Hyph] secret code right in front of the word that doesn't get hyphenated (but wrapped to the next line instead).

More stuff

WordPerfect maintains a *hot* zone made up of a left and right hyphenation zone that determines when a word is up for hyphenation. To be a candidate for hyphenation, a word must start within the left zone and extend beyond the right zone. To change how often WordPerfect bugs you to hyphenate words, you can monkey around with the size of the left and/or right zones. To change these, open the Line Format dialog box and then choose 7. Hyphenation Zone. Change the percentages in the left and/or right text boxes (increasing the zone percentages to do less hyphenating or decreasing them to hyphenate more words).

Indent

Moves the left edge of an entire paragraph one tab stop to the right, creating an indent that sets it off from normal text. Be sure that the cursor is positioned at the very beginning of the paragraph before you indent it.

Menus

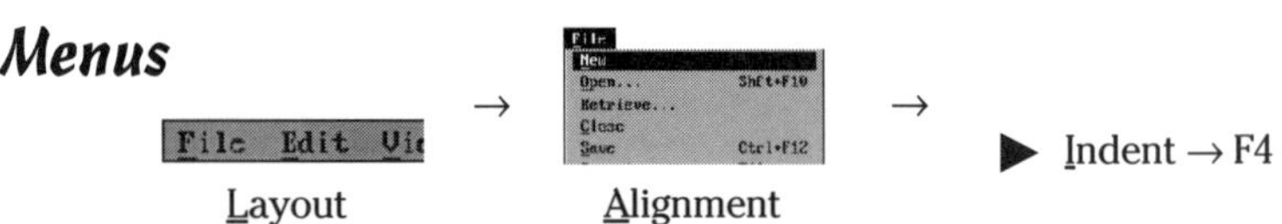

Layout → Alignment → ▶ Indent → F4

For function key freaks

(→ Indent)

Secret codes

When you indent a paragraph, WordPerfect inserts the secret code `[Lft Indent]` at the cursor's position in the line. To remove an indent that you inserted by accident, position the cursor on the [Lft Indent] code in the Reveal Codes window and press Del.

Insert Filename

Enables you to insert the document's filename (with or without its inscrutable path name) into your document. You can use this nifty feature to add the filename to your header or footer so that you can cross-reference the printout with its disk file.

Menus

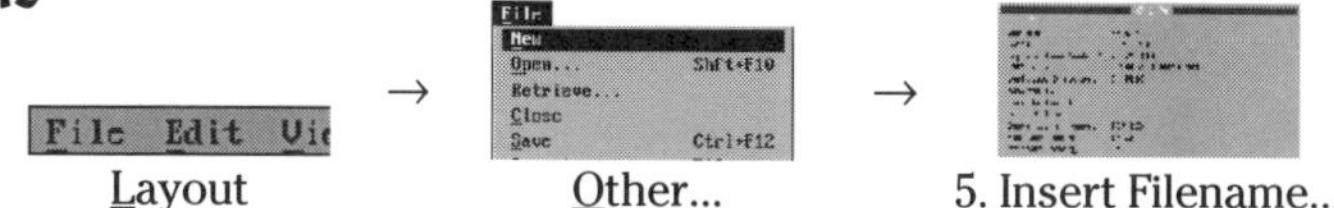

Layout → Other... → 5. Insert Filename...

For function key freaks

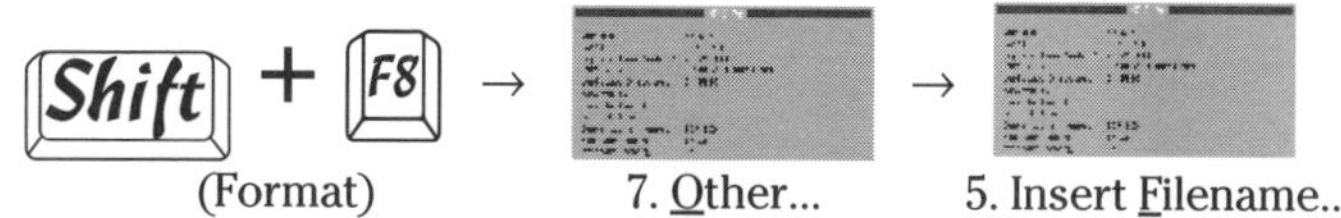

(Format) → 7. Other... → 5. Insert Filename...

The Insert Filename dialog box

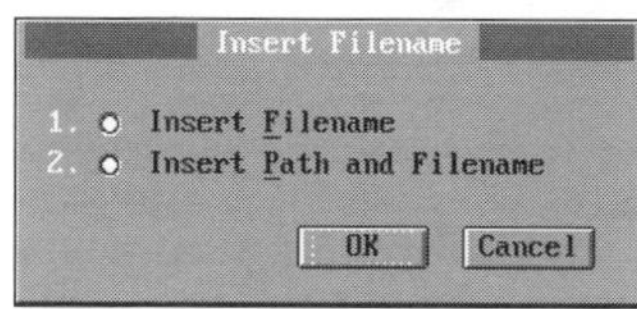

To insert just the filename of your document, choose 1. Insert Filename in the Insert Filename dialog box. To insert the directory path (starting with the drive letter) as part of the filename, choose 2. Insert Path and Filename instead.

Secret codes

When you use the Insert Filename feature to insert the document name (with or without path), WordPerfect inserts a `[Filename]` secret code in the text. If you position the cursor on this secret code, it expands to show the name of the document (including the pathname, when you use that option).

More stuff

Because WordPerfect inserts a secret code that produces the filename, the program automatically updates the filename if you rename the document with the Save As command on the File menu. You can even use this feature to insert the filename before you save the document the first time.

Justification

Changes the way paragraphs are aligned in the document. You can choose between Left (which gives you a flush left, ragged right margin), Center (which centers all lines between the left and right margins), Full (which gives you a flush left and flush right margin), and Full, All Lines justification (which forces-justifies even the last, short line of each paragraph so that it is flush left and right like all the other full lines).

Menus

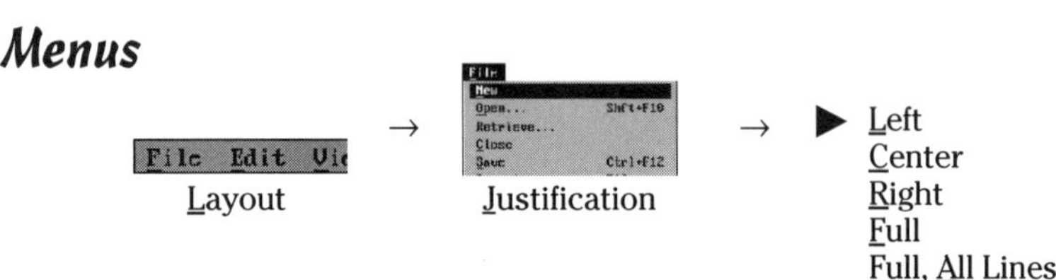

Layout → Justification → ▶ Left
Center
Right
Full
Full, All Lines

For function key freaks

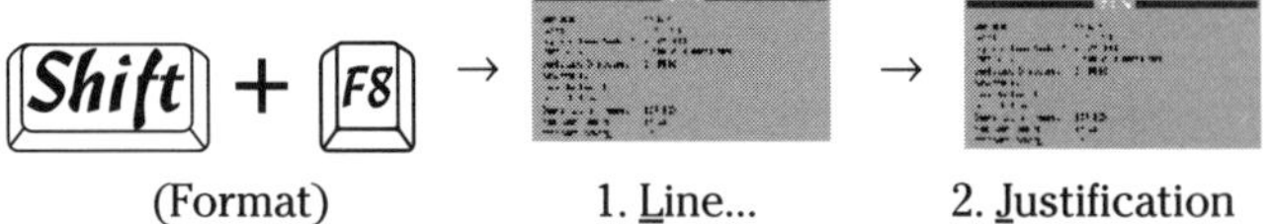

Shift + F8 (Format) → 1. Line... → 2. Justification
1. Left
2. Center
3. Right
4. Full
5. Full, All Lines

Secret codes

When you change the justification in the document, WordPerfect inserts a [Just] secret code. If you position the cursor on this secret code, WordPerfect expands it to indicate the type of justification that is in effect.

More stuff

Unlike changes in alignment with the Center or Flush Left commands — which affect text only in the current line up to the hard return ([HRt] secret code) that begins the next line — changes in the justification of a document affect all text from the [Just] secret code onward. Therefore the only way to return text to normal left justification after changing to another justification is to position the cursor where the text should return to normal and follow the steps to insert the [Just:Left] secret code.

Labels

Formats addresses for a whole bunch of different mailing labels that you can get for a printer when using labels to address your mail.

Menus

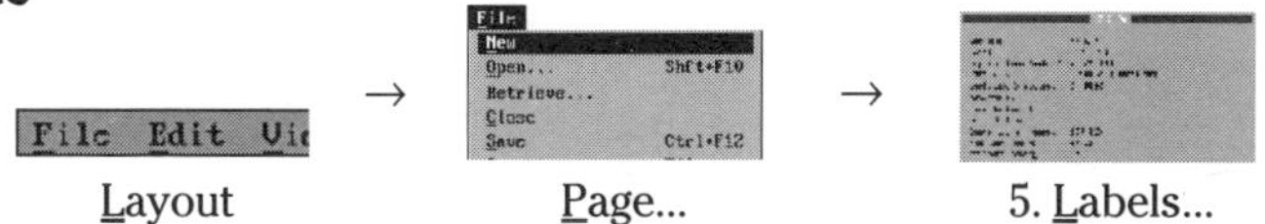

Layout → Page... → 5. Labels...

For function key freaks

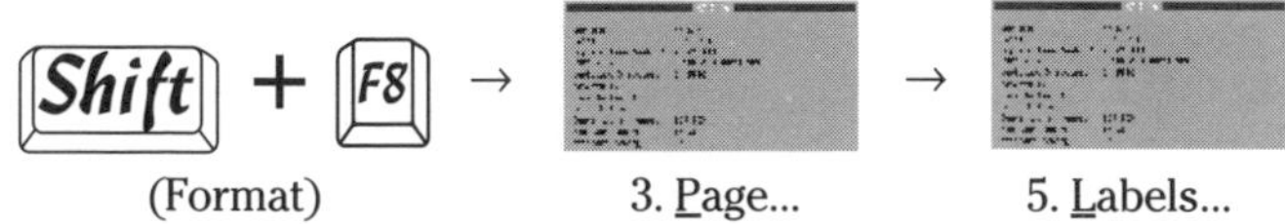

(Format) → 3. Page... → 5. Labels...

The Labels dialog box

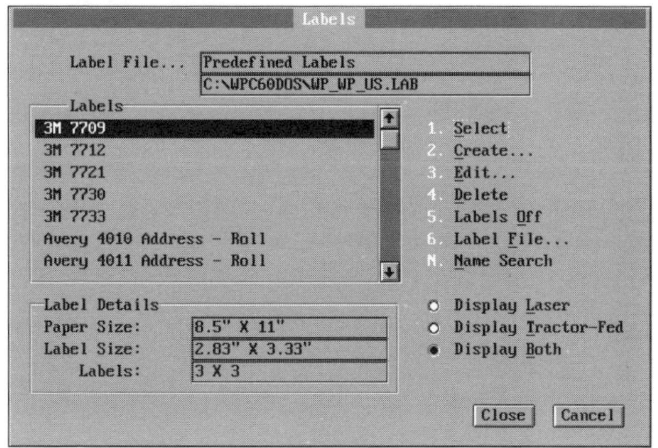

Option or Button	*Function*
1. Select	Selects the labels highlighted in the Labels list box.
2. Create	Enables you to create a new label definition if none of the predefined labels work.

3. Edit...	Enables you to modify the predefined label definition that's selected in the Labels list box if its definition requires some modification.
4. Labels Off	Turns off labels in a document and returns you to the normal paper size and type for your printer (usually letter size).
5. Label File	Enables you to select, create, or edit a new file of label definitions for use with your printer. The file you select here shows up in the Label File text boxes at the top of the Labels dialog box (by default, this file is WP_WP_US.LAB).
N. Name Search	Enables you to select a label definition in the Labels list box by typing the first few characters of its name.
Display Laser	Displays only the label definitions in the Labels list box that are for laser printers.
Display Tractor-Fed	Displays only the tractor-fed label definitions in the Labels list box.
Display Both	Displays both laser and tractor fed label definitions in the Labels list box (this is the default).

Secret codes

When you select a labels definition, WordPerfect inserts two Secret codes back to back:

```
[Labels Form][Paper Sz/Typ]
```

If you position the cursor on the [Labels Form] Secret code in the Reveal Codes window, the code lists the predefined label form selected. If you position the cursor on the [Paper Sz/Typ] Secret code, it expands to list the paper size and type used with the particular labels form.

When you turn off labels in a document, WordPerfect inserts a [Labels Form:Off] Secret code in the document along with a [Paper Sz/Typ] Secret code that returns the paper size to whatever's normal for your printer (often letter paper).

More stuff

When you select a labels form that has multiple labels on a single physical page, WordPerfect treats each label as its own page on the screen. (In other words, the Page indicator changes as you go from label to label.) Therefore, to start filling in a new label, press Ctrl+Enter (Hard Page). To see how each individual label will look, get into page mode (by choosing Page Mode on the View menu). To see how a whole page of labels will print, open the Print Preview window (by choosing Print Preview on the File menu).

Line Draw

Enables you to draw simple lines and boxes in your document.

Menus

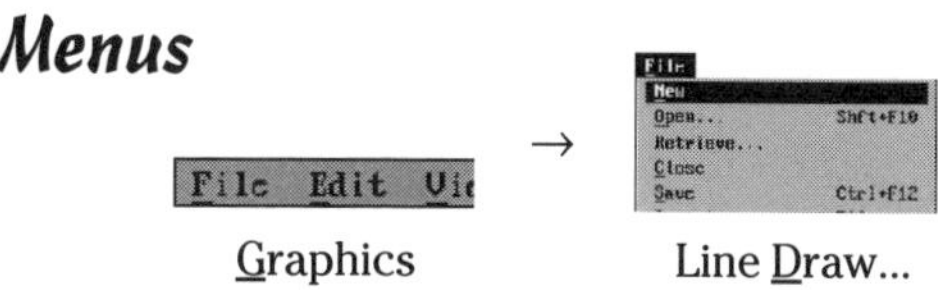

Graphics → Line Draw...

For function key freaks

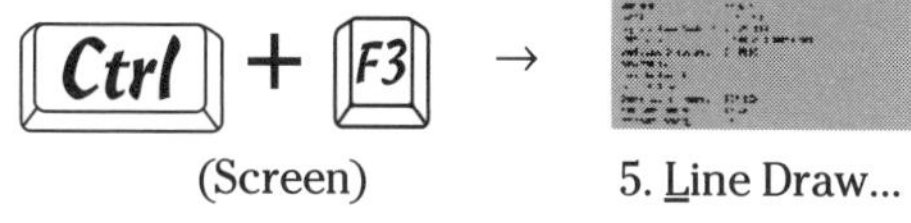

Ctrl + F3 (Screen) → 5. Line Draw...

Using Line Draw

Line Draw makes WordPerfect into a kind of Etch-a-Sketch whereby you can use your arrow keys to draw lines and boxes in your document. Although Line Draw makes it a snap to draw lines and boxes, you have to be careful when mixing these graphics with text (as when creating an organizational chart). The key to using Line Draw, therefore, is to use only a monospaced font, like good old Courier, and make sure that WordPerfect is in Typeover mode (not its natural Insert mode — see Typeover) when you type information in a box.

To create lines and boxes with Line Draw, follow these steps:

1. Position the cursor at the place in the document where you want the line drawing to appear.
2. Choose Line Draw on the Graphics menu — (or press Ctrl+F3 (Screen) and choose 5. Line Draw). WordPerfect opens the Line Draw dialog box at the bottom of the screen

and removes the pull-down menus, ribbon, and any other such stuff from the top of the screen.

3. By default, WordPerfect selects a single line graphics character for drawing. To draw with a double line, choose option 2. @| |. To draw with an asterisk, choose option 3. *. To draw with another graphics character, choose option 4. Change and then choose the option of the character you want to use (1. through 8.) in the Change Line Draw Character. To draw with another keyboard character (such as $ or @), choose 9. User-defined. Then type the character you want to use. The graphics character or keyboard character you select with the 4. Change option then replaces the * after option 3. in the Line Draw dialog box.
4. To start drawing, press the arrow keys. WordPerfect draws lines in the direction of the arrow key, using the Line Draw character you've selected.
5. If you make a mistake when drawing, choose 5. Erase, and then press the opposite arrow key to erase all or part of the line you messed up.
6. If you need to have a break in your drawing, choose 6. Move. Move the cursor to the place where the drawing should recommence and then select the option for the character you want to draw with (1., 2., or 3.). Choosing Move is like picking up your pen so that nothing takes place as you move the cursor with the arrow keys.
7. When you've finished your line-drawing masterpiece, choose Close or press F7 to close the Line Draw dialog box and return to your document.

More stuff

If you have a printer capable of printing graphics, you can create boxes and lines in a document with the Graphics Boxes and Graphics Lines features — see Graphics (Boxes) and Graphics (Lines) for details. In addition, you can also use the Borders feature (see Borders) to put border lines around paragraphs, pages, or columns of document text.

Line Height

Enables you to control how much blank space WordPerfect puts between each line of text on a page (something WordPerfect normally takes care of automatically).

Menus

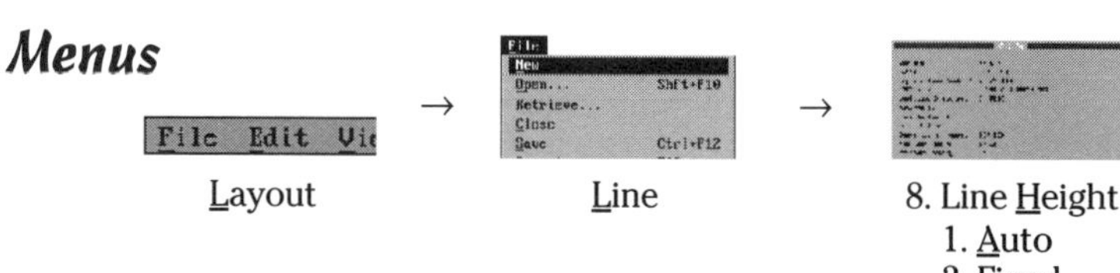

Layout → Line → 8. Line Height
1. Auto
2. Fixed

For function key freaks

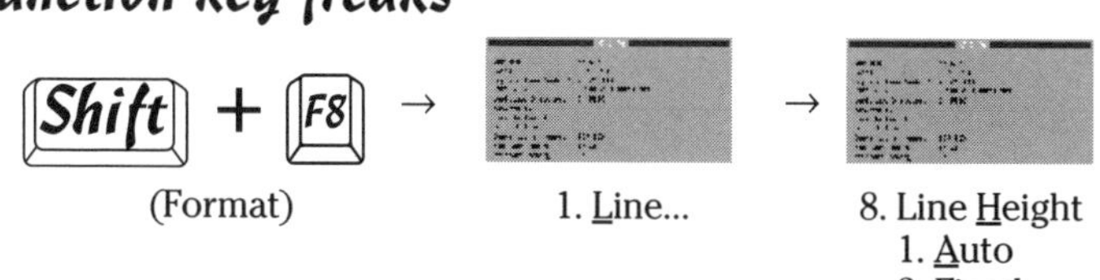

(Format) → 1. Line... → 8. Line Height
1. Auto
2. Fixed

Secret codes

When you set a fixed line height for your text, WordPerfect inserts a `[Ln Height]` Secret code in the document. If you position the cursor on this Secret code, it expands to display the new line height. For example, if you fix the line height at 1/4 inch, the expanded Secret code appears as `[Ln Height:0.25"]`when you highlight it in the Reveal Codes window.

More stuff

Most of the time, you won't have to monkey with the line height because WordPerfect automatically increases this as necessary to accommodate the largest font that you use in a line.

Position the cursor at the beginning of the first line you want to fix and choose 8. Line Height in the Line Format dialog box. Next, choose 2. Fixed, enter the new measurement, and press Enter. To have WordPerfect once more determine the best line height for your text, choose 1. Auto in the same dialog box.

Line Numbering

Numbers the lines on each page of your document.

Menus

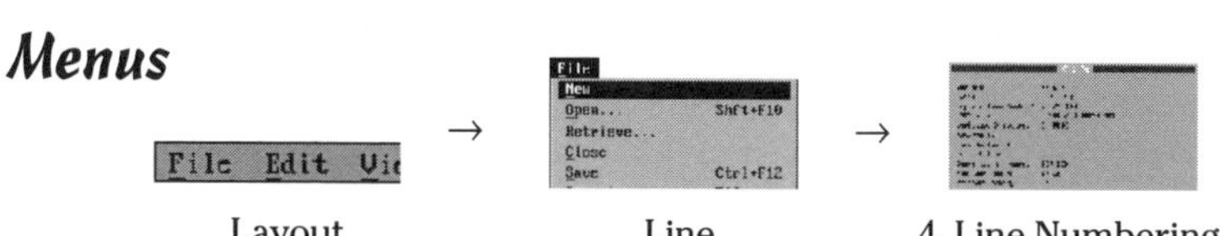

Layout → Line → 4. Line Numbering...

For function key freaks

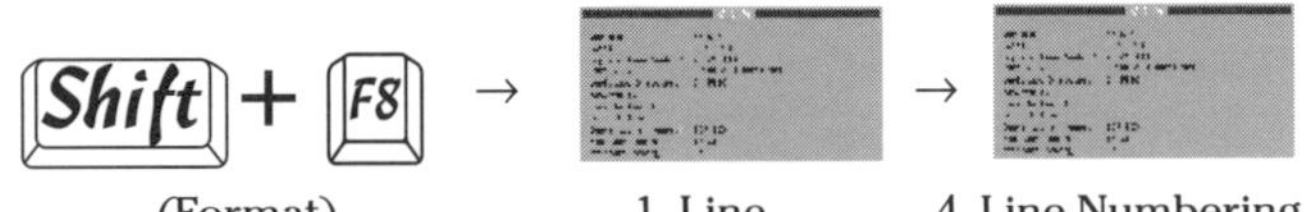

The Line Numbering Format dialog box

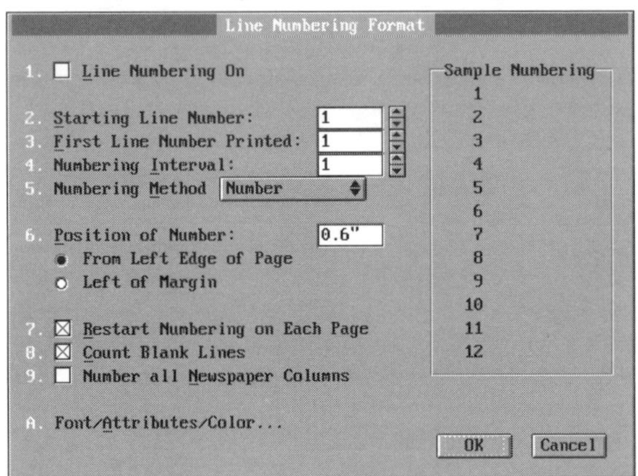

Option or Button	*Function*
1. Line Numbering On	Enables you to turn on and off line numbering at the current line. If this check box has an X in it, line numbering is turned on. If it's empty, line number is off.
2. Starting Line Number	Enables you to change the starting line (1 by default).
3. First Line Number Printed	Enables you to select the first line number to be printed in the document (1 by default).
4. Numbering Interval	Enables you to change the interval between the numbers printed in the document (1 by default).
5. Numbering Method	Enables you to select a new numbering method: Number (the default), Lower Letter, Upper Letter, Lower Roman, or Upper Roman.

6. Position of Number	Enables you to change the position of the line numbers. You can position the numbers from either the left edge of the page or from the left margin.
7. Restart Numbering Each Page	Enables you to have WordPerfect restart the numbering (from the Starting Line Number) on each new page of the document.
8. Count Blank Lines	Enables you to determine whether or not blank lines are counted in the line numbering. (Blank lines are counted by default.)
9. Number all Newspaper Columns	Enables you to determine whether each newspaper column on the page gets line numbers.
A. Font/Attributes/Color...	Enables you to select a new font, attributes, and color for the line numbers.

Secret codes

When you turn on line numbering in the document, WordPerfect inserts a [Ln Num] Secret code at the beginning of the current line that turns on line numbering from that line onward. (If you position the cursor on this code, it expands to [Ln Num:On] in Reveal Codes.) When you turn off line numbering in the document, WordPerfect inserts a [Ln Num: Off] Secret code at the beginning of the current line.

More stuff

Line numbering is one of those elements that doesn't show up on the screen in any display mode (not even in page mode where you'd surely think it would). The only way to see your line numbers prior to printing the document is in the Print Preview window (opened by choosing Print Preview on the File menu).

Line Spacing

Changes the line spacing of the text in your document.

Menus

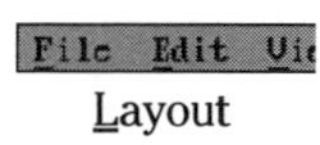

Layout

→

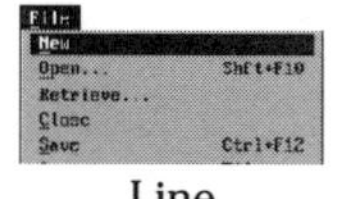

Line

→

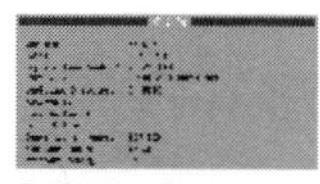

3. Line Spacing

For function key freaks

Shift + F8 → →

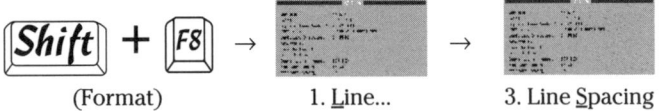

(Format) 1. Line... 3. Line Spacing

Secret codes

When you change the line spacing, WordPerfect inserts a [Ln Spacing] Secret code at the beginning of the current line. If you position the cursor on this Secret code, it expands to show the new spacing. For example, if you set the spacing to double spacing and you then open Reveal Codes and put the cursor on the [Ln Spacing] Secret code, it shows up as [Ln Spacing:2.0] in the Reveal Codes window.

More stuff

When setting the line spacing for your document, WordPerfect lets you enter values that are smaller than ½-line increments. Keep in mind, however, that your printer may not be able to deal with anything smaller. Whenever possible, WordPerfect displays the new line spacing on the screen more or less as it will print.

Macros

Enables you to record WordPerfect commands that perform a routine task automatically and at a much faster rate than you could possibly do it manually.

Menus

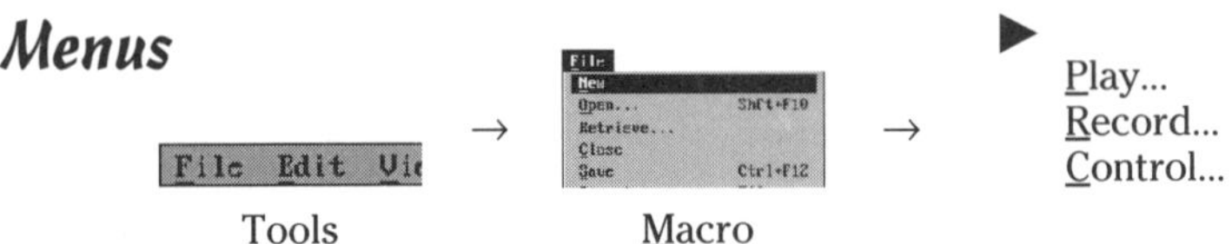

Tools → Macro → Play... / Record... / Control...

For function key freaks

To play a macro:

Alt + F10

(Macro Play)

To record a new macro:

Ctrl + F10

(Macro Record)

To display the Macro Control dialog box:

(Macro Control)

Recording macros

Recording macros in WordPerfect is like recording cassette tapes or videotapes. After you turn on the macro recorder, WordPerfect records the result of each action, such as typing some text or choosing some new format settings. You can use the macro recorder to record a straight series of WordPerfect commands (like changing the top margin to two inches and the line spacing to double spacing), a straight series of words or phrases (such as *Abercrombie, Fitch, Abercrombie and Phelps*), or a combination of commands and text (such as entering the company name *Baggins and Bilbo, Inc.*, and then centering and boldfacing this text before inserting two blank lines).

To record a macro, follow these steps:

1. Position the cursor at the point in your document where it's safe (and possible) to execute all the WordPerfect commands you want to record in your macro.
2. Choose the Macro command from the Tools menu and then choose Record. Or simply press Ctrl+F10.
3. In the Record Macro dialog box, enter a name for the macro and choose OK. The name can be as long as eight characters and must represent a valid filename with no extension. (WordPerfect automatically assigns the extension .WPM to the filename you enter.) To make it easier to play back the macro, you can assign Alt plus a single letter key as the filename. For example, if you enter **alta** as the filename, you can then play the macro simply by pressing Alt+A.
4. Enter the keystrokes and commands you want to record. WordPerfect displays the message `Recording Macro` to remind you that you're in macro recording mode. If you need to reposition the cursor during macro recording, use the keyboard, not the mouse.
5. When you're finished, choose the Macro option from the Tools menu and then choose Stop (or press Ctrl+F10 again). WordPerfect compiles the macro and stores it in a file with a name that corresponds to the macro's name.

Playing back macros

To play back an Alt+letter key macro, you simply press Alt plus the letter key. To play back a macro with a regular filename, choose the Macro command from the Tools menu and then choose Play. Or simply press Alt+F10 (Play Macro). Then type the macro's filename (without its .WPM extension) and press Enter or choose OK.

When you play back a macro, WordPerfect plays back each command in the sequence in which it was recorded. If you find that your macro is not behaving as expected, you can stop the playback by pressing the Esc key. Because of the potential danger in playing back an untested macro, you should always make sure that you save the current document before you play back a macro for the first time. That way, should the macro wreak havoc in your document before you can shut it down with the Esc key, you can always close the trashed document without saving your changes and then open the previously saved version on disk.

More stuff

If you're a mouse maniac, you can use the mouse when recording macros to choose the WordPerfect commands that you want on the pull-down menus and in the dialog boxes. However, if you want to record cursor movements as part of the macro, you must abandon the mouse and switch to the cursor movement keys because WordPerfect can't record the repositioning of the cursor in the text by clicking the mouse or with the scroll bars.

Margins

Enables you to set new left, right, top, and bottom margins for your document. Also enables you to indent the first line or the left or right margin of each paragraph without changing the left and right margin settings.

Menus

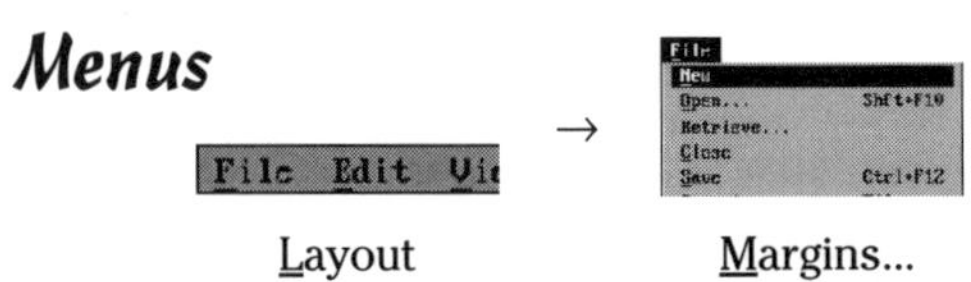

Layout → Margins...

For function key freaks

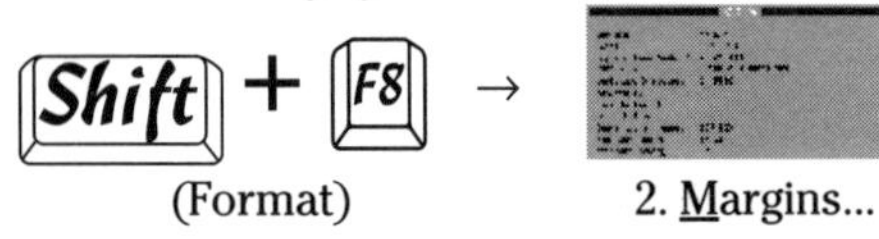

(Format) → 2. Margins...

The Margin Format dialog box

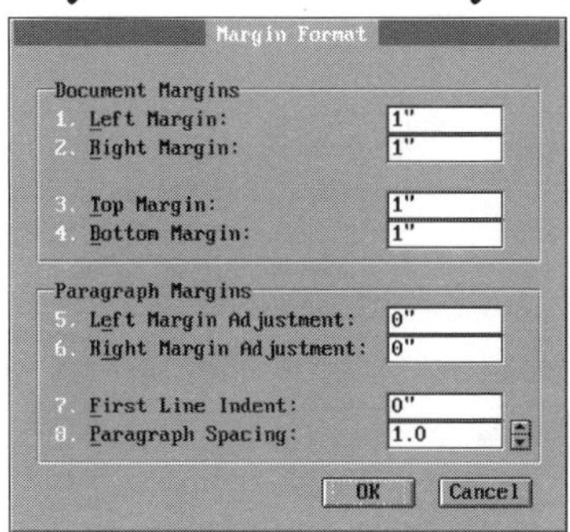

Option or Button	*Function*
1. Left Margin	Enables you to set a new left margin.
2. Right Margin	Enables you to set a new right margin.
3. Top Margin	Enables you to set a new top margin.
4. Bottom Margin	Enables you to set a new bottom margin.
5. Left Margin Adjustment	Enables you to indent the left margin of each paragraph by a set amount without changing the left margin setting.
6. Right Margin Adjustment	Enables you to indent the right margin of each paragraph by a set amount without changing the right margin setting.
7. First Line Indent	Enables you to indent the first line of each paragraph by a set amount without having to press Tab each time.
8. Paragraph Spacing	Enables you to set the spacing between each paragraph of text.

Secret codes

When you change the margin settings, WordPerfect inserts Secret codes specific to the margin you changed at the beginning of the current paragraph. For example, if you were to increase the left margin to 1 1/2 inches and the top margin to 2 inches at the beginning of page 2 in your document, you see two Secret codes when you open the Reveal Codes window:

```
[Lft Mar][Top Mar]
```

If you position the cursor on the [Lft Mar] Secret code, it becomes [Lft Mar:1.5"]. If you position the cursor on the [Top Mar] Secret code, it becomes [Top Mar:2"].

More stuff

You can see the changes you make to the left and right margins on the screen in any display mode. To see the changes you make to the top and bottom margins, you need to switch to page mode or open the Print Preview window (by choosing Print Preview on the File menu).

Merge

Generates *personalized* form letters and other documents that consist of *canned* text plus variable information that is dropped into the letter from a data file.

Menus

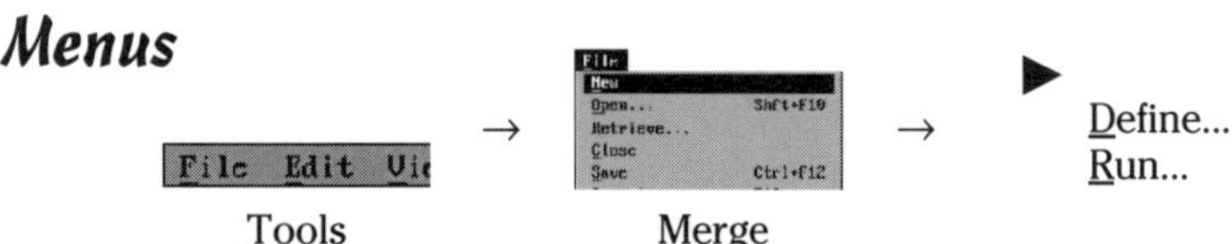

For function key freaks

To define a new form or data file: To run a merge:

(Merge Codes) (Merge/Sort)

Creating a table data file

Before you can perform a merge, you must create a data file that contains the data records (for example, the names and addresses of clients) to use in the merge and a form file that indicates *where* the information in each record is to be merged. The easiest way to create a data file is to set it up as a WordPerfect table, as follows:

1. If the current document window isn't empty, open a new document with the New command on the File menu.
2. Choose the Merge command on the Tools menu. Then select the Define command on the cascading menu or press Shift+F9 (Merge Codes) to open the Merge Codes dialog box.
3. Choose the 3. Data [Table] option.
4. Choose 1. Create a Table with Field Names.

5. Enter the descriptive name for each piece of information (field) you need to keep track of in the Field Name text box. Press Enter after typing each field name in order to add it to the Field Name List box. When you're finished adding field names, choose the OK button to close the Field Names dialog box and create the table. If you made a mistake in entering the field names, press the F7 (Exit) to exit the Field Name text box. Then select the 2. Field Name List option to select the last field name in the list and activate the 1. Insert Field Name, 2. Add Field Name at the End, 3. Edit Field Name, and 4. Delete Field Name options. After editing the field names with the appropriate options, choose the OK button or press F7 (Exit) followed by the Enter key.
6. Fill out the first record in the data file table. After you finish entering information in a field, press Tab to advance to the next field. If you need to back up to edit a previous field, press Shift+Tab (Backtab). When you finish entering the information for the last field, press Tab to add a blank row to the data table and advance the cursor to the first field.
7. If you need to adjust the widths of the columns in the data file table, choose the Tables command on the Layout menu; then choose Edit. Use the ← and → keys to select the column; then press Ctrl+→ to widen the column or Ctrl+← to narrow it. When you finish adjusting the column widths, choose the Close button or press the F7 (Exit) key.
8. Continue filling out the records until you've added all your records for the data file table.
9. Save the file with the Save or Save As command on the File menu (or press Shift+F10). When naming your data file, you can add an extension such as .DTA to differentiate this file from other standard documents.

Creating a form file

After you create a data file with the data records, you need to create the form file that indicates how and where each piece of information (field) from the data file is used. The form file contains both *boilerplate* text and field codes (which say *put this piece of information from each record right here*). To create a form file, follow these steps:

1. If the current document window isn't empty, open a new document with the New command on the File menu.
2. Choose the Merge command on the Tools menu. Then select the Define command on the cascading menu, or press Shift+F9 (Merge Codes) to open the Merge Codes dialog box.

3. Choose the 1. Form option; then choose the OK button in the Merge Codes (Form File) dialog box or press Enter.
4. Type the standard text in your form document, inserting FIELD merge codes at each place in the text where you want WordPerfect to merge information from records in the data file. Be sure to include all necessary punctuation and spaces between FIELD codes.
5. To insert a FIELD merge code in the text of the form file, press Shift+F9 (Merge Codes). Then choose the 1. Field option and type the name of the field in the Field text box. If you don't remember the field names, choose the List Field Names...F5 button (or press F5). Type in the name of the data file and press Enter or use the File List...F5 button to select the filename. After selecting the data file, highlight the field name you want to use in the List Field Names dialog box and press Enter to insert the field into the Field text box of the Parameter Entry dialog box. Then press Enter again to insert the field code into the document. (The next time you need to insert another field code, you can speed up the selection process by pressing Shift+F9, typing 1 or F, pressing F5, highlighting the field name, and pressing Enter twice in a row.)
6. When you finish composing the form document by combining the canned text with the appropriate field names, save the file with the Save or Save As command on the File menu (or press Shift+F10). When naming your data file, you can add an extension such as .FRM (for form file) to differentiate this form file from other standard documents.

Merging the data and form file

After you have created your data file and form file, you're ready to rock 'n' roll (well, at least to perform the merge). To perform the standard merge, follow these steps:

1. Choose the Merge command on the Tools menu; then select the Run command on the cascading menu — or press Ctrl+F9 (Merge/Sort) and choose the 1. Merge option to open the Run Merge dialog box.
2. Choose the 1. Form File option; then enter the name of the form file to use and press Enter. If you don't know the filename, select it in the drop-down list box (opened by pressing ↓ or clicking the down-arrow button) or use the File List...F5 button to select the file in the List File dialog box.
3. As soon as you designate the form file to use, WordPerfect automatically puts the name of the data file associated with that form file in the Data File text box. (Data files become associated with form files through a previous selection or

when selecting fields in the List Fields dialog box.) If you didn't associate a data file with the form file or if you want to use a different data file, choose the 2. Data File option and enter the correct filename in the Data File text box.

4. Current Document is the default Output option, which puts the merged forms generated by merging the data file with the form file in the current document window. If you don't want the merged forms in the current document window (because it may already contain a document), choose the 3. Output option. Then choose either Unused Document (to put the files in a blank document window), Printer (to send them directly to the printer), or File (to save them in a new file). If you choose File, you must then enter the name for the new file in the Merge Output File dialog box and choose OK.
5. If you need to change any of the merge default settings (such as removing blank lines caused by empty fields, selecting only certain records, or generating envelopes for each merged form), choose the Data File Options and change the settings in the expanded Run Merge dialog box.
6. Choose the Merge button to start the merge. WordPerfect keeps you informed of its progress on the status bar as it merges information from the record in the data file with copies of the form file, creating a new merged form for each record used.

More stuff

Keep in mind that you can have WordPerfect generate an envelope for each form letter you generate in the merge. To do this, choose the Data File Options button. Then select 8. Generate an Envelope for Each Data Record and insert the appropriate data file field codes into the Mailing Address area of the Envelope dialog box. WordPerfect then generates an envelope for each record in your data file during the merge (placing these envelopes after the form letters that are generated).

To create mailing labels for your form letters, you need to create a form file that uses a label form (see Labels) with the appropriate data file fields inserted into the first label only. Then, perform a merge using this label form file and the data file to which the fields refer.

New (Document)

Opens a brand new document in another document editing window.

Menus

→
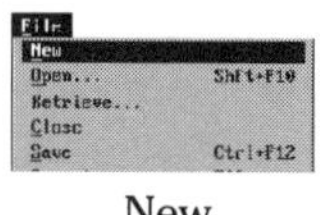

File New

More stuff

When you use the New command on the File menu, WordPerfect opens a new document editing window, its number indicated on the status bar after the Doc indicator (as in Doc 1, Doc 2, and so on). If you have enough memory, WordPerfect 6 lets you work on up to nine new documents at one time — proving beyond a shadow of a doubt that you really are overworked! See Windows for ideas on arranging the document windows on the screen.

Open (Document)

Opens the document you specify that has been saved on disk into a brand new document window (by choosing the default Open into New Document option) or into the current window, combining the current window's text with that of the opened document it now contains (by choosing the Retrieve into Current Document option).

Menus

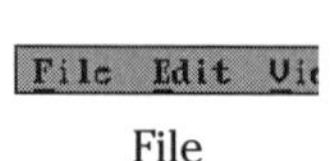

→

File Open...

For function key freaks

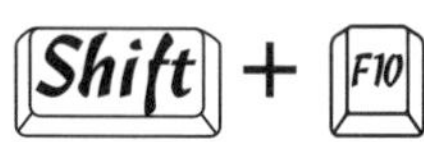

(Open/Retrieve)

The Open Document dialog box

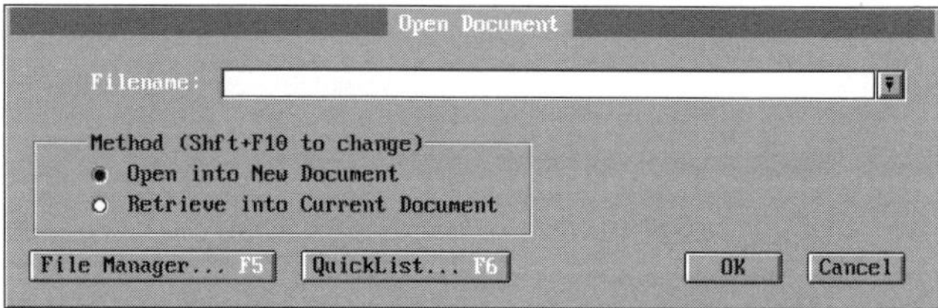

Option or Button	Function
1. Filename	Enables you to enter the filename of the document you want to open. Include the pathname of the file if it's not in the current directory. To select one of the last four files you've opened, choose the drop-down list button and then select the filename from the list.
2. Method (Shft+F10 to change) 1. Open into New Document 2. Retrieve into Current Document	Enables you to select between opening a file in its own document editing window or retrieving it into the current window and combining its text with whatever text WordPerfect finds there.
File Manager... F5	Enables you to open the Specify File Manager List dialog box where you can select a new directory before you open the File Manager in order to select the file you want to open (see File Manager).
QuickList... F6	Enables you to select a new directory or file that's been given an alias in the QuickList dialog box (see QuickList).

More stuff

If you try to open a file not created with WordPerfect 6.0, the program opens the File Format dialog box where the most likely file format is highlighted. If the correct format is highlighted, choose Select. Otherwise, highlight the correct format in the List box and then choose Select.

Outline

Creates outlines in your document just like your teacher had you make. When you create an outline, WordPerfect automatically numbers the different levels for you. You can combine headings at various levels (up to eight total) with regular body text. You can also collapse the outline to hide all the body text so that only the outline headings are displayed, and then later you can expand the outline to show everything.

Menus

Tools → Outline ▶ Outline Options...

For function key freaks

To display the Outline dialog box:

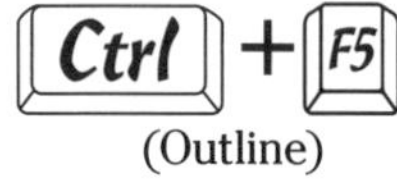

(Outline)

To promote a heading to the next level:

To demote a heading to the previous level:

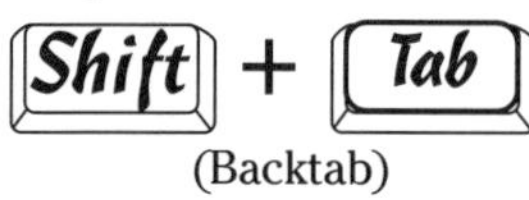

(Backtab)

To convert text to an outline item or an outline item to text:

Ctrl + T

To display the Outline button bar and enable its command letters:

Ctrl + O

Creating an outline

Use the outline feature to create formal outlines that would make your English teacher proud. A formal outline can have up to eight successive outline levels. WordPerfect automatically numbers and formats the entries in each level according to the outline style that you choose. To create an outline, just follow these steps:

1. Position the cursor at the beginning of the line where you want the initial first-level heading in your outline to appear.
2. Choose the Outline command on the Tools menu. Then choose the Begin New Outline option on the cascading menu — or press the Ctrl+F5 (Outline) key and choose the 1. Begin New Outline option.
3. Highlight the style that you want (Bullets, Headings, Legal, Legal 2, Outline, or the default Paragraph) in the Outline Style List dialog box. Then choose the 1. Select option or press the Enter key.
4. WordPerfect inserts the first number or symbol for Level 1 headings and indents the text in accordance with the outline style that you selected.

5. Type the heading and press Enter. WordPerfect then inserts the second number or symbol used for Level 1 headings.
6. Type in the second first-level heading and press Enter. If you need to enter the initial second-level heading instead, press Tab to demote the outline level and to change the style of numbers, letters, or symbols. Then type the initial second-level heading and press Enter.
7. WordPerfect enters the next number, letter, or symbol in the sequence for the current outline level. Continue to enter all the headings that you need at that level, terminating each one with the Enter key. Press the Tab key to demote the outline level before entering the heading for the next lower level. To enter a heading at a higher level, press Shift+Tab (Backtab) until you've promoted the level sufficiently before entering the heading.
8. When you've finished entering the last heading for your outline, choose the Outline command on the Tools menu. Then choose the End Outline option on the cascading menu before terminating the heading with the Enter key. Or press the Ctrl+F5 (Outline) key, choose the 5. End Outline option, and press Enter.

The Outline dialog box

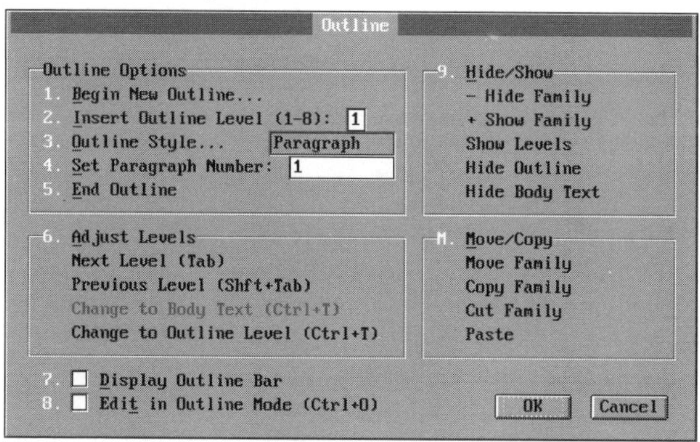

To open the Outline dialog box, choose Outline on the Tools menu and then select Outline Options on the cascading menu. Or simply press Ctrl+F5 (Outline). WordPerfect displays the Outline dialog box with the following options:

Option or Button	*Function*
1. Begin New Outline...	Turns on outlining by displaying the Outline Style List dialog box where you highlight the style you want to use. Choose 1. Select. After outlining is turned on, pressing Enter inserts the next number, letter or symbol at the current outline level. Pressing Tab selects the next lower outline level style (demotes it) and pressing Shift+Tab selects the next higher outline level style (promotes it). See 5. End Outline.
2. Insert Outline Level (1–8)	Enables you to decide the particular outline level (between 1 and 8) to use, overriding whatever level WordPerfect normally assigns.
3. Outline Style...	Opens the Outline Style List dialog box where you can specify a new outline style, create a new style, or edit one of the existing styles.
4. Set Paragraph Number	Enables you to specify a new number for a particular level by overriding the number that WordPerfect normally gives.
5. End Outline	Turns off outlining so that Enter, Tab, and Shift+Tab work normally again. See 1. Begin New Outline... earlier in this list.
6. Adjust Levels	Enables you to modify the outline level either by promoting it with 1. Next Level (Tab), demoting it with 2. Previous Level (Shft+Tab), converting the outline to normal text with 3. Change to Body Text (Ctrl+T), or by converting body text to an outline level with 4. Change to Outline Level (Ctrl+T).
7. Display Outline Bar	Displays the outline button bar that contains buttons for doing such things as changing outline levels, choosing the level to be displayed, selecting a new outline style, and more.
8. Edit in Outline Mode	Enables you to select buttons on the (Ctrl+O) Outline button bar by typing mnemonic letters so that you can use this button bar even if you won't go near a mouse.

9. Hide/Show	Enables you to hide or redisplay the current outline family, which includes the current outline level plus all subsidiary levels, with 1. -Hide Family or 2. + Show Family. The option also specifies which outline level to display with 3. Show Levels, hides all outline levels and displays only body text with 4. Hide Outline, or hides all the body text and displays only the outline levels with 5. Hide Body Text.
M. Move/Copy	Enables you to move the current outline family with 1. Move Family or 3. Cut Family and 4. Paste, or lets you copy the family with 2. Copy Family.

Using the Outline button bar

When working with an outline, you can use the buttons on the Outline button bar to make short work of your outline. If you display this button bar by pressing Ctrl+O rather than the 7. Display Outline Bar option, WordPerfect allows you to choose the buttons either by clicking them or typing the command (mnemonic) letter. Otherwise, you're stuck with clicking.

Overstrike

Creates a compound character by printing two characters in the same column position to make your printer appear to be able to print fancy symbols and foreign language characters. For example, with overstrike you can create the accented letter *ñ* used in certain Spanish words like *mañana* (created by printing the *tilde* in the same column as the *n*).

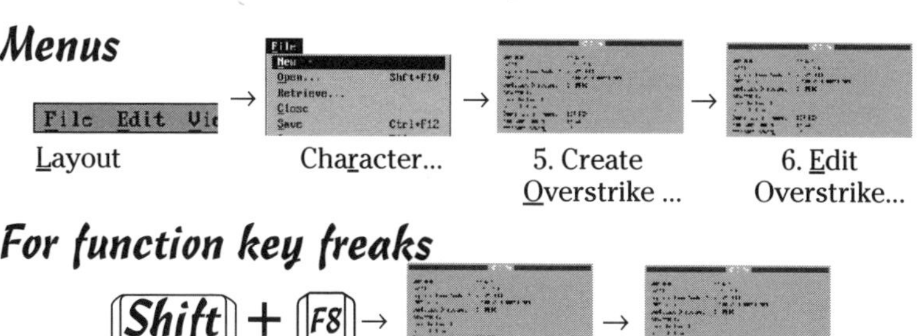

Menus

Layout → Character... → 5. Create Overstrike ... → 6. Edit Overstrike...

For function key freaks

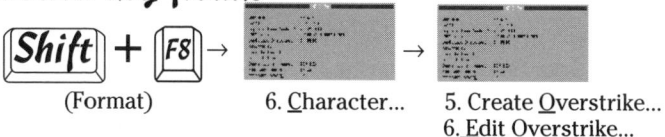

Shift + F8 (Format) → 6. Character... → 5. Create Overstrike... 6. Edit Overstrike...

Using Overstrike

To create an overstrike character, follow these steps:

1. Choose the Character command on the Layout menu — or press Shift+F8 (Format) and then choose the 6. Character option — to open the Character Format dialog box.
2. Select the 5. Create Overstrike option to open the Create Overstrike dialog box.
3. To apply an attribute like bold or italics to the overstrike character you're creating, choose the Attributes... Ctrl+F8 button (or press Ctrl+F8) and then select the desired position, size, or appearance option in the Overstrike Attributes dialog box (WordPerfect inserts the appropriate Secret code in the Create Overstrike dialog box).
4. Type the two characters that are to be printed in the same position in the Overstrike Characters text box (in either order) and then press Enter.
5. Choose the OK button or press Enter again to insert the overstrike character into your document.

To edit a character created with overstrike, position the cursor on or immediately after the composite character. Then open the Character Format dialog box and choose 6. Edit Overstrike.

Secret codes

Suppose that you've used Overstrike to create the character *ñ* in the word *mañana.* In the Reveal Codes window, you see `ma[Ovrstk]ana`. If you position the cursor on the [Ovrstrk] Secret code, it expands to [Ovrstk:n~].

More stuff

In Text mode, only one of the two characters appears on the screen, so use graphics or page mode to see the composite character.

The WP Character feature has pretty much replaced Overstrike for creating special symbols and characters, unless you're using a printer that's incapable of printing graphics (on which the WP Characters rely).

Page Break

Inserts a hard (or manual) page break at the cursor's position. Use this command anytime you need to force some text onto a new page.

Menus

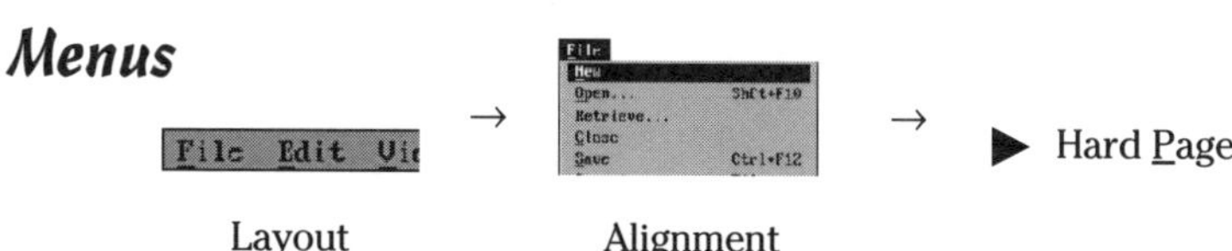

→ ▶ Hard Page

Layout Alignment

For function key freaks

Ctrl + Enter

Secret codes

The Secret code a for hard page break that you insert in the document is [HPg]. The Secret code for a soft page break that WordPerfect automatically inserts in the document is [SPg].

You can delete a hard page break by finding its Secret code in the Reveal Codes window and zapping it. The only way to get rid of a soft page break is to change the format settings that affect how many lines fit on the page, such as the Paper Size/Type or Line Spacing.

More stuff

Be careful that you don't insert hard page breaks until after you've made all your editing changes in the document (so you don't end up with blank pages or pages with just a little bit of text when you print the document).

WordPerfect provides a number of commands for keeping certain text together on a page no matter how you edit the text (see Block Protect, Conditional End of Page, and Widow/Orphan for details) so that you don't have to use hard page breaks to keep text together.

Page Mode

Displays your document text in a special graphics mode that includes the white space for the top and bottom margins plus any special stuff like a header, footer, or footnotes that occur at the top and bottom of the page which normally are not visible.

Menus

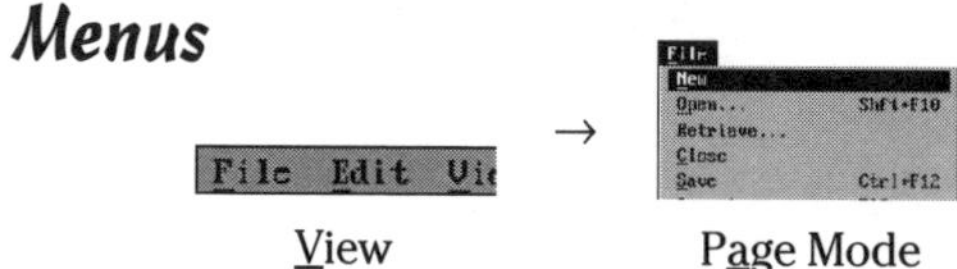

View Page Mode

For function key freaks

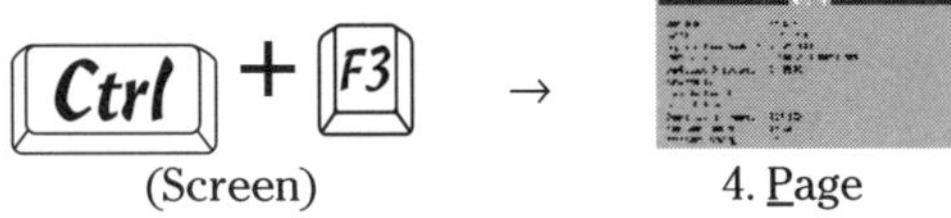

(Screen) 4. Page

More stuff

Switch to page display mode when you want to see the relationship between the body text and the top and bottom margins or when you want to see special elements like headers and footers on the screen. Note, however, that although you can edit any body text in page mode, WordPerfect doesn't allow you to make any changes to the header, footer, or the footnote displayed on the screen (you can look but you can't touch!). See also Display Modes, Graphics Mode, and Text Mode.

Page Numbering

Adds page numbers to your document that WordPerfect automatically keeps up-to-date as you edit the pages of the document.

Menus

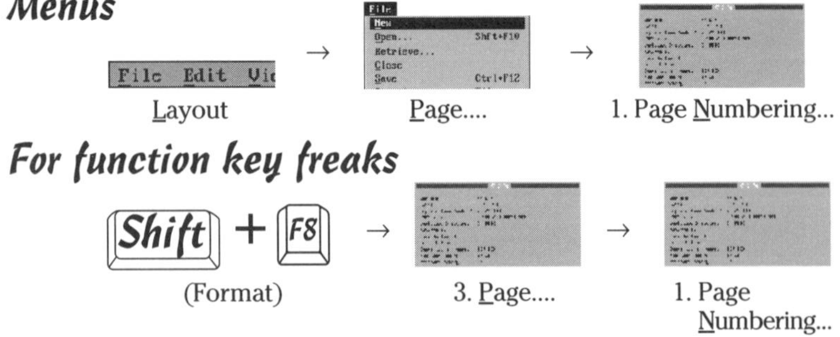

Layout → Page.... → 1. Page Numbering...

For function key freaks

Shift + F8 (Format) → 3. Page.... → 1. Page Numbering...

The Page Numbering dialog box

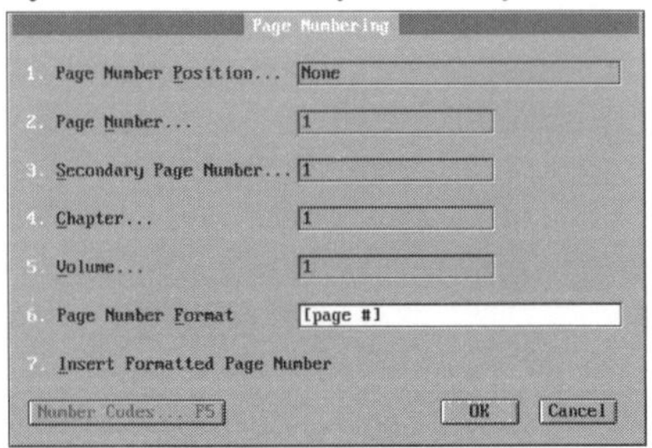

Page Numbering

1. Page Number Position... None
2. Page Number... 1
3. Secondary Page Number... 1
4. Chapter... 1
5. Volume... 1
6. Page Number Format [page #]
7. Insert Formatted Page Number

Number Codes... F5 OK Cancel

Option or Button	*Function*
1. Page Number Position...	Enables you to select the position of the page number and its font, attributes, and color.
2. Page Number...	Enables you to select a new starting page number and/or select a new numbering style.
3. Secondary Page Number...	Enables you to select a new starting page number and/or select a numbering style for a secondary page number, such as in Page 1 (formally Page 2), in which 2 is the starting number for the secondary page numbers.
4. Chapter...	Enables you to select a new starting page number and/or select a numbering style for a chapter (or other such section) in your document, as in Chapter 3 - Page 1, in which 3 is the starting number for the chapter. Note that chapter numbers aren't automatically incremented by WordPerfect.
5. Volume...	Enables you to select a new starting page number and/or select a numbering style for a volume (or other such section) in your document, as in Volume 5, Chapter 1 - Page 1, in which 5 is the starting number for the volume. Note that volume numbers aren't automatically incremented by WordPerfect.
6. Page Number Format	Enables you to insert text and codes that tell WordPerfect how the page numbers appear in the document (see Number Codes... F5 later in this list).
7. Insert Formatted Page Number	Inserts a page number using the current number settings (including formatting) in the text of the document at the cursor's position.
Number Codes... F5	Enables you to select a code for the page number, secondary page number, chapter number, or volume number and insert it in the Page Number Format text box after you've selected 6. Page Number Format (see previous).

Secret codes

Suppose that you've added page numbers to the top right part of your entire document, starting with page number 10 instead of the normal page 1. In Reveal Codes, you'd see two Secret codes at the top of the first page

```
[Pg Num Set][Pg Num Pos]
```

When you position the cursor on the [Pg Num Set] code, it expands to [Pg Num Set:10]. When you position the cursor on the [Pg Num Pos] code, it expands to [Pg Num Pos:TopRight].

More stuff

Be sure that the cursor is somewhere on the first page to display the page number (page 1, if the whole document needs page numbers) before you select the Page Numbering command.

Instead of using the Page Numbering command to number the pages in your document, you can create a header or footer that displays the page number by selecting the 7. Insert Formatted Page Number option in the Page Numbering dialog box after you've opened the Header or Footer window (see Header/Footer for details). You can also use this same option to insert the current page number into the body text of the document.

Paper Size/Type

Enables you to select a new paper size for all or particular pages of your document.

Menus

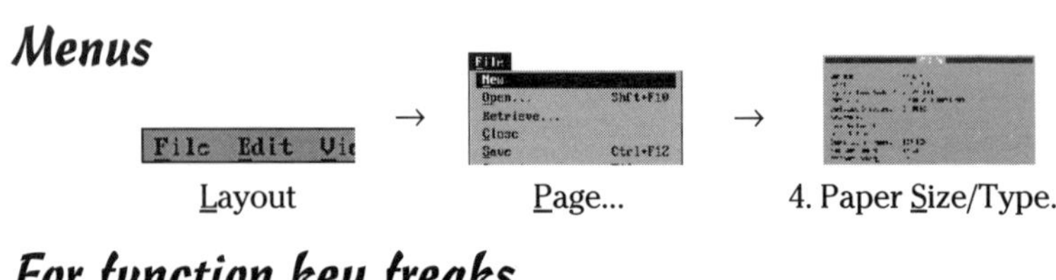

Layout → Page... → 4. Paper Size/Type...

For function key freaks

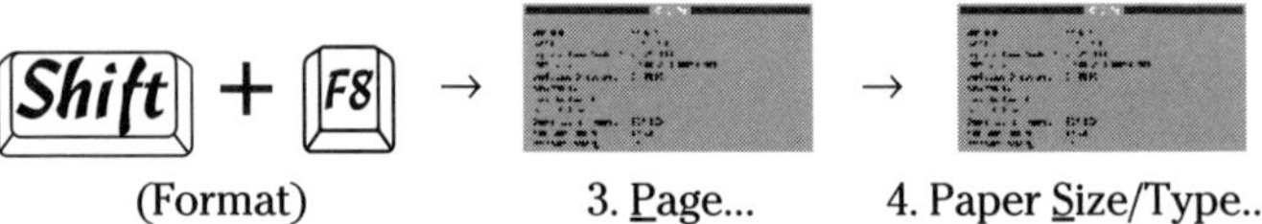

Shift + F8 (Format) → 3. Page... → 4. Paper Size/Type...

The Paper/Size Type dialog box

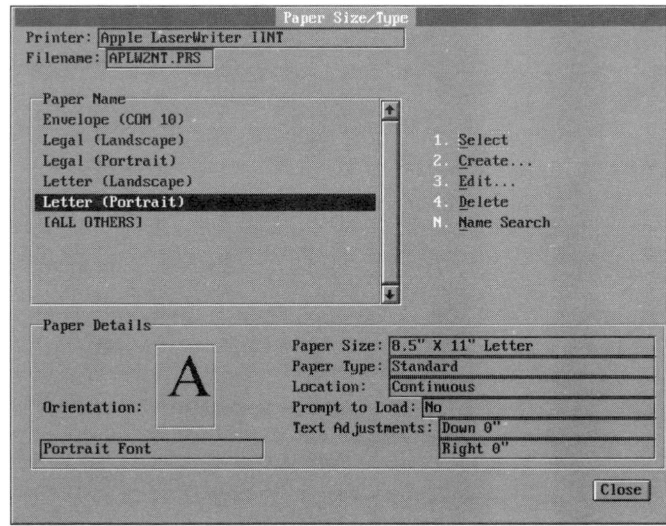

Option or Button	*Function*
1. Select	Selects the paper highlighted in the Paper Name list box and returns you to the Page Format dialog box.
2. Create...	Enables you to create a new paper size and type to use (see "Creating a custom paper size/type" later in this chapter).
3. Edit...	Enables you to edit the paper definition that's highlighted in the Paper Name list box.
4. Delete	Enables you to delete the paper definition that's highlighted in the Paper Name list box.
N Name Search	Enables you to highlight a paper name by typing the first few characters of its name.

Creating a custom paper size/type

If none of the predefined paper sizes for your printer will do, you can create a custom paper size and type by choosing the 2. Create option in the Paper Size/Type dialog box. When you do, WordPerfect opens a Create Paper Size/Type dialog box with the following options:

Option or Button	Function
1, Paper Name	Enables you to change the name of the paper size/type definition that you chose with the Create option.
2. Paper Type	Enables you to select what type of paper the new paper definition uses.
3. Paper Size...	Enables you to select the size of the paper used by the new paper definition.
4. Paper Location...	Enables you to indicate whether the paper is manually fed to the printer or is available on a continuous basis.
5. Prompt to Load	Directs WordPerfect to prompt you to load new paper each time you print with this paper definition.
6. Orientation...	Enables you to choose between portrait and landscape printing, either by using a font that prints in the new orientation or, if your printer is incapable of such acrobatics, a form turned in a wide or narrow orientation.
7. Adjust Text	Enables you to adjust where the printing commences on the page in relation to either the top, left, or right side of the page.

Secret codes

Assume that you selected Letter (Landscape) paper size/type for your new document so that the print runs with the long side of the paper. In Reveal Codes, you'd see `[Paper Sz/Typ]` at the top of the page. If you position the cursor on this Secret code, it expands to [Paper Sz/Typ:11" x 8.5",Letter (Landscape)]

More stuff

Be sure that the cursor's somewhere on the page whose size needs changing before you select a new paper size/type in the Paper Size/Type dialog box. To change the size of a new page in the document, insert a hard page (Ctrl+Enter) and then change the paper size/type.

Print

Prints all or part of the document in the current document editing window.

Menus

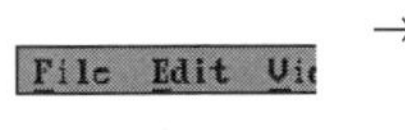

→

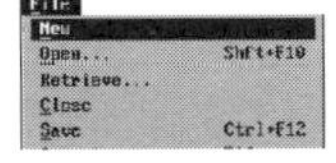

File Print/Fax...

For function key freaks

(Print/Fax)

For mouse maniacs

If necessary, select the WPMAIN button bar by choosing the Button Bar Setup command on the View menu. Choose the Select command on the cascading menu. Highlight WPMAIN in the Button Bars list box and choose the 1. Select option or OK. Then click the Print button.

The Print/Fax dialog box

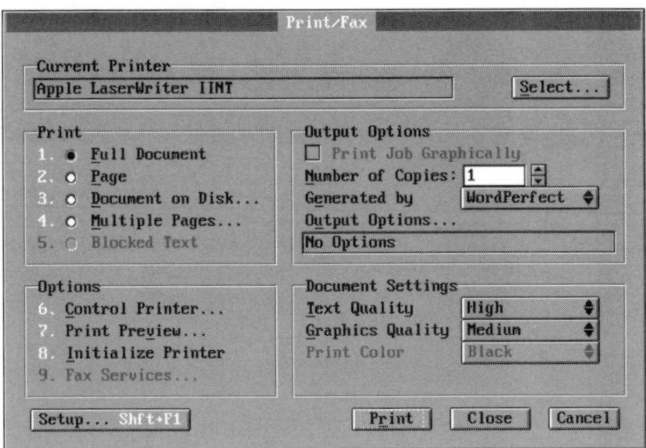

Option or Button	*Function*
Select...	Enables you to select a new printer to use by highlighting its name in the Select Printer dialog box and choosing 1. Select.
1. Full Document	Prints all pages of the document.
2. Page	Prints only the current page of the document (the page with the cursor when you opened the Print dialog box).

Option or Button	*Function (continued)*
3. Document on Disk...	Prints a document that you haven't yet opened in a document window after you indicate the filename.
4. Multiple Pages...	Enables you to specify which pages of the document to print (see "Printing Just Part of a Document" for details).
5. Blocked Text	Prints only the text marked as a block at the time you opened the Print dialog box (this radio button is automatically selected when a block is highlighted).
6. Control Printer...	Enables you to cancel the print job or bump it up in the queue. Also, enables you to start the printing if you're using a paper definition that calls for manually feeding the paper or for prompting you to load the paper.
7. Print Preview...	Opens the Print Preview windows that show you how each page of the document will appear in the printout (see Print Preview).
8. Fax Services...	Enables you to send a WordPerfect file as a fax if you have a fax/modem card in your computer and have installed it with WordPerfect.
Print Job Graphically	Prints the entire document (text and all) as one big graphic. You don't have to fool with option except in the rare cases where graphics in your printed document don't match the way they appear in the Print Preview window.
Number of Copies	Enables you to set the number of copies of the printout.
Generated by	Enables you to determine whether WordPerfect generates the copies (meaning they'll all be collated) or your printer generates them (meaning you'll have to collate them yourself).
Output Options...	These Output Options are available only for some real hot shot printers. They give you even greater control over how multiple copies of documents come out of the printer (however, this is real techy stuff that's better left to someone who really knows the printer).

Text Quality	Enables you to determine the print quality of the text in the document (High, Medium, Draft, or Do Not Print). You can use Draft to get a quick and dirty printout. You can use Do Not Print to print the text in the document separate from the graphics (necessary when your printer doesn't have enough memory to print both at the same time).
Graphics Quality	Enables you to determine the print quality of the graphics in the document (High, Medium, Draft, or Do Not Print). You can use Do Not Print to print the graphics in the document separate from the text (necessary when your printer doesn't have enough memory to print both at the same time).
Print Color	Enables you to select full color or black-and-white for printing a document with a color printer.
Setup... Shft+F1	Enables you to change the default settings for many of the options in the Print/Fax dialog box, including the number of copies, text and graphics quality, and the redline method used by the printer.

Printing just part of a document

When you only need to print a part of your document. When you select the 4. Multiple Pages option. WordPerfect displays the Print Multiple Pages dialog box.

When specifying the pages (or labels when printing with a labels paper size and type — see Labels for details) to print with the 1. Page/Label Range option, be sure that you enter the page numbers in numerical order. To specify a range of a pages, use a hyphen as follows:

–10 Print from the beginning to page 10.

10– Print from page 10 on to the last page.

3–10 Print pages 3 through 10.

To specify individual pages, place a comma between the page numbers, as in `4,10,23` to print only pages 4, 10, and 23 in the document. You can also combine ranges and individual pages, as in `3-7,9,25` to print the range of pages 3 through 7, plus pages 9 and 23.

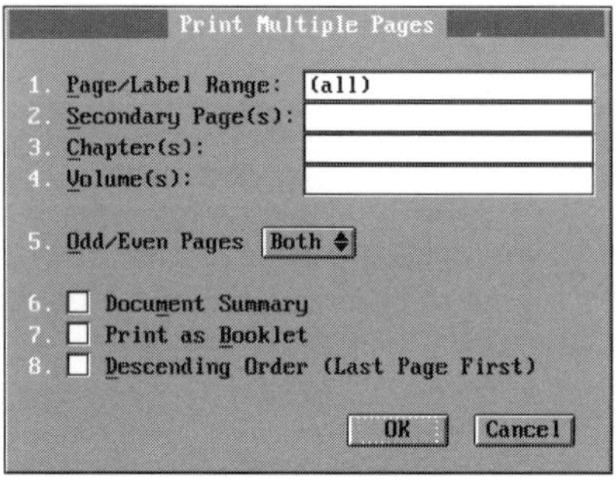

Print Multiple Pages

1. Page/Label Range: (all)
2. Secondary Page(s):
3. Chapter(s):
4. Volume(s):

5. Odd/Even Pages Both

6. Document Summary
7. Print as Booklet
8. Descending Order (Last Page First)

OK Cancel

Option or Button	*Function*
1. Page/Label Range	Enables you to specify the pages (or labels, when printing with a label form) to be printed.
2. Secondary Page(s)	Enables you to specify which secondary pages to print (see Page Numbering).
3. Chapter(s)	Enables you to specify which chapters to print (see Page Numbering).
4. Volume(s)	Enables you to specify which volumes to print (see Page Numbering).
5. Odd/Even Pages	Enables you to specify that only odd or only even pages in the print/label range be printed.
6. Document Summary	Enables you to specify that the document summary be printed with the pages (see Document Summary).
7. Print as Booklet	Gets WordPerfect to figure out how to arrange the pages when assembling a booklet that has more than one document page printed on each sheet of paper (see Subdivide Pages).
8. Descending Order (Last Page First)	Enables you to have WordPerfect print the range of pages in reverse order (from highest to lowest).

Controlling the print job

As soon as you select the Print button in the Print/Fax dialog box, WordPerfect sends the document to the printer as a numbered print job. After that, if you need to intervene in the printing in any way, you must do so in the Control Printer dialog box (opened by selecting the 6. Control Printer option in the Print/Fax dialog box).

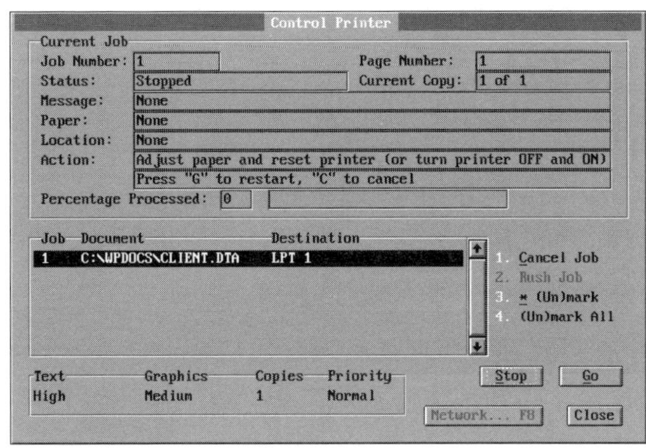

Option or Button	*Function*
1. Cancel Job	Enables you to cancel the printing of the print jobs you've marked or the one you've highlighted in the list box.
2. Rush Job	Enables you to send the highlighted print job to the top of the list so that it gets printed ahead of the others in the print list.
3. * (Un)mark	Enables you to mark (or unmark) the individual print job in the list box.
4. (Un)mark All	Enables you to mark (or unmark) all the print jobs in the list box.
Stop	Enables you to stop the printing of the current print job.
Go	Enables you to start the printing of the current print job.
Network... F8	Enables you to display all the print jobs in the network print queue if you're using WordPerfect on a Novell network.

Print Preview

Shows you on the screen how the pages of your document will look when you print them.

Menus

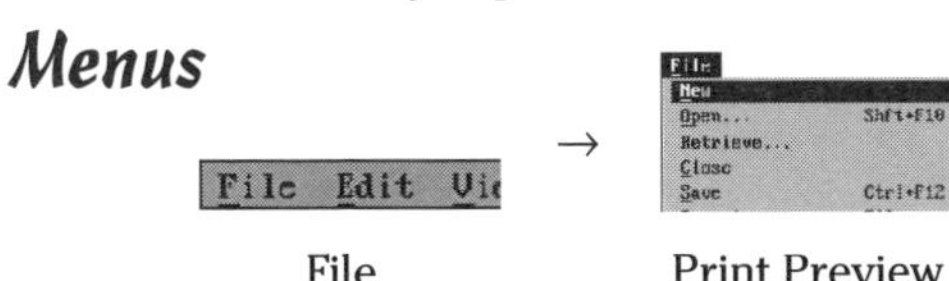

File → Print Preview

For function key freaks

(Print) 7. Print Preview...

The Print Preview window

When you select the Print Preview command, WordPerfect displays the current page in the Print Preview command. The program also automatically displays the Print Preview button bar at the top of the screen. You can then select the print preview options you want to use either by selecting them on the pull-down menus or by clicking the appropriate buttons as follows:

Pull-Down Menu	Button	Function
File		
Setup...	Setup	Lets you control whether graphics appear in black and white or color in the Print Preview window.
Close (F7)	Close	Closes the Print Preview window and returns you to the document editing window.
View		
100@% View	Zoom100@%	Enables you to view the page at the actual printed size.
200@% View	Zoom200@%	Enables you to view the page at twice the actual size.
Zoom In	Zoom In	Enables you to increase the display of the page by 25@%.
Zoom Out	Zoom Out	Enables you to decrease the display of the page by 25@%.
Zoom Area	—	Enables you to zoom in on a particular area of the page. Drag the magnifying glass to include the area you want to zoom in on or use the arrow keys to move the magnifying glass to the middle of the area and press Enter.
Select Area...	—	Enables you to select the area of the page to displayed in the Print Preview window. Drag the selection box over the area you want to zoom in or use the arrow keys to move this box and then press Enter.

Menu item	Button	Description
Reset	—	Enables you to reset the view in the Print Preview window to the way it was when you first opened this window after you've been fooling around with different View settings.
Full Page	FullPage	Displays the entire current page in the Print Preview window.
Facing Pages	FacngPgs	Displays a two-page spread with the even page on the left and the odd page on the right.
Thumbnails >		Displays little tiny versions of consecutive pages, according to the number of pages you select.
1 Page	—	
2 Page	—	
4 Page	—	
8 Page	Thumb 8	
32 Page	Thumb 32	
Other...	—	Choose the Other option and enter the number of pages to display when none of the predefined page number options will do.
Button Bar	—	Enables you to turn on and off the display of the button Print Preview button bar.
Button Bar Setup >	—	Enables you to edit the contents of the Print Preview button bar or change how this button bar is displayed in the Print Preview window.
Edit...	BBar Edit	
Options..	BBar Opt	
Pages		
Go To Page...	GoToPage	Enables you to select the number of the page to be displayed in the Print Preview window.
Previous Page	PrevPage	Enables you to display the previous page in the document in the Print Preview window.
Next Page	NextPage	Enables you to display the next page of the document in the Print Preview window.

More stuff

Keep in mind that unlike when you're in graphics or page mode in the normal document editing window, you can do no editing in the Print Preview window.

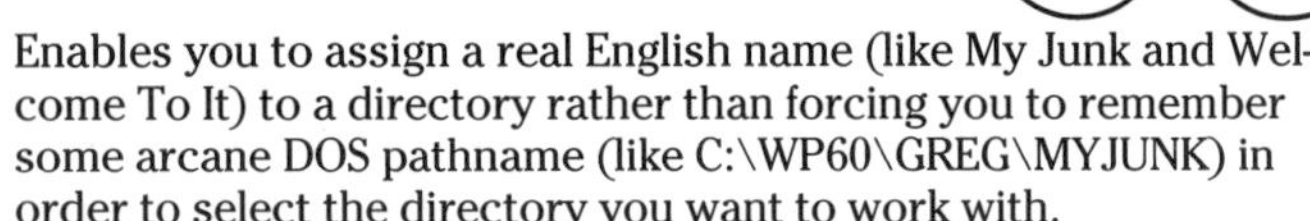

QuickList

Enables you to assign a real English name (like My Junk and Welcome To It) to a directory rather than forcing you to remember some arcane DOS pathname (like C:\WP60\GREG\MYJUNK) in order to select the directory you want to work with.

Creating a QuickList

You can create a QuickList entry that indicates the location of a favorite directory or an oft-used file on your hard disk. To create a QuickList entry, follow these steps:

1. Choose the File Manager command on the File menu — or press the F5 (File Manager) key — to open the Specify File Manager List dialog box.
2. Select the QuickList... F6 button to open the QuickList dialog box.
3. Choose the 2. Create option to open the Create QuickList Entry dialog box.
4. Type an alias for the directory or file you're adding to the QuickList that completely describes its contents or function (such as *My Junk and Welcome to It*) and press Enter (refer to the Examples area in this dialog box for help).
5. Type in the pathname of the directory you're adding and press Enter, or select it with the Directory Tree... F8 button. If you're adding a filename, type the pathname including the filename and press Enter.
6. WordPerfect closes the Create QuickList Entry dialog box and returns you to the QuickList dialog box, where your new QuickList entry is highlighted. To insert the directory or the filename assigned to this alias, choose the 1. Select option. Otherwise, choose the Close button to return to the Specify File Manager List dialog box without changing the directory.

More stuff

After creating a QuickList item for a directory or file that you use a lot (but can never remember where it's located), you can select its directory or filename by choosing the QuickList... F6 button whenever you open a dialog box that needs a directory (like the Specify File Manager List dialog box) or a filename (like Open Document dialog box). Then highlight its alias in the QuickList dialog box. Choose 5. Use as Pattern if you're selecting a directory and you want its pathname inserted into the open dialog box (as with the Specify File Manager List dialog box) or choose 1. Select if you're indicating a document that you want to use (as with the Open Document dialog box).

Redline/Strikeout

Marks editing changes in your document. Redline is used to indicate the text that has been added since the last revision; strikeout is used to indicate the text that should be deleted.

Menus

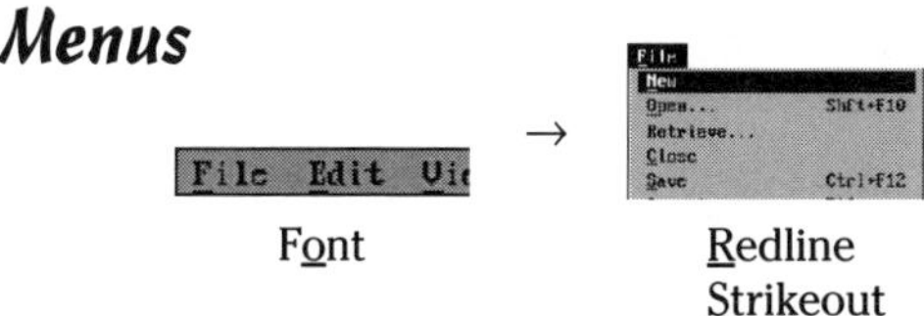

Font → Redline, Strikeout

For function key freaks

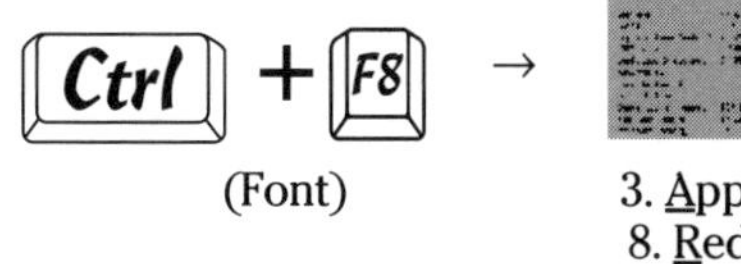

(Font) → 3. Appearance, 8. Redline, 9. Strikeout

Marking and removing redline and strikeout

You apply redline and strikeout attributes to text just as you apply bold or underlining. To add redline or strikeout to text as you type it, position the cursor where the redlined or strikeout text is to be inserted, open the Font menu, select the attribute to turn it on, and type your text. To turn off redline or strikeout, open the Font menu and select the attribute again. Or choose the Normal command (or press → to move beyond the code that turns off the attribute).

To add redlining or strikeout to existing text, mark the text as a block — see Block (Text) for details — and then select the appropriate attribute on the Font menu.

Although redline and strikeout text go on like any other attribute, the really slick part is how you remove them from the text. Just keep in mind when using the following method that WordPerfect removes the redline attribute without bothering the text, but when it comes to removing strikeout, the program gets rid of both the attribute *and* the text (a kind of superdelete). This means that if you want to retain the strikeout text but lose the strikeout attribute, you have to get into Reveal Codes and delete the [StkOut On] or [StkOut Off] Secret code.

With the cursor anywhere in the document, choose the File menu, choose the Compare Documents and Remove Markings commands — or press Alt+F5 (Mark) and select 9. Remove Markings. To get rid of both the redline and strikeout, choose the 1. Remove Redline Markings and Strikeout Text radio button. To get rid of just the strikeout text and leave the redlining, choose the 2. Remove Strikeout Text Only option. Choose OK or press Enter.

If you ever mess up and remove redline markings and/or strikeout text only to discover you that you had no business doing that, choose the Undo command on the Edit menu (or press Ctrl+Z) right away to bring back the markings and deleted text.

Changing the way redlining prints

Although strikeout always prints as text with a line running through the middle of it, the way redlined text normally prints depends on what printer you're using. For example, with dot matrix printers, WordPerfect indicates redlining by printing a vertical bar (|) next to the lines in the margins. On many black and white laser printers, however, redlining is shown by printing the actual redlined text in a shade of gray to contrast with the normal black text.

To change how redlining prints in the document, choose the Document command on the Layout menu, or press Shift+F8 (Format), and then select 4. Document. Select the 5. Redline Method option to open its drop-down list. After choosing Left, Alternating, or Right as the redline method, the 6. Redline Character option becomes available. To switch to some other character besides the vertical bar (|), choose 6. Redline Character and then enter the new character in its text box. When entering a new character, you can insert a character from the WordPerfect Characters dialog box opened by pressing Ctrl+W (see WordPerfect Characters). Choose the OK button or press Enter.

Secret codes

Let's say that you've used redlining and strikeout to show your boss how you've edited a key phrase (what percentage you get for a cost-of-living raise) in your new contract. The original line reads:

Employee shall receive an annual cost of living raise of not less than three percent of her annual salary.

In your edited version, you mark the *three* in the phrase *three percent* with strikeout and then insert *five* marked with redlining. In Reveal Codes, you see

```
[StkOut On]three[StkOut Off][Redln
On]five[Redln Off] percent
```

More stuff

WordPerfect uses redline and strikeout to automatically mark differences between the version of a document as edited on-screen and an earlier version on disk when you use the Compare Documents feature (see Compare Documents for details).

Repeat

Repeats a keystroke or action, such as moving the cursor or deleting a character a set number of times.

Menus

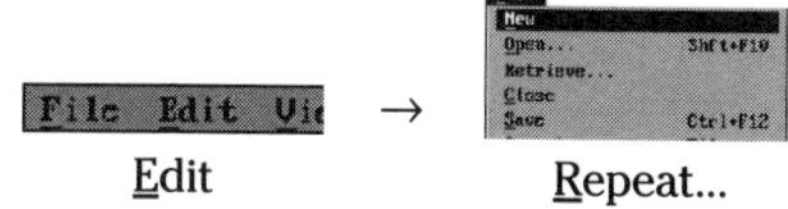

Edit Repeat...

For function key freaks

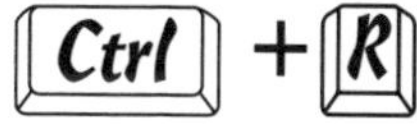

Could you repeat that please?

Repeat is one of those WordPerfect features that seems really neat when you first hear about it but is easy to overlook when you're actually editing. WordPerfect originally added this feature to make it easy to insert a string of characters like ———— or ******** in your document.

To repeat a character, press Ctrl+R and then type the single character you want to repeat when you see the Repeat dialog box. By default, WordPerfect repeats the character you type eight times. If you want more or less repetitions, type a new number in the Count text box before you type the character to be repeated.

You can use the Repeat feature to repeat certain keystrokes as well as to type characters. For example, you can delete the next eight characters in a document by pressing Ctrl+R and then pressing Del. In addition to deletions and cursor movements, you can also repeat macros the number of times set in the Repeat dialog box by pressing Ctrl+R, pressing Alt+F10 (Macro Play), and then entering the name of the macro (see Macros).

Reveal Codes

Opens the Reveal Codes window at the bottom of the document editing window where you can view as well as edit all those wacky Secret codes that WordPerfect insists on putting into your document as you edit and format its text.

Menus

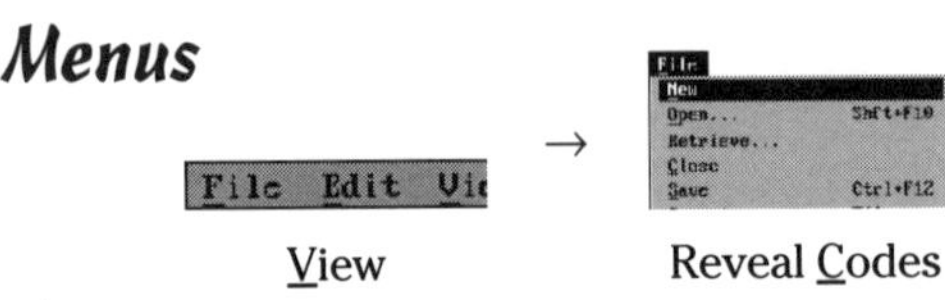

View → Reveal Codes

For function key freaks

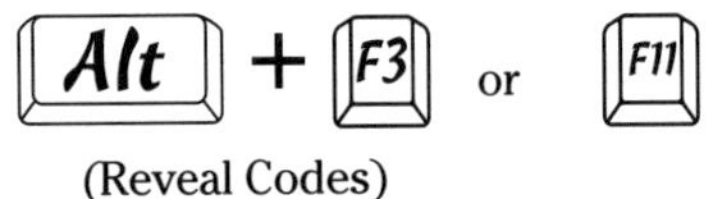

(Reveal Codes)

Using Reveal Codes

WordPerfect's Reveal Codes gives you a behind-the-scenes look at the placement of all the formatting codes that tell your printer how to produce all those special effects in your document, such as new margins, tabs, bold, centering for a line of text, a new Large font size for a title, paragraph borders around your footer text, and so on.

Of course, this information is of absolutely no interest to a normal human being unless something goes wrong in the formatting of the document and you can't figure how to fix it in the normal editing window. That's the time when you need to *get under the hood,* so to speak, by opening the Reveal Codes window to do your editing with all those little Secret codes in full view.

When editing with the Reveal Codes window open, use the regular document editing window above it to find your general place in the document and then concentrate on what's happening in the Reveal Codes window when making your changes. You mouse maniacs need to remember that you can't use the mouse to reposition the cursor (that block) in the Reveal Codes window — only the cursor movement keys work. To delete a code, position the cursor on the code and press Del or position the cursor on the character to the immediate right of the code and press Backspace. To move a code, you need to delete it, move the cursor to the place in the document where you want to insert it, and then press Esc to use Undo (see Undo) to bring it back.

More stuff

You can change the size of the Reveal Codes window by choosing the Screen Setup command on the View menu. Then choose the 3. Reveal Codes option, followed by the 2. Window Percentage option. Normally, the Reveal Codes window takes up 25 percent of the screen area. To change this percentage, enter the new value (between 5 and 95) in the text box.

If you want WordPerfect to show the expanded form of all Secret codes in the Reveal Codes window, even when the cursor's not on the code, choose the 1. Display Details option to put an X in its check box in the Screen Setup dialog box as well.

Ribbon

Displays a special bar called the *ribbon* at the top of the document editing screen. The ribbon contains a series of buttons that you mouse maniacs can use to change things like the Zoom view, justification, and font in your document.

Menus

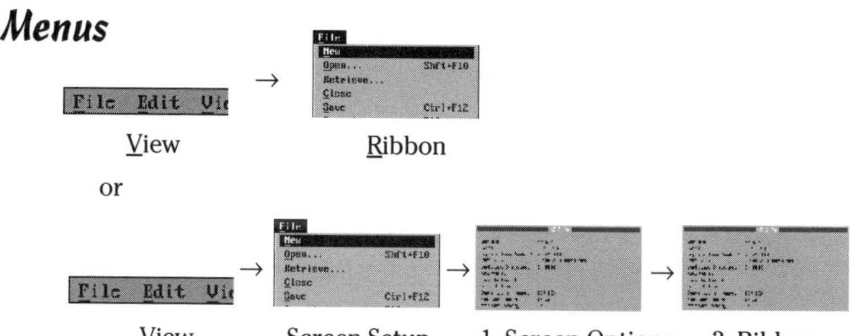

View → Ribbon

or

View → Screen Setup... → 1. Screen Options → 3. Ribbon

Using the ribbon

The ribbon contains the following six buttons: *Zoom* button that enables you to change the magnification of the screen display when using WordPerfect in graphics or page display mode (see Zoom). *Styles* button that enables you to select a new style for the text (see Styles). *Column* button that enables you to set between 1 and 24 newspaper columns in your document (see Columns). *Justification* button that enables you to choose between Left, Right, Centered, and Full justification for your text (see Justification). *Font* button that enables you to select a new font for your text (see Font). *Font size* button that enables you to change the size of the font (see Font).

Each of the buttons on the ribbon has a drop-down list button attached to it. To select a new setting with a particular button, just click on its drop-down list button and then either drag to the new setting you want to select, or use the scroll bar to display it and then click on the option.

Save

Enables you to save your changes to a document on disk so that you have a copy of the document for future use. The first time you save, you must give the document a new filename. After that, you can use this command to save your changes to that file as you continue to work.

Menus

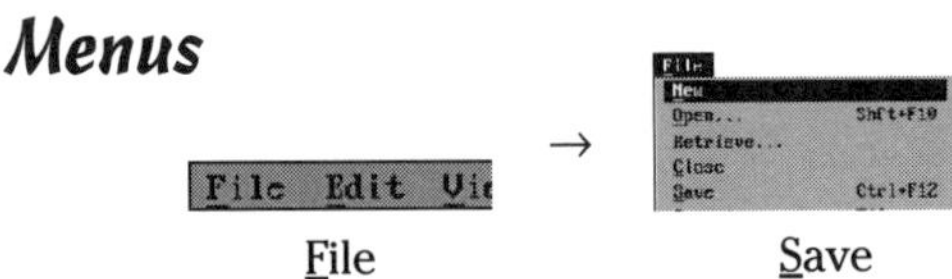

File → Save

For function key freaks

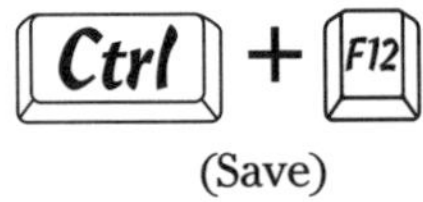

(Save)

Saving a file for the first time

To save a file for the first time, you need to go through the whole following rigmarole. After that, however, you only have to choose Save on the File menu to save your changes (WordPerfect doesn't bother with filenames, passwords, and that kind of stuff).

1. Choose Save on the File menu or press F10 (Save As) to display the Save Document dialog box.
2. To see what directory your new file will be saved in, press F5 (File Manager) or choose the File List...F5 button. The directory shown in the Directory text box of the Select List dialog box that appears is the one where your new file will be saved. After noting the directory, choose Cancel or press Esc to return to the Save Document window.
3. Type the name for your new file in the Filename text box (up to eight characters for the main filename and three characters for an optional filename extension, separated from the main filename with a period). If the directory shown in the Select List dialog box is not where you want

the new file to reside, be sure to precede the filename with the correct directory path in the Filename text box.

4. To assign a password to your file, choose the Password... F8 button or press the F8 key. Carefully type the password (keep in mind that passwords are case sensitive) in the Enter Password text box, then choose OK or press Enter. Retype the password in the Re-enter Password text box exactly as you just entered it in the Enter Password text box. Then choose OK or press Enter again.
5. Choose the OK button or press Enter when you return to the Save Document dialog box. WordPerfect then saves the document, and the filename (including the path if you entered one) appears on the left side of the status bar.

Save As

Enables you to change the name or location of your WordPerfect document or to even save it in a different file format so that coworkers who are less fortunate than you are (who have to use some *other* word processor) can have access to your document.

Menus

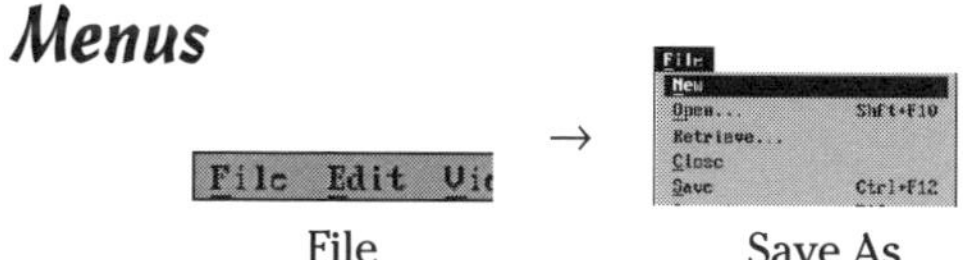

File Save As

For function key freaks

(Save As)

The Save Document dialog box

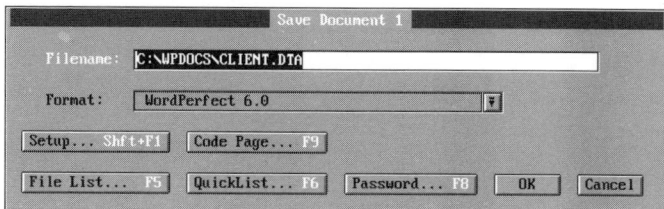

Save Document 1

Filename: C:\WPDOCS\CLIENT.DTA

Format: WordPerfect 6.0

Setup... Shft+F1 | Code Page... F9

File List... F5 | QuickList... F6 | Password... F8 | OK | Cancel

Option or button	Function
1. Filename:	Enables you to change the filename of your document. To make a copy under the same filename, but in a new directory, just type in a new pathname, leaving the filename unchanged.
2. Format:	Enables you to save the document in another file format (WordPerfect 6.0 supports a bunch of them). Just select the new format in the drop-down list.
Setup... Shft+F1	Enables you to modify the Fast Save default (which speeds up saving by saving the document in an unformatted state) and the file format default (which is WordPerfect 6.0, of course).
File List... F5	Enables you to select the directory in which to save the document by using the File Manager (see File Manager).
Code Page... F9	Enables you to select a code page for a foreign language when saving a document for use in a foreign language version of WordPerfect or in some other word processor.
QuickList... F6	Enables you to select the directory in which to save the new file using a QuickList alias (see QuickList).
Password... F8	Enables you to password-protect your file. To add a password, you must be able to duplicate the password twice in a row. When entering a password, remember that passwords are case sensitive. Don't mess with passwords unless you're really sure that you won't forget the password. (It's a good idea to write down the password and store it in a secure place so that coworkers can get into the file should you suddenly decide to chuck it all and go live in Tahiti.)

More stuff

Use the Save instead of the Save As command on the File menu when your intention is to save the editing and formatting changes you've made to the document with the same filename. Use Save As only when you need to save a copy of the document with a new filename and/or in a new directory, in another file format for use with another word processor, or if someone convinces you that you need to add a password to the document.

Screen Setup

Enables you to control how the WordPerfect display appears on your screen. The options you choose in the Screen Setup dialog box remain in effect each time you start WordPerfect.

Menus

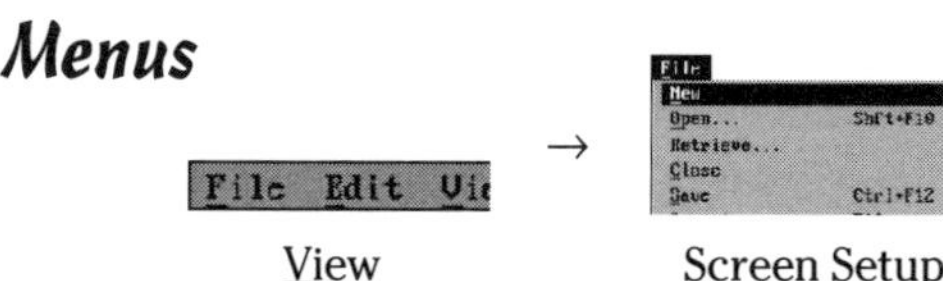

View → Screen Setup

For function key freaks

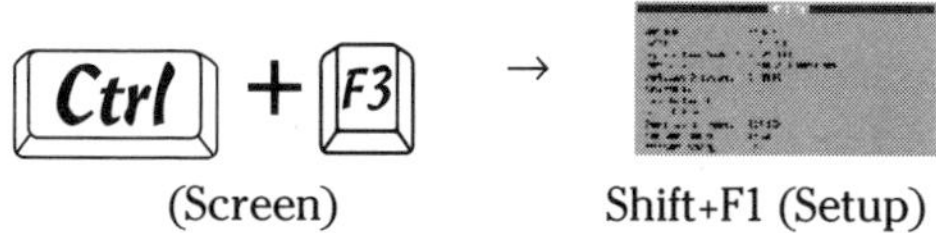

(Screen) → Shift+F1 (Setup)

The Screen Setup dialog box

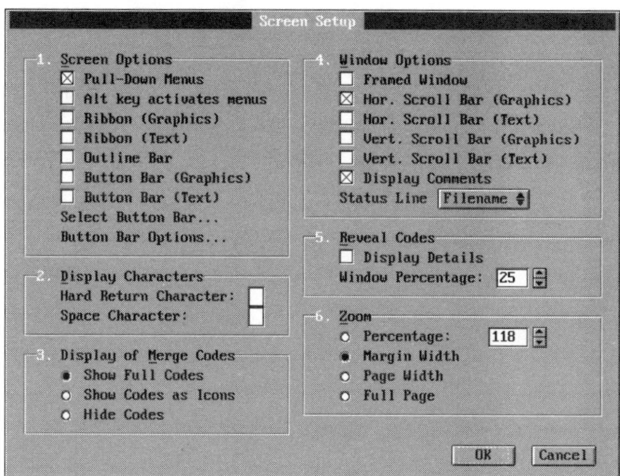

Option or button	*Function*
1. Screen	Enables you to display or hide various screen components such as the pull-down menus, ribbon, and button bar. Make sure that each screen option you want displayed contains an X in its check box.

2. Display Characters	Enables you to select a character to represent hard returns and spaces on the screen. When entering a character, you can select a character in one of the WordPerfect character sets by pressing Ctrl+W (see WordPerfect Characters).
3. Display of Merge Codes	Enables you to determine how merge codes are displayed in form and data files (see Merge).
4. Window Options	Enables you to control how the document windows you open in WordPerfect appear on the screen. These window elements include, for example, a frame with sizing buttons around the window and with horizontal and vertical scroll bars. Make sure that each window option you want displayed contains an X in its check box.
5. Reveal Codes	Enables you to control whether or not the current settings in Secret codes are displayed at all times (rather than expanding when you put the cursor on the code in the Reveal Codes window) and determine what percentage of the screen is taken up by the Reveal Codes window.
6. Zoom	Enables you to choose between the Margin Width, Page Width, and Full Page Zoom options or enter a Zoom percentage of your own.

Search and Replace

Enables you to quickly locate certain text in the document. If you use the Replace command, you can have WordPerfect replace the search text with other text, either on a case-by-case basis or globally throughout the entire document.

Menus

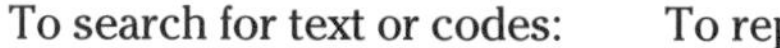

To search for text or codes: To replace text or codes:

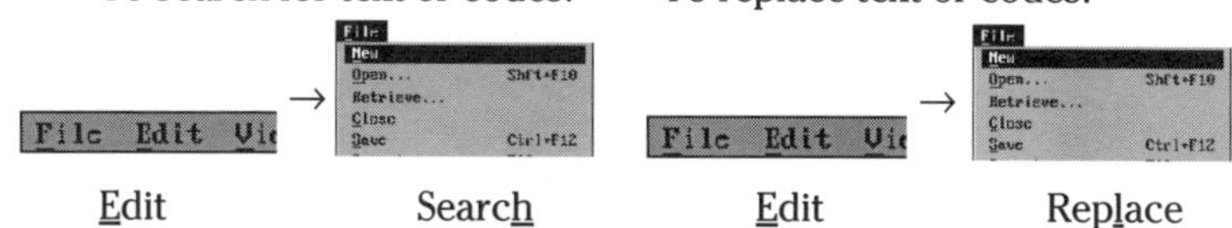

Edit Search (h) — Edit Replace (l)

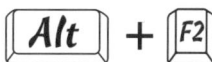

For function key freaks

To search for text or codes: To replace text or codes:

(→ Search) (Replace)

The Search dialog box

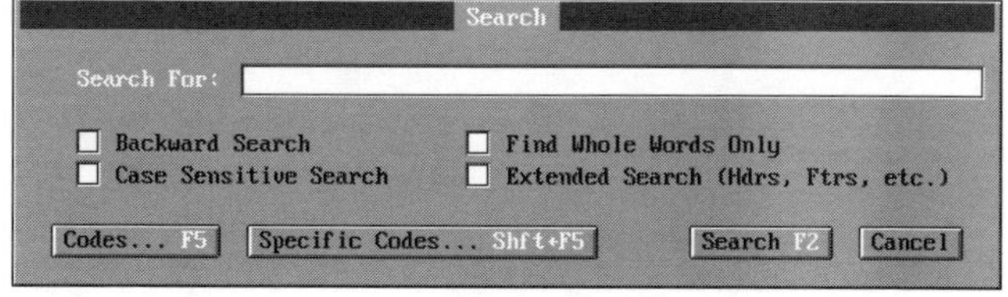

Option or button	*Function*
1. Search For	Enables you to enter the search text and/or Secret codes that you want to locate in the document.
2. Backward Search	Conducts the search backwards in the document from the cursor's current position to the beginning.
3. Case Sensitive	Conducts a case-sensitive search in which only words and phrases that use the same capitalization are located.
4. Find Whole Words Only	Restricts the search to occurrences of the search text in whole words only so that WordPerfect does not stop when the search text occurs within other words or phrases.
5. Extended Search (Hdrs, Ftrs, and so on)	Searches every part of the document, including the text in your headers, footers, and footnotes.

Codes... F5	Enables you to select the Secret codes that you want to search for in the text. To insert a Secret code in the Search For text box, highlight the name of the code in the Search Codes dialog box and then choose Select.
Specific Codes... Shift+F5	Enables you to search for specific Secret code settings for a select list of Secret codes (such as a left margin setting of 1½ inches or a 24-point font size).
Search F2	Starts the search or continues the search when a match is located in the text.

The Replace dialog box

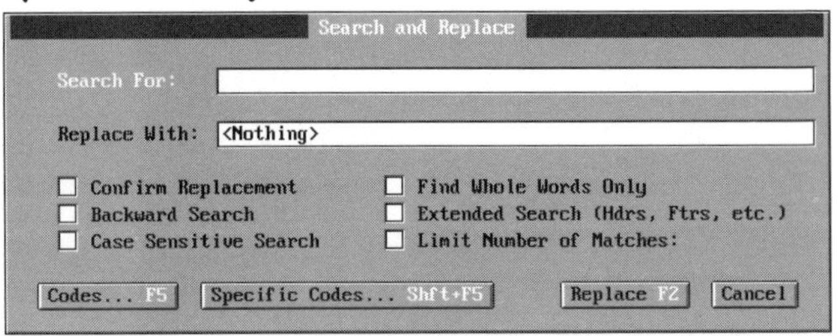

Option or button	Function
1. Search For:	Enables you to enter the search text and/or Secret codes that you want to replace in the document.
2. Replace With:	Enables you to enter the replacement text and/or codes.
3. Confirm Replacement	Indicates that you want WordPerfect to have you confirm each replacement made in the document (this is by far the safest option).
4. Backward Search	Conducts the search and replace operation backwards in the document from the cursor's current position to the beginning (normally, this operation is conducted forward from the cursor).
5. Case Sensitive Search	Conducts a case-sensitive search whereby only words and phrases that use the same capitalization are located.

6. Find Whole Words Only	Restricts the search to occurrences of the search text in whole words only so that WordPerfect does not stop when the search text occurs within other words or phrases.
7. Extended Search (Hdrs, Ftrs, etc.)	Searches every part of the document, including the text in your headers, footers, and footnotes, when conducting the search and replace operation.
8. Limit Number of Matches:	Enables you to limit the number of occurrences that will be searched and replaced.
Codes...F5	Enables you to select the Secret codes that you want to search for and replace in the text. To insert a Secret code in the Search For or Replace With text box, highlight the name of the code in the Search Codes dialog box and then choose Select.
Specific Codes...Shft+F5	Enables you to replace the settings of particular codes during a search and replace operation (such as searching for a 2-inch top margin and replacing it with a 1-inch top margin).
Replace F2	Begins the search and replace operation.

More stuff

When searching for text, you can reverse the direction of the search from a forward to a backward search by pressing Shift+F2 (← Search), rather than having to select 2. Backward Search in the Search dialog box.

When conducting a global search and replace operation, always protect yourself by saving the document prior to starting the procedure.

Sort

Enables you to rearrange text in alphabetical or numerical order. In WordPerfect, you can sort lines of text (like simple lists), paragraphs, records in a merge data file (see Merge), or rows in a table (see Tables).

Menus

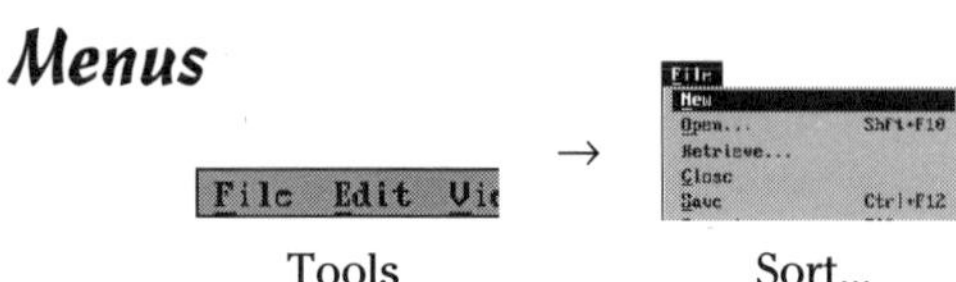

Tools Sort...

For function key freaks

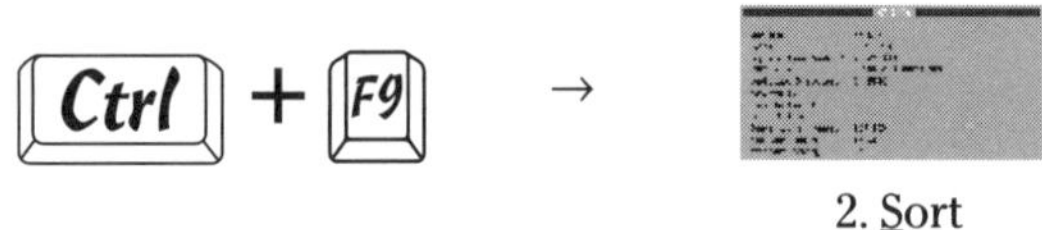

2. Sort

Sorting information in WordPerfect

Sorting is based on *keys* that indicate what information should be used in alphabetizing or reordering the information numerically. For example, if you want to sort a bunch of lines containing your coworkers' names and telephone numbers alphabetically by last name, you would tell WordPerfect to use the last name of each person as the sorting key. When sorting information with Word-Perfect, you can define more than one sorting key. If your list of names and telephone numbers contains several Smiths and Joneses, you can define a second key that indicates how the duplicates are to be arranged (by first name, for example).

The Sort dialog box

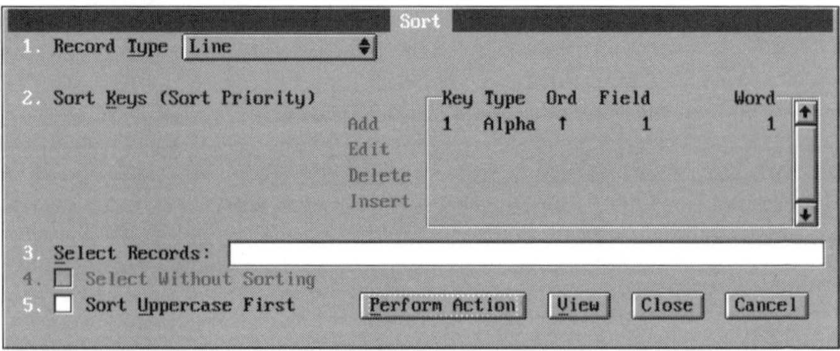

Option or button	Function
1. Record Type	Enables you to change the type of record (Line, Paragraph, Parallel Column, Merge Data File, or Table) to be sorted. Normally, you don't need to fuss with this because WordPerfect usually can tell what type of records you're working with and supplies the correct record type.

2. Sort Keys (Sort Priority)	Enables you to define all of the sort keys you need to use to get the information arranged the way you want it.
3. Select Records	Enables you to create a condition for any of the sort keys you've defined that determines which information is sorted. Use this option with extreme caution because WordPerfect retains and sorts only the records that meet your condition, discarding all the others.
4. Select Without Sorting	Selects the information that meets your selection condition (see preceding) without bothering to sort the information. Use this option with extreme caution: you can lose data because WordPerfect saves only the records that meet your condition, discarding all the others.
5. Sort Uppercase First	Puts uppercase letters ahead of lowercase letters when performing an alphanumeric sort.
Perform Action	Starts the sorting operation.
View	Returns you temporarily to your document, where you can examine the text. When you're ready to return to the Sort dialog box, press F7 (Exit).

More stuff

The key to understanding sorting in WordPerfect is to understand how the program divides different types of information into *fields* and *records* with different types of sorts: In a *Line sort*, each line terminated by a hard return is a record, which can be subdivided into fields (separated by Tabs) and words (separated by spaces, slashes (/), or hyphens). In a *Paragraph sort*, each paragraph that ends in two or more hard returns is a record, which can be subdivided into lines (separated by soft returns), fields (separated by Tabs), and words (separated by spaces, slashes (/), or hyphens). In a *Merge Data File*, each record ends with an ENDRECORD merge code, which can subdivided into fields (separated by ENDFIELD codes), lines (separated by hard returns), and words (separated by spaces, slashes (/), or hyphens). In *Parallel Columns*, each record is a row of parallel columns (see Columns), which can be subdivided into columns (separated by a hard page), lines (separated by soft or hard returns), and words (separated by spaces, slashes (/), or hyphens). In a *table*, each record is a row, which can be subdivided into cells (numbered from left to right starting with 1), lines (separated by hard returns), and words (separated by spaces, slashes (/), or hyphens).

Speller

Enables you to eliminate all those embarrassing spelling errors. The WordPerfect Speller also locates double words and words with weird capitalization.

Menus

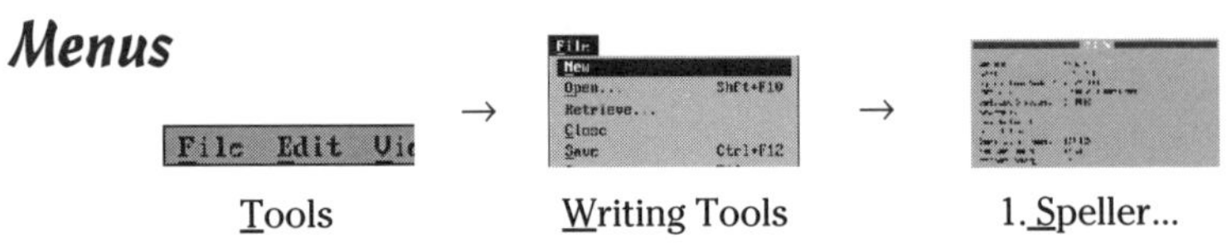

Tools → Writing Tools → 1. Speller...

For function key freaks

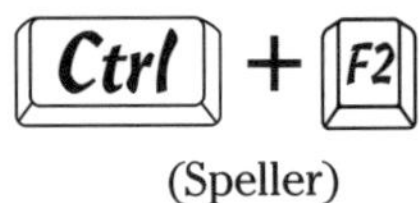

(Speller)

Spell checking a document

To check the spelling of a word or page in your document, position the cursor somewhere in that word or on that page. To check the spelling from a particular word in the text to the end of the document, position the cursor on that word. To check the spelling of the entire document, you can position the cursor anywhere in the document. Choose the Writing Tools command on the Tools menu and then select the 1. Speller option — or press the Ctrl+F2 (Spell) key. By default, the program selects the 3. Document option in the Speller dialog box. To check the entire document (including the text in the header, footer, footnotes, and endnotes, as well as the body text of the document), just press the Enter key. To spell check less than the whole document, choose the appropriate option (1. Word, 2. Page, or 4. From Cursor). After selecting the option representing the amount of the document to check, WordPerfect starts checking each word in the section of text specified. When the Speller locates a word that it can't find in its dictionary, it highlights the word in the text and then opens the Word Not Found dialog box, usually with a list box of suggested spellings. If you have another supplementary dictionary you want the Speller to use when performing the spell check, choose the 8. Select Dictionary option, highlight the name of the dictionary you want to use in the Add To dialog box, and choose the Select button.

To *replace* the unknown word highlighted in the text with one of the words in the Suggestions list box, type its letter or highlight the word and choose the 7. Replace Word option. To *skip* this unknown word this one time only and continue the spell check, choose the 1. Skip Once option. To *skip* this unknown word and every other occurrence of it in the document, choose the 2. Skip in this Document option. To *add* the unknown word to the dictionary so that the Speller skips it in this and every other document, choose the 3. Add to Dictionary option. To *edit* an unknown word in the text, choose the 4. Edit Word option and then press the F7 (Exit) key or Enter after you finish changing it.

When no suggestions for the unknown word are offered in the Word Not Found dialog box, you can enter a best-guess spelling for the unknown word and have the Speller look that up by choosing the 5. Look Up option. Then enter the alternate word to be looked up (you can use the * and ? wildcard characters to stand in for any unknown characters) in the Word or Word Pattern text box and press the Enter key. To then replace the unknown word with one of the suggestions inserted in the Look Up Word dialog box, type its letter or highlight the word and press Enter. If no suggestions are produced for the word or word pattern you entered, press the Esc key twice to return to the Word Not Found dialog box.

When the Speller locates the occurrence of a duplicate word in the text, it highlights the duplicate word in the document and displays the Duplicate Word Found dialog box. To leave the duplicate word in the text, select the 1. 2. Skip Duplicate Word option. To delete the duplicate word, choose the 3. Delete Duplicate Word option. To edit the duplicate word in the text, choose the 4. Edit Word option and then press the F7 (Exit) key or the Enter key when you're done modifying it. To leave the word as it was entered and disable this type of checking, choose the 5. Disable Duplicate Word Checking option. When the Speller locates a word that uses irregular capitalization, it highlights this word in the document and then displays the Irregular Case dialog box. To leave the word in the text as entered, select the 1. 2. Skip Duplicate Word option. To replace the word with one of the spellings in the Suggestions list box, highlight the word and then select the 3. Replace Word option or press Enter. To edit the word highlighted in the text, choose the 4. Edit Word option and then press the F7 (Exit) key or the Enter key when you're done changing it. To leave the duplicate word and disable this type of checking, choose the 5. Disable Case Checking option. When the Speller encounters a word with numbers in it (such as *B-52* or *RX7*), it highlights the unknown word and displays the Word Not Found dialog box with the Speller's suggestions for it (if any are found). To skip this word and ignore all the other words with numbers in the text to be checked, choose the 6. Ignore Numbers option to put an X in its check box.

When the Speller finishes checking the document (or the part you indicated), it displays a Spell Check Completed dialog box. Choose the OK button or press Enter to close the Speller window and return to the document, where you can save the changes made to spelling in the document by choosing the Save or Save As command on the File menu.

The Word Not Found dialog box

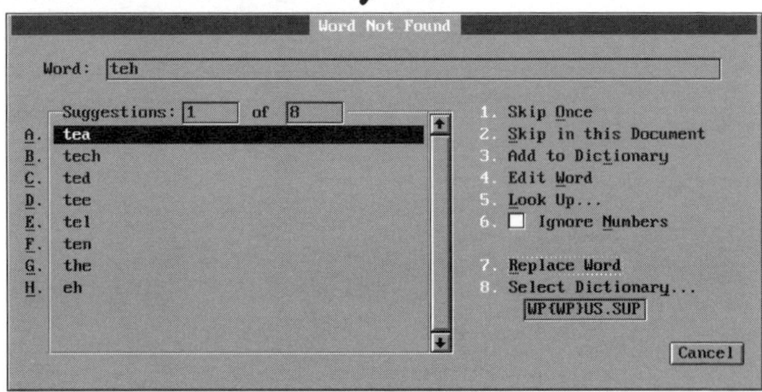

Option or button	*Function*
1. Skip Once	Tells the Speller to skip only this occurrence of the unknown word so that it flags the next occurrence (if any).
2. Skip in this Document	Tells the Speller to skip this and all subsequent occurrences of the unknown word in the document.
3. Add to Dictionary	Adds the unknown term to your supplemental dictionary.
4. Edit Word	Enables you to edit the unknown word (helpful when the Speller has no suggestions and you have an idea of how the word should be spelled).
5. Lookup...	Enables you to look up a word in the Speller's dictionary.
6. Ignore Numbers	Tells the Speller to not bother flagging unknown words that contain numbers.
7. Replace Word	Tells the Speller to replace the word flagged as unknown in the text with the suggestion that is highlighted in the Word Not Found dialog box.
8. Select Dictionary	Enables you to select a new supplemental dictionary to be used in the spell checking.

More stuff

If you want to limit the spell checking to just a particular section of text that you've changed, mark that text as a block — see Block (Text) for details — and then select the Speller by pressing Ctrl+F2.

Styles

Enables you to format parts of a document in the same manner simply by applying the appropriate style rather than having to go through all individual formatting commands each time.

Menus

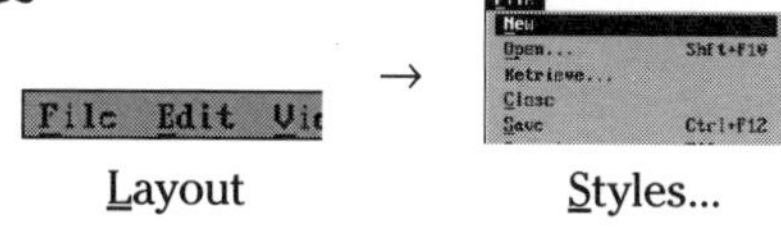

Layout → Styles...

For function key freaks

(Styles)

Creating a style by example

Although you can create a style for your document from scratch by choosing each of the format settings from the WordPerfect pull-down menu after choosing the 4. Style Contents option in the Edit Style dialog box, the easiest way by far to create the style by example is as follows:

1. Format the document text exactly as you want it to appear in the style, including fonts, sizes, attributes, alignment, justification, and the like.
2. Mark the formatted text as a block — see Block (Text) for details. If you're creating a paragraph style, select the entire formatted paragraph as a block. If you're creating a character style, select just the characters that you've formatted.
3. If you want to create a character style rather than a paragraph style, choose the 2. Style Type option and change the setting from the default of Paragraph Style to Character Style in the drop-down list box.

4. Choose the 2. Create option to open the Create Style dialog box and then enter a new style name (up to 12 characters long) and press Enter.
5. If you want to create an open or character style rather than a paragraph style, choose the 2. Style Type option and change the setting from the default of Paragraph Style to Open Style or Character Style in the drop-down list box.
6. Choose the 3. Create From Current Paragraph (or 3. Create from Current Character if you chose Character Style) to put an X in its check box.
7. Choose the OK button to open the Edit Style dialog box. WordPerfect shows the codes picked up from the formatted block in the Style Contents box in the Edit Style box.
8. To add an optional description that identifies the function of the style in the Style List dialog box, choose the 2. Description option and then type a short description and press Enter.
9. If you want to modify the Secret codes that are inserted in the document when you turn off the style (normally, WordPerfect merely turns off the codes that the style turns on), choose the 5. Show Style Off Codes option to put a comment in the middle of the Style Contents box. The comment indicates that codes above the comment are inserted when the style is turned on, and that codes below are inserted when the style is turned off.
10. If you need to edit the contents of the style, choose the 4. Style Contents option. To remove a Secret code, position the cursor on the code and then press the Del key. To insert a new code when the style is turned on, position the cursor somewhere before the comment and select the appropriate WordPerfect command that inserts the Secret code either with the pull-down menus or the function keys. To insert a new Secret code when the style is turned off, position the cursor somewhere after the comment and select the appropriate WordPerfect command. When you finish editing the codes, press the F7 (Exit) key.
11. If you want to alter how the Enter key functions in the style, choose the 6. Enter Key Action... Off/On option to open the Enter Key Action dialog box. If you're creating a paragraph style, the 3. Turn Style Off and Back On option is the default, but you can choose the 2. Turn Style Off or 4. Turn Style Off and Link to options instead. If you're creating a character style, the 1. Insert a Hard Return is the default, but you can choose the 2. Turn Style Off, the 3. Turn Style Off and Back On, or the 4. Turn Style Off and Link to options instead.

12. If you choose the 3. Turn Style Off and Back On option, you must select the name of the style that is to be turned on as soon as you press Enter in the drop-down list box that appears. Then press Enter.
13. Choose the OK button or press Enter again to close the Edit Style box and return to the Style List dialog box, where the new style now appears in the list in alphabetical order.
14. To apply the new style to the text marked as a block, choose the 1. Select option. To return to the document without applying the new style, choose the Close button instead. If you apply the style with the 1. Select option, you may have to open the Reveal Codes window and remove some duplicate codes. For example, if your style picks a [Lft Indent] code from the formatted marked block, WordPerfect indents your text twice when you apply the style to the block: once from the example formatting and another time from the style.

The Edit Style dialog box

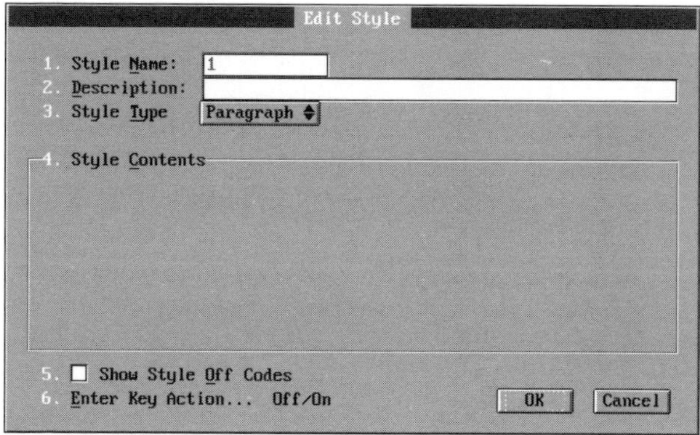

Option or button	*Function*
1. Style Name	Enables you to change the name of the style (you must give the style a name when you first create it).
2. Description	Enables you to add a description that tells you what the style does.
3. Style Type	Enables you to change the style type (Paragraph Style, Character Style, or Open Style).

Option or button	Function
4. Style Contents	Enables you to change the contents of the style by inserting or deleting the Secret codes (you do this by choosing the appropriate commands on the pull-down menus or by pressing the right function keys). Press F7 (Exit) when you're finished making your modifications.
5. Show Style Off Codes	Inserts a comment in the Style Contents area. All Secret codes above the comment are inserted when the style is turned on, and all codes below are inserted as soon as you turn off the style.
6. Enter Key Action... Off/On	Enables you to change the way the Enter key works after turning on the style (Insert a Hard Return, Turn Style Off, Turn Style Off and Back On, or Turn Style Off and Link to).

More stuff

To turn on a style or remove a style, position the cursor at the place where the style's formatting is to take hold and open the Style List dialog box (by choosing Styles on the Layout menu or by pressing Alt+F8).

Subdivide Pages

Enables you to get more than one page of text printed on a single sheet of paper. You can use this feature to create name tags, notes, and small ads that don't take up the whole sheet of paper. After you print your smaller pages on physical sheets of paper, you can cut them apart.

Menus

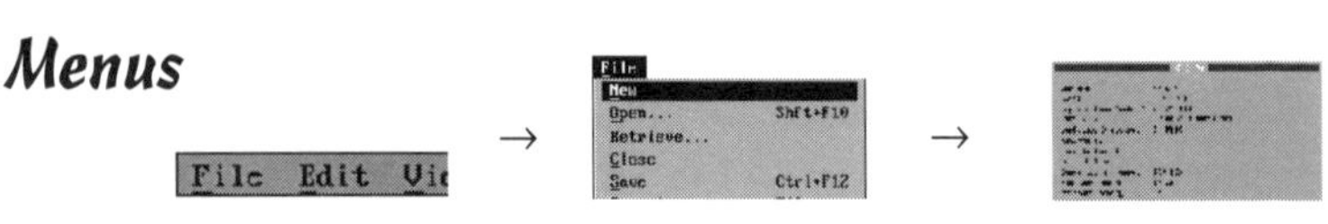

Layout → Page → 6. Subdivide Page...

For function key freaks

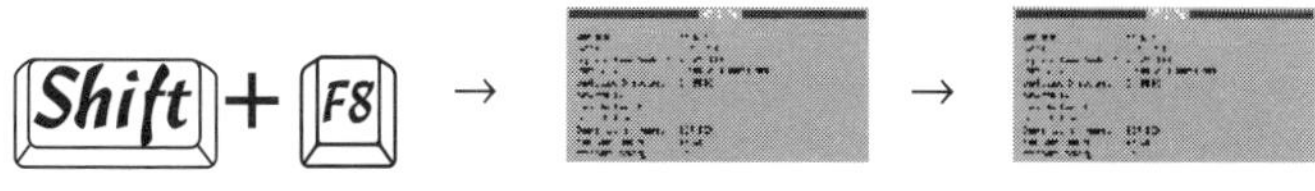

(Format) → 3. Page... → 6. Subdivide Page...

More stuff

When you choose 6. Subdivide Page in the Page dialog box, WordPerfect opens the Subdivide Page dialog box, in which you need to enter the number of columns and rows in which to divide the physical page. The columns correspond to the number of vertical subdivisions across the page, while the rows correspond to the number of horizontal subdivisions.

Suppress

Enables you to stop the printing of a header, footer, or page number on a single page of the document.

Menus

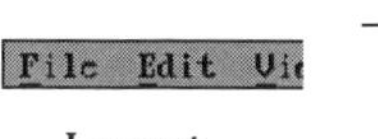

Layout → Page → 9. Suppress... (Page Numbering, Headers, and so on)

For function key freaks

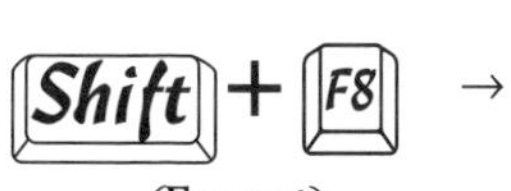

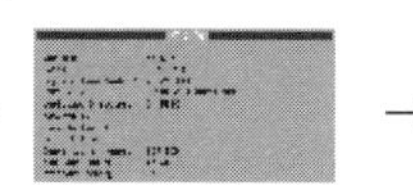

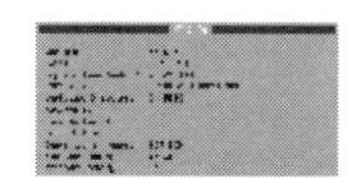

(Format) → 3. Page... → 9. Suppress... (Page Numbering, Headers, and so on)

The Suppress dialog box

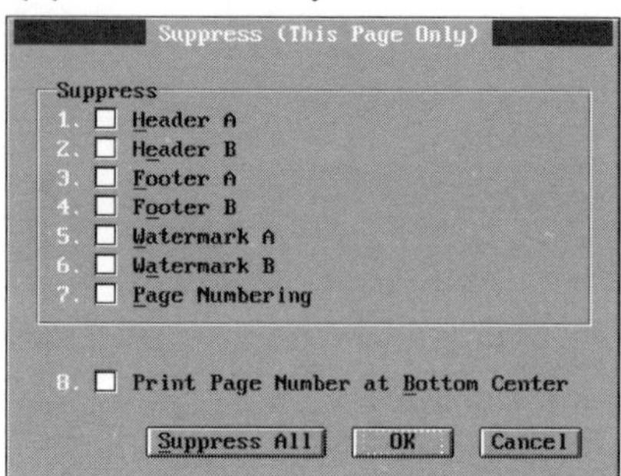

Option or button	Function
1. Header A	Suppresses the display of the first header on the current page.
2. Header B	Suppresses the display of the second header on the current page.
3. Footer A	Suppresses the display of the first footer on the current page.
4. Footer B	Suppresses the display of the second footer on the current page.
5. Watermark A	Suppresses the display of the first watermark on the current page.
6. Watermark B	Suppresses the display of the second watermark on the current page.
7. Page Numbering	Suppresses the display of the page number on the current page.
8. Print Page Number Bottom Center	Prints the page number centered at the at bottom of the current page.

Secret codes

When you use this command, WordPerfect inserts a

```
[Suppress]
```

Secret code at the top of the current page. If you open the Reveal Codes window and put the cursor on this code, the code expands to show what page element is suppressed. To reinstate this page element, delete the [Suppress] code.

More stuff

Before choosing this command, remember to position the cursor somewhere on the page where the page element is to be temporarily suspended.

Switch

Enables you to switch between the documents you have open in different document windows. You can use the Switch command on the Window menu (Shift+F3) to go back and forth between the current window and the next window you have open, or you can use the Switch to command (F3) to select a particular window by number.

Menus

To switch between the current document window and the next document window:

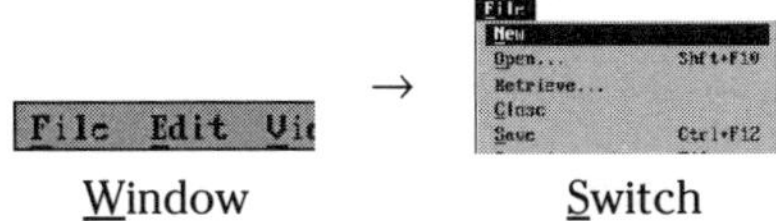

Window → Switch

To switch to a particular document window by its number:

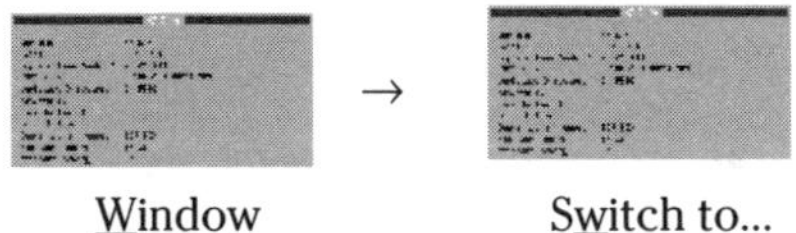

Window → Switch to...

For function key freaks

To switch between the current document window and the next document window:

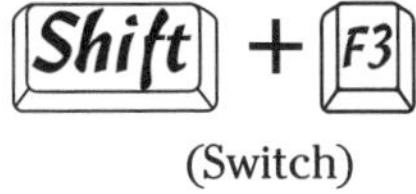

(Switch)

To switch to a particular document window by its number:

(Switch To)

More stuff

Instead of using the Switch to command or function key and then choosing the number of the document window to activate, you can press the Home key followed by the number of the window.

Tab Set

Enables you to change the tabs in your document.

Menus

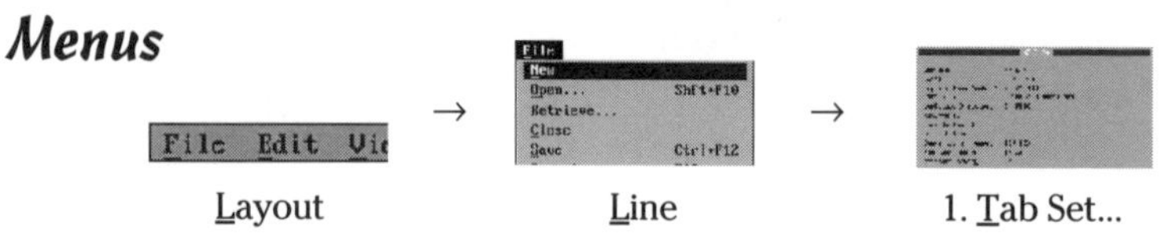

Layout → Line → 1. Tab Set...

For function key freaks

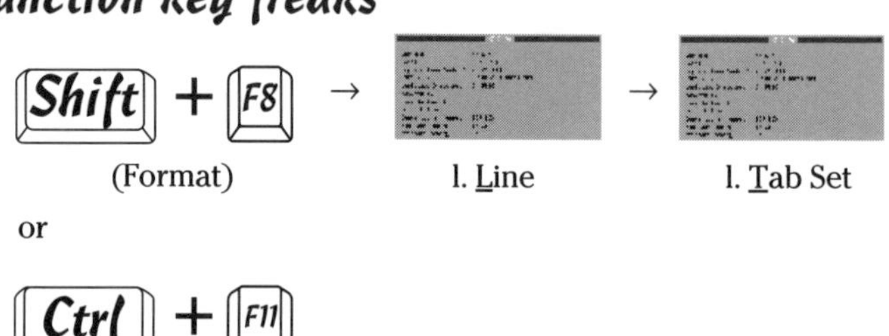

(Format) → 1. Line → 1. Tab Set

or

Ctrl + F11

(Tab Set)

The Tab Set dialog box

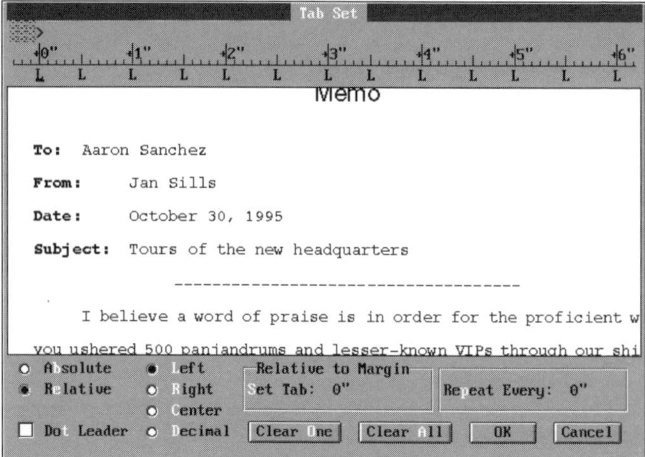

Tab Set
Memo
To: Aaron Sanchez
From: Jan Sills
Date: October 30, 1995
Subject: Tours of the new headquarters
I believe a word of praise is in order for the proficient w
you ushered 500 panjandrums and lesser-known VIPs through our shi
Absolute
Relative
Left
Right
Center
Decimal
Relative to Margin
Set Tab: 0"
Repeat Every: 0"
Dot Leader
Clear One
Clear All
OK
Cancel

Option or button	*Function*
Absolute or Relative	Enables you to switch between absolute tabs, which are measured from the edge of the page, and relative tabs, which are measured from the left margin and are automatically adjusted when you change the left margin setting.
Dot Leader	Adds dot leaders (a string of periods like .....) to the tab (dot leaders appear in front of the tab stop when you press the Tab key).
Left, Right, Center, or Decimal	Enables you to select the type of tab you want to set. Left tabs left-justify the text on the tab stop. Right tabs right-justify the text. Center tabs center the text on the tab stop. Decimal tabs align the decimal point (period) on the tab stop, while right-justifying all characters before the decimal point and left-justifying all characters after the decimal point.
Set Tab	Sets a tab on the ruler at the position you enter in the Set Tab text box.
Repeat Every	Repeats tabs uniformly across the ruler; the tabs are separated by the measurement you enter in the Repeat Every text box.
Clear One	Deletes the current tab from the ruler.
Clear All	Deletes all the tabs on the ruler.

More stuff

Instead of going through the rigmarole of changing tabs, you can change a left tab to another type on the fly as you're typing your text. Suppose that you want to center a heading over the third tab stop on the current document. To convert the third Left tab to a Center tab without bothering with the Tab Set dialog box and its options, press the Tab key twice and then, instead of pressing Tab a third time, press Home, Shift+F6 (Center) key. Doing this operation converts just this tab to a centered tab so that the heading you type is centered on this one tab stop.

WordPerfect refers to a tab converted to another type in this manner as a *hard tab.* You can create the following types of hard tabs in WordPerfect:

Type of Hard Tab	*Keystroke*
Hard left tab	Home, Tab
Hard center tab	Home, Shift+F6 (Center)
Hard right tab	Home, Alt+F6 (Flush Right)
Hard decimal tab	Home, Ctrl+F6 (Tab Align)

Tables

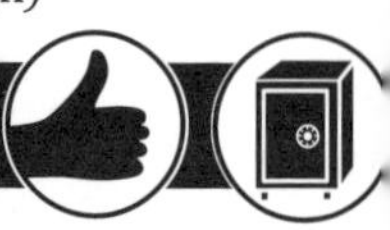

Enables you to set text in a tabular format using a layout of columns and rows, much like a spreadsheet. In fact, WordPerfect tables not only superficially resemble spreadsheets but can even accommodate worksheets created with spreadsheet software and can perform most of the very same functions. Moreover, the boxes formed by the intersection of a column and a row in a table are called cells (like in a spreadsheet). Each has a cell address that corresponds to the letter of its column (from A to Z, doubled afterwards as in AB, AC, and so on) and the number of its row (numbered from 1 down the table) so that the first cell in the upper left-hand corner is A1 (because it's in column A and row 1).

Menus

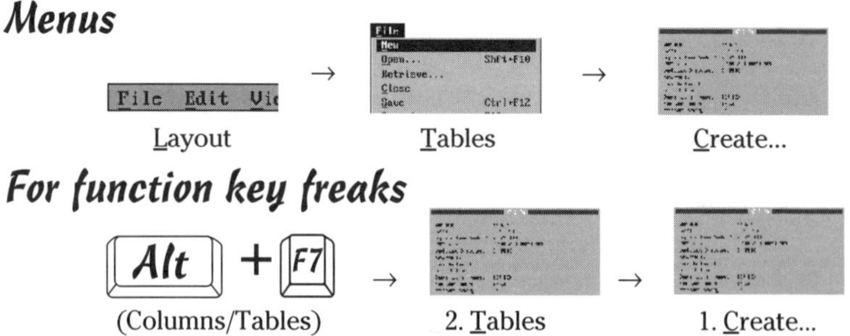

Creating a table

To create a table, you must first indicate the number of columns and rows you want the table to have by following these steps:

1. Move the cursor to the beginning of the new line in the document where the table is to appear.
2. Choose the Tables command on the Layout menu and then choose Create. Or press Alt+F7 (Columns/Tables), choose 2. Tables, and then choose 1. Create.
3. By default, WordPerfect creates a table with three columns and 1 row. To accept this default table size, choose the OK button. To create a table with more columns and rows, enter the new number of columns and rows and then choose OK.

Editing a table

When you choose OK to create a new table structure, WordPerfect automatically opens the special Table Edit window where you can use the following options to edit the structure, by changing either the structure or the formatting of the information you enter into its cells, columns, and rows. In addition to the options shown in this table, you can modify the width of the current column (the one with the cursor) by holding down the Ctrl key as you press the → key. To narrow the width of the current column, press Ctrl+← instead.

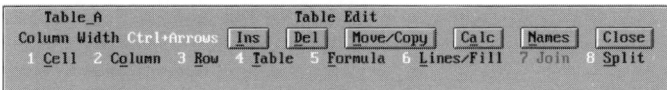

```
Table_A                          Table Edit
Column Width Ctrl+Arrows  Ins  Del  Move/Copy  Calc  Names  Close
 1 Cell  2 Column  3 Row  4 Table  5 Formula  6 Lines/Fill  7 Join  8 Split
```

Option or button	*Function*
1 Cell	Enables you to change the formatting of the cells that you've currently selected.
2 Column	Enables you to change the format and margins of the current column in table.
3 Row	Enables you to change the margins, height, and number of lines of text in the current row of the table.
4 Table	Enables you to change the formatting of all the table cells, the margin settings of all the columns, or the position of the table on the page.
5 Formula	Enables you to create a formula that performs a specific calculation involving the values you enter in the cells referred to (by cell address or name) in the formula.
6 Lines/Fill	Enables you to select the line and fill pattern for the current cell or block of cells or the entire table.
7 Join	Joins together the cells that you've selected.
8 Split	Breaks apart a joined cell (see preceding) into its original separate cells.
Ins	Enables you to insert blank columns or rows in the table either before or after the cursor's current position in the table.
Del	Enables you to delete the current column, row, or block of cells.

Move/Copy	Enables you to move or copy the information and/or formatting from the current cell, block of cells, row, or column to another part of the table.
Calc	Recalculates all the formulas in the table, assuring that your numbers are all up-to-date.
Names	Enables you to assign English names to the current cell, block of a cells, column, row, or the table itself. You can then use these names in the formulas you create.
Close	Closes the Table Edit window and returns you to the normal document editing window.

Entering text in a table

After creating the table structure and exiting Table Edit mode, you can enter text in the various cells of the table. To enter text, just position the cursor in the cell and then begin typing. To advance to the next cell to the right, press the Tab key. To return to the previous cell, press Shift+Tab (Back Tab). When you reach the last cell in a row, press Tab to move to the cell at the beginning of the next row. If you press Tab when the cursor is in the very last cell of a table, WordPerfect adds a blank row of cells to the table and positions the cursor in the first cell in this new row.

Editing a table

You can edit the text you enter in the cells of your table as you would edit regular document text. If you need to edit the structure of table or the appearance and formatting of its cells, however, you must return to Table Edit mode by choosing Tables on the Layout menu followed by Edit (or you can just press Alt+F11). When you're finished editing the structure and the formatting of the table, choose the Close button or press F7 (Exit) to return to the document editing window, where you can continue editing the contents of the table.

More stuff

You can convert a table created with tabs or parallel columns (see Columns) into a WordPerfect table. To do this, mark the lines of the tabular table or parallel columns as a block, and then choose Tables on the Layout menu followed by Create. Choose 1. Tabular Text or 2 Parallel Columns in the Create Table from Block dialog box and then choose OK. WordPerfect then creates a table structure that includes all of the information in your tabular table or parallel columns and puts you in Table Edit mode. If need be, modify the column widths (with Ctrl+→ or Ctrl+←) in the table and change any of the formatting. Then choose the Close button or press F7 (Exit).

Text Mode

Displays all text in a single (monospaced) font without headers, footers, or footnotes and indicates all graphics boxes by place holders that tell only the box number. Text attributes like bold and underline are indicated onscreen by various combinations of colors and intensities.

Menus

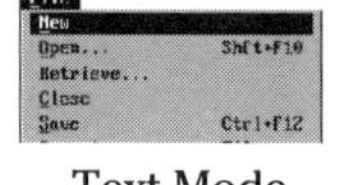

View → Text Mode

For function key freaks

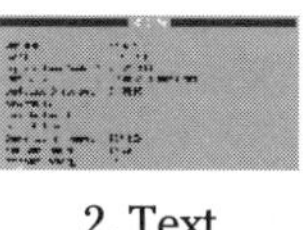

(Screen) → 2. Text

Thesaurus

Enables you to find synonyms (words with similar meanings) and antonyms (words with opposite meanings) for a lot of the words that you overuse in the document.

Menus

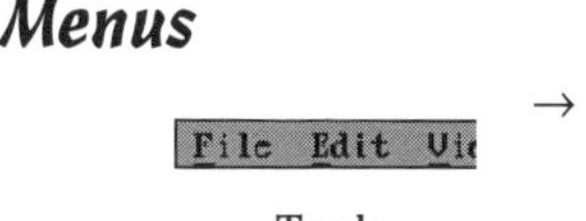

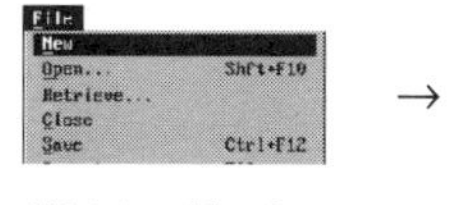

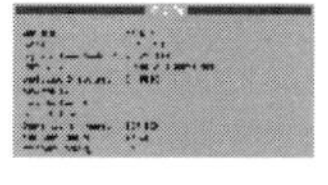

Tools → Writing Tools... → 2. Thesaurus...

For function key freaks

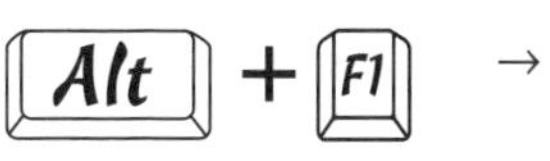

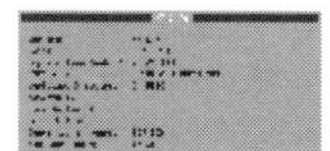

(Writing Tools) → 2. Thesaurus...

The Thesaurus dialog box

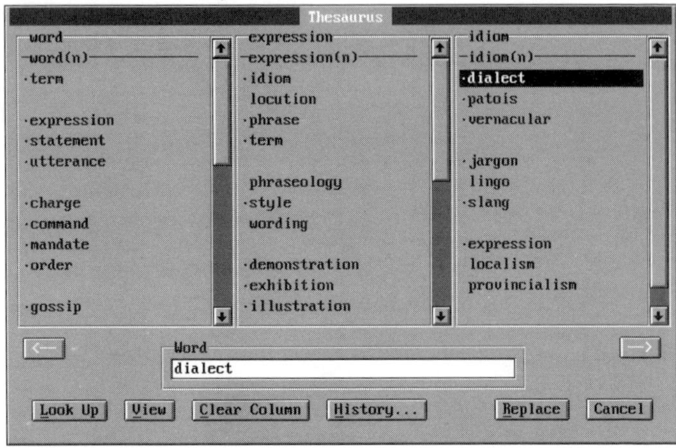

Option or button	Function
←	Moves you through the previous *headwords* (words that have synonyms in the Thesaurus file indicated by a period in front of the word) that you've selected in the Thesaurus one column to the left at a time.
→	Moves you through the previous headwords you've selected in the Thesaurus dialog box one column to the right at a time.
Look Up	Enables you to look up a word in the Thesaurus.
View	Returns temporarily to the document, where you can examine the context of the word you're trying to replace. When finished, press F7 (Exit) to re-activate the Thesaurus dialog box and its options.
Clear Column	Clears the current column of all synonyms and antonyms.
History	Shows you a list of each of the headwords you've looked up. To bring back a headword, highlight it and then choose the Select button.
Replace	Replaces the word highlighted in the document text with the synonym or antonym highlighted in the Thesaurus dialog box.

More stuff

To look up a word in the Thesaurus, position the cursor somewhere in the word and then open the Thesaurus text box. When you replace a word with a synonym or antonym in the Thesaurus, WordPerfect makes no attempt to match the original case or number in the text.

Typeover

Opposite mode of the default Insert mode. The new characters you type eat up the existing characters on the line rather pushing them to the right (as is the case in Insert mode). You can switch between Insert and Typeover mode by pressing the Ins key. WordPerfect always tells you when you've switched into Typeover mode by replacing the filename or font name on the status bar with the message *Typeover.*

Undelete

Restores any of the last three text deletions in your document at the cursor's current position.

Menus

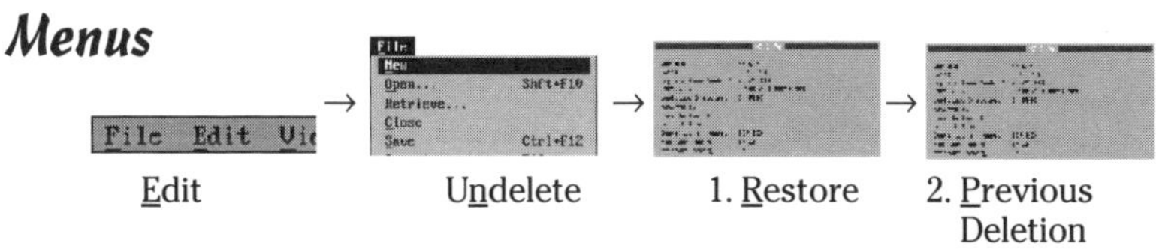

Edit → Undelete → 1. Restore → 2. Previous Deletion

For function key freaks

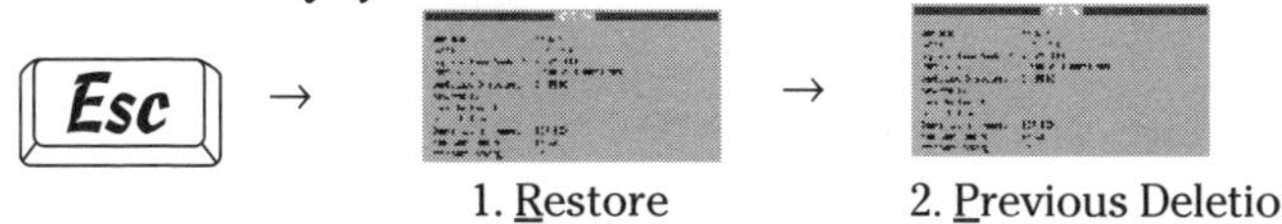

Esc → 1. Restore → 2. Previous Deletion

More stuff

When you press the Esc key (or choose Undelete on the Edit menu) and no pull-down menu or dialog box is open, WordPerfect displays the Undelete dialog box and displays the last deletion you made in the document as highlighted text at the cursor's position. To restore this text to the document, choose 1. Restore. To see a previous deletion (up to the third from last one made), choose 2. Previous Deletion and, when the text you want to restore appears, choose 1. Restore. If the text never appears, press Esc to close the Undelete dialog box.

Underline

Underlines selected text in the document.

Menus

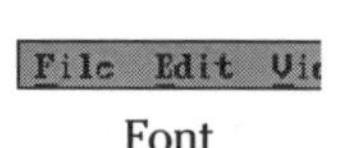

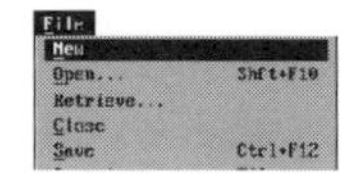

Font → Underline

For function key freaks

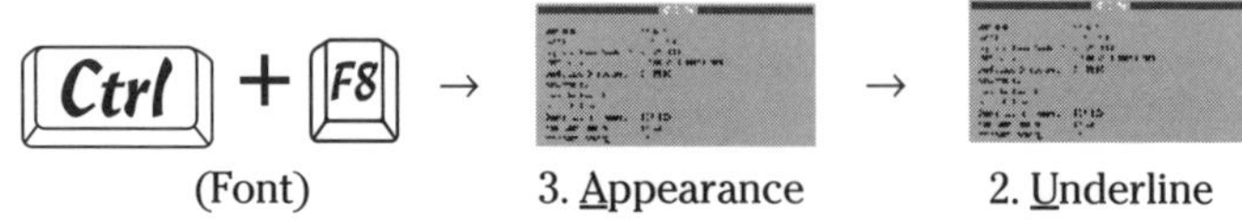

(Font) → 3. Appearance → 2. Underline

or

(Underline)

Secret codes

Lets say that you underline just the word *Thrills* in the heading

Cheap Thrills for All!

in your document. When you open Reveal Codes, you see

```
Cheap [Und On]Thrills[Und Off] for All!
```

More stuff

You can underline text before or after you type it just as you can do with bold and italics (see Bold for the general idea). To get rid of underlining in the text, open the Reveal Codes window and delete either the [Und On] or the [Und Off] Secret code that encloses the text.

Undo

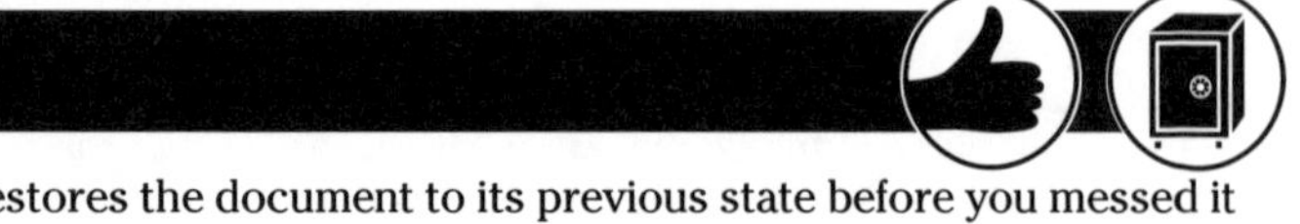

Restores the document to its previous state before you messed it up.

Menus

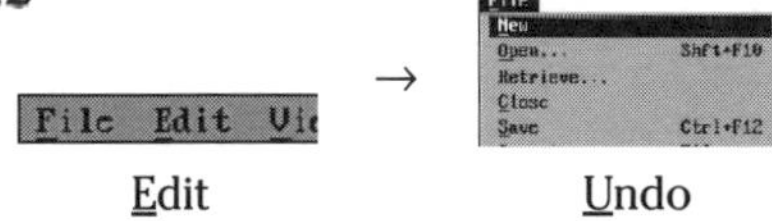

Edit → Undo

For function key freaks

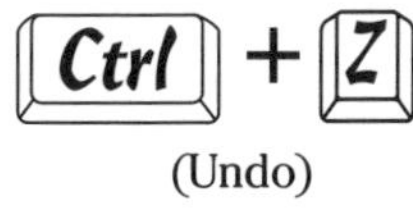

(Undo)

More stuff

Be sure that you use the Undo feature *right* after you make your boo-boo in the document. Don't try anything else because this just might make it impossible to right the situation.

Watermark

Enables you to insert *background* text or graphics in a document so that other text printed over the watermark can still be read.

Menus

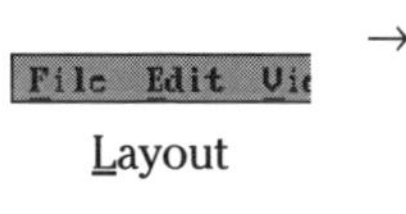

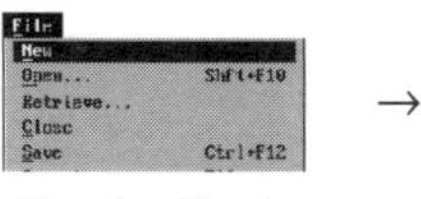

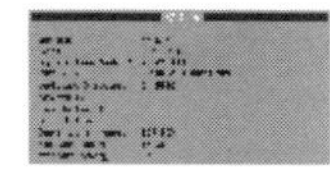

Layout → Header/Footer /Watermark... → 3. Watermarks

For function key freaks

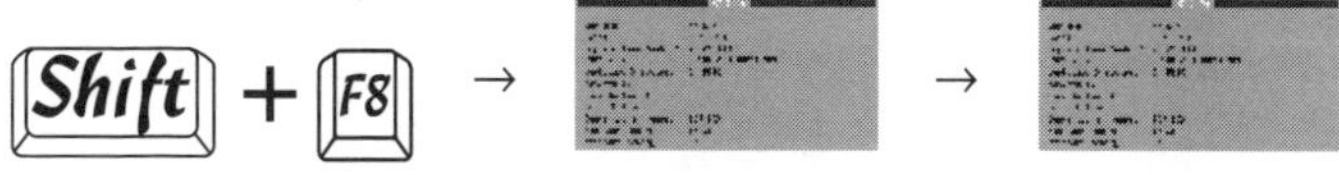

(Format) → 5. Header/Footer /Watermark... → 3. Watermarks

Creating a Watermark

Creating a watermark is very similar to creating a header or footer (that's why they put it on the same menu). To create a watermark, follow these steps:

1. Locate the cursor on the first page that is to have a watermark.

2. Choose the Header/Footer/Watermark command on the Layout menu or press Shift+F8 (Format). Then choose 5. Header/Footer/Watermark to open the Header/Footer/Watermark dialog box.
3. Choose 3. Watermarks in the Header/Footer/Watermark dialog box.
4. Choose 1. Watermark A to create your first watermark or 2. Watermark B to create your second.
5. By default, WordPerfect adds a watermark to all pages in the document. To add the watermark to even pages only, choose 2. Even Pages. To add the watermark to odd pages only, choose 3. Odd Pages.
6. Choose the Create button to open the Watermark window, where you enter and format the text for your watermark just as you would the text for any header or footer (see Headers and Footers); or, add a graphic image by choosing the Retrieve Image command on the Graphics menu. Note that the text and graphic images you add to the Watermark window appear in light gray on the screen to approximate their appearance in the printed document.
7. When you've finished entering and formatting the watermark text or adding the watermark image, press F7 (Exit) to close the Watermark window and return to your document
8. To see how the watermark will appear in the document when you print it, choose Print Preview on the File menu or press Shift+F7 (Print) and then 7. Print Preview (the watermark does not appear onscreen either in graphics or page display mode).

   Remember that you can suppress the printing of a watermark on a specific page just as you can suppress a header or footer (see Suppress for details).

Widow/Orphan

Ensures that no single line of a paragraph is allowed to appear alone at the very bottom or top of a page without the rest of the paragraph text.

Menus

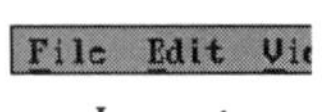

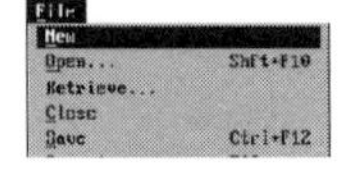

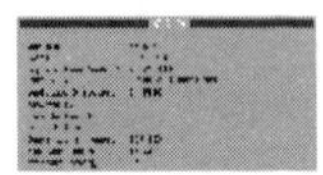

Layout → Other... → 3. Window/Orphan Protect

For function key freaks

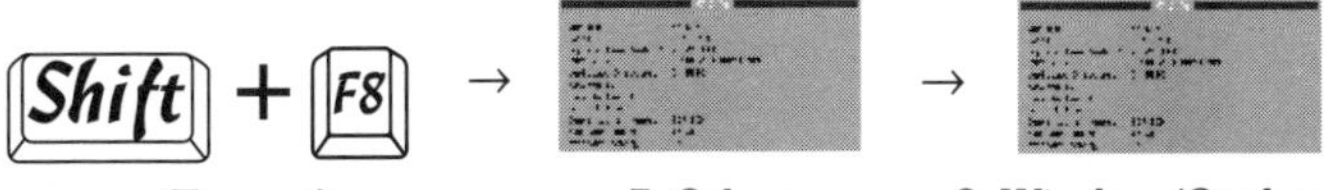

(Format) 7. Other... 3. Window/Orphan Protect

Secret codes

When you turn on Widow/Orphan control, WordPerfect inserts a

```
[Wid/Orph]
```

Secret code at the cursor's position in the text. If you position the cursor on this code, it expands to [Wid/Orph:On]. If you turn off Widow/Orphan protection at some point in the document, the program inserts a [Wid/Orph:Off] Secret code.

Window

The Window commands enables you to control the size and arrangement of the document windows you have open and to select the one you want to edit.

Menus

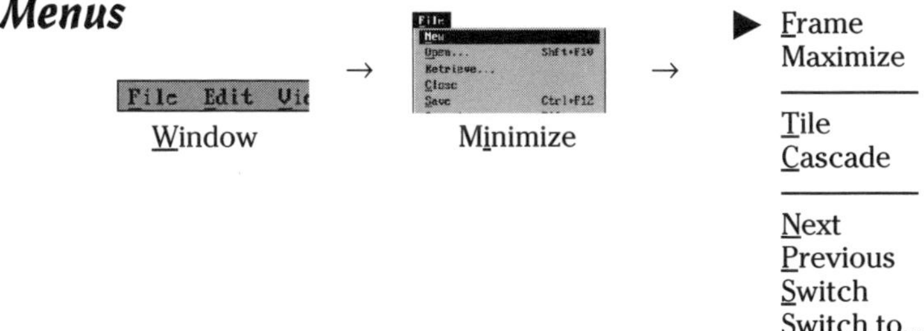

Window → Minimize → Frame, Maximize, Tile, Cascade, Next, Previous, Switch, Switch to...

More stuff

The first three commands on the Window menu let you control the size of the current document window.

Choose the Tile and Cascade commands to arrange all the open windows (you can have up to a maximum of nine if your computer has enough memory).

Use the Next, Previous, Switch, and Switch to commands to activate the various windows that you have open.

WordPerfect Characters

Enables you to insert special characters (like foreign language, math, and science symbols) not available from the regular keyboard.

Menus

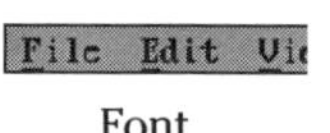 → 

Font → WP Characters...

For function key freaks

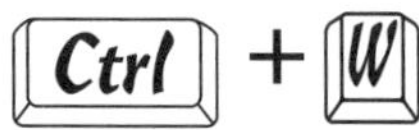

More stuff

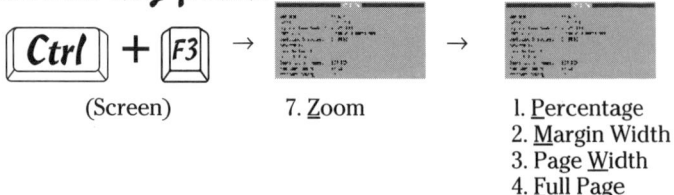

To insert a WordPerfect character into the text of your document or into a text box in a dialog box, open the WordPerfect Characters dialog box (you must do this by pressing Ctrl+W when you're in a dialog box). Then choose 2. Set and highlight the set you want to use and choose 3. Characters and highlight the character before you choose Insert.

Zoom

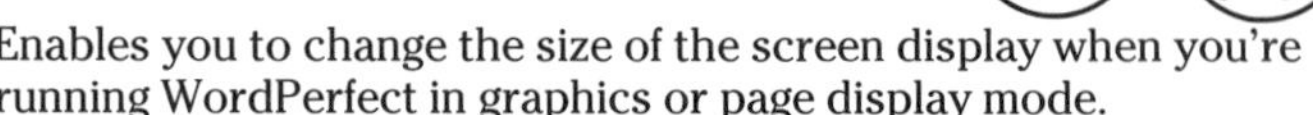

Enables you to change the size of the screen display when you're running WordPerfect in graphics or page display mode.

Menus

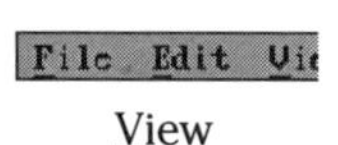 → 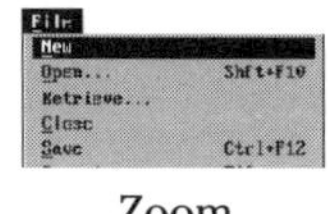

View → Zoom

50@%	200@%
75@%	300%
100@%	Margin Width
125@%	Page Width
150@%	Full Page

For function key freaks

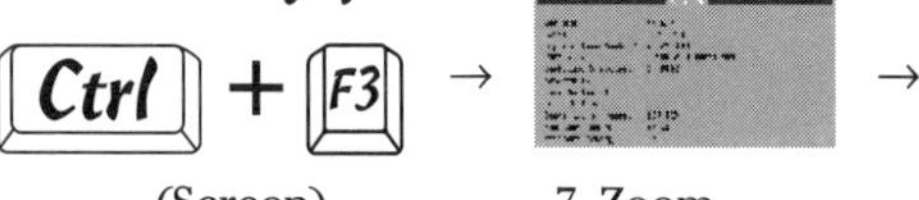

(Screen) → 7. Zoom →

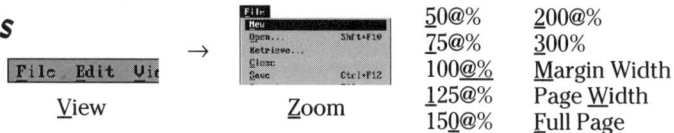

1. Percentage
2. Margin Width
3. Page Width
4. Full Page

IDG BOOKS WORLDWIDE REGISTRATION CARD

RETURN THIS REGISTRATION CARD FOR FREE CATALOG

Title of this book: WordPerfect for DOS For Dummies Quick Reference

My overall rating of this book: ❑ Very good [1] ❑ Good [2] ❑ Satisfactory [3] ❑ Fair [4] ❑ Poor [5]

How I first heard about this book:

❑ Found in bookstore; name: [6]
❑ Book review: [7]
❑ Advertisement: [8]
❑ Catalog: [9]
❑ Word of mouth; heard about book from friend, co-worker, etc.: [10]
❑ Other: [11]

What I liked most about this book:

What I would change, add, delete, etc., in future editions of this book:

Other comments:

Number of computer books I purchase in a year: ❑ 1 [12] ❑ 2-5 [13] ❑ 6-10 [14] ❑ More than 10 [15]

I would characterize my computer skills as: ❑ Beginner [16] ❑ Intermediate [17] ❑ Advanced [18] ❑ Professional [19]

I use ❑ DOS [20] ❑ Windows [21] ❑ OS/2 [22] ❑ Unix [23] ❑ Macintosh [24] ❑ Other: [25] ______ (please specify)

I would be interested in new books on the following subjects:
(please check all that apply, and use the spaces provided to identify specific software)

❑ Word processing: [26]
❑ Spreadsheets: [27]
❑ Data bases: [28]
❑ Desktop publishing: [29]
❑ File Utilities: [30]
❑ Money management: [31]
❑ Networking: [32]
❑ Programming languages: [33]
❑ Other: [34]

I use a PC at (please check all that apply): ❑ home [35] ❑ work [36] ❑ school [37] ❑ other: [38] ______

The disks I prefer to use are ❑ 5.25 [39] ❑ 3.5 [40] ❑ other: [41] ______

I have a CD ROM: ❑ yes [42] ❑ no [43]

I plan to buy or upgrade computer hardware this year: ❑ yes [44] ❑ no [45]

I plan to buy or upgrade computer software this year: ❑ yes [46] ❑ no [47]

Name: Business title: [48]

Type of Business: [49]

Address (❑ home [50] ❑ work [51]/Company name:)

Street/Suite#

City [52]/State [53]/Zipcode [54]: Country [55]

❑ **I liked this book!**
You may quote me by name in future IDG Books Worldwide promotional materials.

My daytime phone number is ______

IDG BOOKS

THE WORLD OF COMPUTER KNOWLEDGE

YES!

Please keep me informed about IDG's World of Computer Knowledge. Send me the latest IDG Books catalog.

BUSINESS REPLY MAIL

FIRST CLASS MAIL PERMIT NO. 2605 SAN MATEO, CALIFORNIA

IDG Books Worldwide
155 Bovet Rd
San Mateo CA 94402-9833